'AS' Level Computi

P.M. Heathcote B.Sc.(Hons), M.Sc.
S. Langfield B.Sc.(Hons)

Published by
Payne-Gallway Publishers Ltd
26-28 Northgate Street
Ipswich IP1 3DB
Tel 01473 251097
Fax 01473 232758
E-mail info@payne-gallway.co.uk
Web site www.payne-gallway.co.uk

2004

PAYNE-GALLWAY
PUBLISHERS LTD

'AS' Level Computing

Acknowledgements

We are grateful to the AQA Examination Board for permission to use questions from past examination papers.
The answers in the teacher's supplement are the sole responsibility of the authors and have neither been provided nor approved by the examination board.

We would also like to thank the following organisations for permission to reproduce copyright material in the form of articles or photographs.
British Software Alliance
Formic Ltd
The Guardian

Graphics: Richard Chasemore
Cover picture © 2000 "Hill Cottage, Highlands", acrylic on canvas reproduced with the kind permission of Suzanne Gyseman
Cover photography © Mike Kwasniak, 160 Sidegate Lane, Ipswich
Design and artwork by Direction123.com

Fifth Edition 2004
There are no previous editions of 'AS' Level Computing. This is the first half of 'A' Level Computing (5th Edition) ISBN 1 904467 52 0 and is therefore called 'Fifth Edition' to avoid confusion.

A catalogue entry for this book is available from the British Library.

ISBN 1 904467 71 7
Copyright © P.M. Heathcote and S. Langfield 2004

Printed in Malta by
Gutenberg Press Ltd.

Preface

The aim of this book is to provide a comprehensive yet concise textbook covering all the topics studied for an 'AS' Level course in Computing.

The book is divided into 3 sections covering all the material for each paper in the modular scheme offered by the Assessment and Qualifications Alliance (AQA). Within a section, each chapter covers material that can comfortably be taught in one or two lessons, and the chapters are sequenced in such a way that practical sessions can be based around the theory covered in the classroom. Important definitions are emphasised in the text.

Section 1 should be supported by practical experience of programming in a high level language such as Pascal, Delphi, Visual Basic or Java.

Section 2 should be supported by practical skills development in spreadsheets and databases.

Section 3 discusses the documentation requirements for a solution to the practical exercise set each year by AQA. This can be implemented using a programming language or a database, and an example of documentation for a database solution to a typical task is given in Appendix A.

Each chapter contains exercises and questions from past examination papers, so that the student can gain plenty of experience in 'exam technique'. Answers to all the questions are available, to teachers only, in a separate Teacher's Supplement that can be downloaded from our web site **www.payne-gallway.co.uk**.

PAYNE-GALLWAY
P U B L I S H E R S L T D

Contents

Module 1
Computer Systems, Programming and Network Concepts   Page   1

Module 2
Principles of Hardware, Software and Applications   Page   75

Module 3
Practical Systems Development   Page   171

Appendix A
The Practical Exercise   Page   190

Appendix B
AQA 'AS' Level Specification   Page   208

Index
     Page   216

Module 1

Computer Systems, Programming and Network Concepts

In this section:

Chapter 1	Computer Hardware	2
Chapter 2	Classification of Software	8
Chapter 3	Bits and Bytes	12
Chapter 4	Data Representation (Text and Numbers)	16
Chapter 5	Data Representation (Sound and Graphics)	20
Chapter 6	Programming Concepts	24
Chapter 7	Program Design and Maintenance	31
Chapter 8	Dry-run Exercises	39
Chapter 9	Queues and Stacks	44
Chapter 10	Binary Trees	49
Chapter 11	Inside the Computer	52
Chapter 12	Communication Methods	58
Chapter 13	Local Area Networks	63
Chapter 14	Wide Area Networks	68

1

Chapter 1 – Computer Hardware

Introduction

On this course you will be learning about the internal structure of computers, how they operate and how they are used in solving problems. You will also learn the fundamentals of computer programming, and build on your existing knowledge of software packages.

In addition, you will need to develop an awareness of the wider implications for individuals and for society of the increasing use of computers. This is best done by keeping your eyes and ears open, noticing new uses of computers, reading newspapers and magazines which contain computer-related articles, and watching appropriate and relevant television programmes.

This course, with its emphasis on the more technical aspects of computing, including operating systems and programming, is suitable for students who intend to go on to study Computer Science, Computing or Software Engineering at University, or make their career in computing.

Computer systems

A **computer system** consists of **hardware** and **software.**

Hardware: The physical components (electronic circuits) that make up the computer.

Software: The computer programs (sequences of instructions) that tell the computer what to do in response to a command or some event.

In this chapter we'll take an introductory look at hardware.

The components of a computer

All computers, whatever their size or function, have certain basic components. They have input devices for reading data into main memory, a central processing unit (CPU) for processing the data, output devices for printing, displaying or outputting information, and auxiliary storage devices for permanent storage of programs and data.

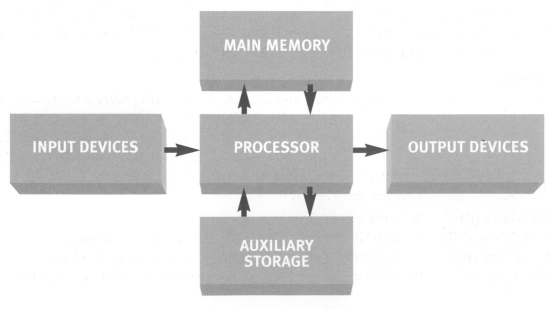

Figure 1.1: Block diagram of a computer system

Types of computer

We are so used to seeing PCs on desktops at home, school, businesses and other organisations that it is easy to forget that there are other types of computer.

Minicomputers are often used as multi-user systems, with hundreds of workstations or terminals attached to a central minicomputer, for example EPOS (Electronic Point of Sale) systems.

Mainframe computers are used by large organisations such as banks, building societies, insurance companies, airlines and government departments. A mainframe may have thousands of terminals attached to it at geographically remote locations, and occupy an entire site with hundreds of disk drives and other hardware units. Frequently, the actual siting of a mainframe computer is kept secret to lessen the danger of a terrorist attack that could cause chaos to an organisation.

Supercomputers are the largest category of computer, costing millions of pounds. They are mostly used by scientific and industrial research departments, government agencies such as NASA, the Weather Centre, Stock Exchanges and by very large commercial organisations.

The processor

The processor has the following functions:
- fetches the next instruction;
- decodes the instruction;
- executes the decoded instruction.

Most computers use integrated circuits, or chips, for their processors and main memory. A chip is about 1cm square and can hold millions of electronic components such as transistors and resistors. The CPU of a microcomputer is called a *microprocessor*. The processor and main memory of a PC are commonly held on a single board called a motherboard.

In 1965 Gordon Moore predicted that the capacity of a computer chip would double every year. He looked at the price/performance ratio of computer chips (the amount of performance available per dollar) over the previous three years and simply projected it forwards. He didn't really believe the rate of improvement would last for long, but in fact to this day chip capacity is still doubling every 18 months or so.

Main memory

The program currently being executed and the data used by this program are held in main memory, which is divided into millions of individually addressable storage units called *bytes*. One byte can hold one character, or it can be used to hold a code representing, for example, a tiny part of a picture, a sound, or part of a computer program instruction. The total number of bytes in main memory is referred to as the computer's memory size. Computer memory sizes are measured as follows:

1 Kilobyte (Kb)	= 1024 bytes		
1 Megabyte (Mb)	= 1024Kb	=	1,048,576 bytes (about 1 million)
1 Gigabyte (Gb)	= 1024Mb	=	1,073,741,824 bytes (about 1 billion)
1 Terabyte (Tb)	= 1024Gb	=	1,099,511,627,776 bytes (about 1 trillion)

1-1

As with processing power, the amount of memory that comes with a standard PC has increased exponentially over the past 20 years. In about 1980, BBC microcomputers with 32K of memory were bought in their thousands for home and school use. In 1981, Bill Gates of Microsoft made his famous remark "640K ought to be enough for anybody". In 2004, a PC with 512Mb of main memory is standard, costing around £1,000 including bundled software.

RAM and ROM

There are basically two kinds of main memory; **Random Access Memory (RAM)** which is the ordinary kind of main memory referred to above, used for storing programs which are currently running and data which is being processed. This type of memory is **volatile** which means that it loses all its contents as soon as the machine is switched off.

Read Only Memory (ROM) is the other type of main memory, and this is non-volatile, with its contents permanently etched into the memory chip at the manufacturing stage. It is used for example to hold the **bootstrap loader**, the program which runs as soon as the computer is switched on and instructs it to load the operating system from disk into main memory (RAM). It may also store fixed data associated with the computer system. In special purpose computers used in video recorders, washing machines and cars, the program instructions are stored in ROM.

Cache memory

Cache memory is a type of very fast memory that is used to improve the speed of a computer, doubling it in some cases. It acts as an intermediate store between the CPU and main memory, and works by storing the most frequently or recently used instructions and data so that it will be very fast to retrieve them again. Thus when an item of data is required, a whole block of data will be read into cache in the expectation that the next piece of data required is likely to be in the same block. The amount of cache memory is generally between 1Kb and 512Kb.

Figure 1.2: How cache memory operates

Disk storage

The most common form of auxiliary storage (also known as *external* or *secondary memory* or *backing store*) is disk. All standalone PCs come equipped with an in-built hard disk, the capacity of which is also measured in bytes. A typical hard disk for a PC stores several gigabytes, and is used for storing software including the operating system, other systems software, application programs and data for long term storage.

Floppy disks consist of a thin sheet of mylar plastic encased in a hard 3½" casing. The standard type of disk in use today has a capacity of 1.44Mb. Flash memory cards or sticks are rapidly replacing floppy disks. These can hold from 32Mb to 1Gb.

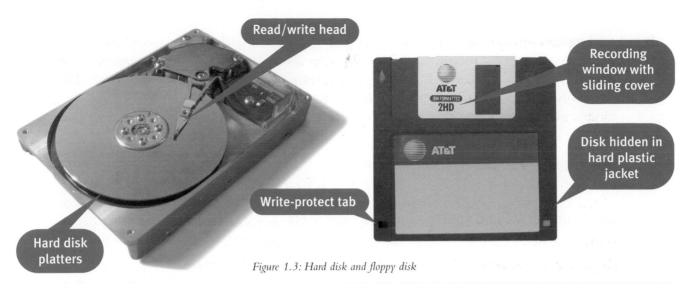

Read/write head

Recording window with sliding cover

Disk hidden in hard plastic jacket

Write-protect tab

Hard disk platters

Figure 1.3: Hard disk and floppy disk

Q1: Two advertisements for computers are shown below. What do the various terms and abbreviations mean? Note how the price has fallen and the specification has increased in less than two years. Is Moore's Law still holding?

1-1

Pentium 4

- Pentium 4 1.6 GHz Processor
- 128MB DDR RAM
- 20GB HDD
- 17" Colour Monitor
- 20/48x CD-ROM Drive
- 16MB Graphics Card
- On-Board Sound
- Midi Tower case
- Windows XP
- MS Works 6.0

£549

exc VAT

Figure 1.4: A high specification PC advertised in May 2002

Pentium 4

- Pentium 4 2.66 GHz Processor
- 256Mb DDR RAM
- 80 GB IDE HDD
- 20/48x CD-ROM Drive
- Integrated Intel Extreme Graphics Card
- Integrated Audio
- 17" Flat Panel Monitor
- Integrated Intel Pro 10/100 Ethernet Card
- Tower case
- Windows XP Home Edition
- MS Works 7.0

£539

exc VAT

Figure 1.5: A high specification PC advertised in March 2004

Input and output devices

Input devices are the means whereby computers can accept data or instructions, and include keyboards, magnetic strip cards, smart cards and magnetic ink character recognition devices for reading the numbers on the bottom of cheques.

Output devices include various types of printer, VDU (Visual Display Unit) and speakers.

Q2: Name some other input and output devices and their uses.

Embedded computers and special-purpose computers

Not all computers are general-purpose computers with a screen, keyboard and disk drive. **Special-purpose** or **dedicated** computers perform a wide variety of tasks from controlling the temperature and humidity in a greenhouse, controlling traffic lights to smooth the flow of traffic or enabling you to use a card at a cash point machine. **Embedded computers** are widely used in household goods, automobiles and in industry. Special purpose computers have the same basic components of input, output, processor and memory, as general purpose computers, but typically the programs that they run are etched permanently into memory (ROM) so that they cannot be altered. These programs are sometimes known as **firmware** – a combination of hardware and software.

1-1

Exercises

1   A computer system is made up of hardware and software. What is meant by
    (a)   hardware;
    (b)   software? (2)
New Question

2   Give an example of
    (a)   an input device;
    (a)   an output device;
    (b)   a storage device. (3)
New Question

3   What is the function of the following components:
    (a)   processor
    (b)   main memory
    (c)   secondary storage? (3)
New Question

4   The table below contains names of several computer system components. For each component, indicate whether it is hardware or software by ticking in the correct column of the table:

1-1

Component	Hardware	Software
Web Browser		
Main memory		
Operating system		
Monitor		
Scanner		

(5)
New Question

Chapter 2 – Classification of Software

Categorising software

Software is the general term used to describe all the programs that run on a computer. There are several categories of software: systems software, general purpose applications (generic) software, special purpose application software, bespoke software. This categorisation is not rigid, however. You will soon discover that very little in computing is black and white; whatever you read, someone will soon come up with an apparently contradictory statement on most topics, leaving you to choose your own truth!

Systems software

Systems software performs tasks needed to run the computer system.

It includes the following types:

1 Operating system. Every computer needs an operating system to act as an interface between the user and the computer hardware. It provides us with a **virtual machine**. An operating system is a set of programs that allows the user to perform tasks without having to know how they are done. For example, a user can give a command to save a file on disk without having to know where the file will be stored or how it will be retrieved again. When a command is given to print a document, the user does not have to be concerned with the details of how the printer works – a program called a device driver takes care of the details.

Application programs are usually written to work with a particular operating system, so that a word processor, which works with Windows, will not work on an Apple Mac, which has a different operating system.

2 Library programs. A library program is available to all users of a multi-user computer system, typically to carry out common tasks required by everyone. For example a routine that searches for lost files or restores corrupted files may be stored in a library. Many of these programs fall into the general category of **utility programs** (see below.)

3 Utility programs. These are programs designed to make life easier for computer users. Utility programs perform common tasks that thousands of computer users need to do at one time or another, such as search for lost files, sort files of data into a particular sequence, copy disk files to magnetic tape for backup purposes and so on.

One common utility is compression software such as PKZip that 'zips' files so that they occupy less space. This is very useful if you want to transmit a graphic or long data file over the Internet, as the transmission time will be much reduced.

Q1: Have you used any utility programs? Where did you get them and what are they used for?

4 Programming language compilers, interpreters and assemblers. Compilers and interpreters are different types of program used to translate the statements in a programming language such as Pascal, Visual Basic or C into a form that the computer can execute. An assembler performs a similar function, translating the statements of a low-level programming language (assembly code) into machine code.

1-2

Applications software

Application software: Software designed to carry out some task for the user that is primarily independent of computers, such as writing a letter or processing orders and invoices.

General purpose application software

All common application packages such as word processing, desktop publishing, spreadsheet, database, computer-aided design (CAD) and presentation packages fall into this category. Most general purpose application software is sold as a package, including a CD containing the software and manuals to help you get started and to be used as a reference.

Figure 2.1: General purpose software

The main productivity tools used by organisations include word processing, spreadsheets, databases, presentation graphics and communications software to enable users to communicate with each other either locally or across the world in an international company.

Complete **software suites** such as Microsoft Office or Sun Star Office offer four or more software products packaged together at a much lower price than buying the packages separately. Microsoft Office, for example, includes Word, Excel, Access, Publisher, a multimedia presentation package called PowerPoint and Microsoft Outlook. The advantage of buying such a suite of programs is that the individual applications are completely compatible so that there is no difficulty importing or exporting data from one package to another, if for example you wish to put a spreadsheet in a word processed report. Also, the packages all have the same look and feel, with the same shortcut keys used for various operations (such as F7 for checking spelling) and this makes learning new software an easier task.

General Purpose Application Software: Software that can be made to do many different tasks.

1-2

Generic and special purpose software

Note that software such as word processing, spreadsheet and database software is sometimes referred to as **generic** software. This simply implies that any of the dozens of spreadsheet packages, for example, can be made to do many different tasks, and is not designed specifically for one type of application.

Special purpose software

Application software such as a payroll, accounts or stock control system, or software such to help fill in an income tax return, for example, is in contrast **special purpose** because it is designed to do one particular task.

Special Purpose Application Software: Software to perform a specific task.

Bespoke software

The software may be designed specifically for one particular organisation, **(bespoke software)** and written especially for them using a programming language or software such as a database management system.

Bespoke Software: Software written to the specification of a particular organisation or customer.

Bespoke or off-the-shelf?

When an organisation decides to computerise an area of its business, a decision has to be made whether to buy an off-the-shelf package or have software specially written. The advantages of buying an off-the-shelf package include the following:

- it is generally a less expensive solution as the cost of developing the software is shared across a wider customer base;
- it may be possible to speak to other users of the package for their evaluation before spending money;
- the software can be bought and installed straight away;
- the software is tried and tested and likely to contain fewer bugs than newly written software;
- the software is usually well documented and additional documentation may be available from other sources;
- training may be available from different providers in common software packages.

Conversely, there are also advantages in buying tailor-made **('bespoke')** software:
- it is designed to do exactly what the user wants;
- it has no unwanted features;
- it can be written to run on specified hardware;
- it can be integrated with existing software;
- there may not be a suitable software package on the market.

Exercises

1 (a) Two classifications of software are System Software and Application Software.

What is meant by:

(i) System Software; (1)

(ii) Application Software? (1)

(b) Give an example of:

(i) System Software; (1)

(ii) Application Software. (1)

AQA CPT1 Qu 2 Jan 2001

2 (a) Application software can be subdivided into general purpose and special purpose.

(i) Give a type of general purpose application software package. (1)

(ii) What is meant by a special purpose application software package? (1)

(b) A large organisation is planning to computerise their payroll. The management have the choice of buying a readily available software package or writing bespoke software.

(i) What is meant by bespoke software? (1)

(ii) Give **one** advantage and **two** disadvantages of bespoke software over readily available software. (3)

AQA CPT1 Qu 5 May 2001

3 Parts of a typical computer operating system may be stored in

(a) External (secondary) memory

(b) Read Only Memory (ROM)

(c) Random Access Memory (RAM)

Explain why **each** type of memory is used by the operating system. (6)

New Question

Chapter 3 – Bits and Bytes

The binary system

All digital computers use the **binary** system for representing data of all types – numbers, characters, sound, pictures and so on. A binary system uses just 2 symbols to represent all information. The symbols could be anything like + and -, or 0 and 1. The great advantage of the binary system is that the digits 1 and 0 can be represented by electrical circuits that can exist in one of two states – current is either flowing or not flowing, and a circuit is either closed or open, on or off, voltage can be high or low.

A closed circuit allowing current to flow represents 1

An open circuit represents 0

Figure 3.1: Electrical circuits can represent 1 or 0

Bits and bytes

A binary digit (1 or 0) is known as a '**bit**', short for **BI**nary digi**T**. In most computers today, bits are grouped together in 8-bit bytes. A byte can hold 256 different combinations of 0s and 1s, which means that, for example, 256 different characters can be represented.

One byte holds one character.

The ASCII code

Over the years, different computer designers have used different sets of codes for representing characters, which has led to great difficulty in transferring information from one computer to another. Most personal computers (PCs) nowadays use the ASCII code (American Standard Code for Information Interchange), but many mainframe computers use a code called EBCDIC (Extended Binary Coded Decimal Interchange Code – pronounced EB-SUH-DICK or EB-SEE-DICK according to taste). EBCDIC uses 8 bits to encode each character.

ASCII originally used a 7-bit code. The 128 different combinations that can be represented in 7 bits are plenty to allow for all the letters, numbers and special symbols. Later, the eighth bit was also used, which allowed an extra 128 characters to be represented. The extra 128 combinations are used for symbols such as Ç, è, ü, ©, ®, Œ, etc. This is known as extended ASCII.

> **Q1**: About how many different combinations of 0s and 1s are required to represent all the keys on a keyboard? (Remember to include uppercase and lowercase letters).

The first 32 ASCII codes are used for simple communications protocols, not characters. For example ACK stands for 'acknowledge' and would be sent by a device to acknowledge receipt of data or communication signal.

The ASCII codes are shown below.

Character	ASCII	Char	ASCII	Char	ASCII	Char	ASCII
NULL	0000000	space	0100000	@	1000000	`	1100000
SOH	0000001	!	0100001	A	1000001	a	1100001
STX	0000010	"	0100010	B	1000010	b	1100010
ETX	0000011	£	0100011	C	1000011	c	1100011
EOT	0000100	$	0100100	D	1000100	d	1100100
ENQ	0000101	%	0100101	E	1000101	e	1100101
ACK	0000110	&	0100110	F	1000110	f	1100110
BEL	0000111	'	0100111	G	1000111	g	1100111
BS	0001000	(	0101000	H	1001000	h	1101000
HT	0001001	)	0101001	I	1001001	i	1101001
LF	0001010	*	0101010	J	1001010	j	1101010
VT	0001011	+	0101011	K	1001011	k	1101011
SF	0001100	,	0101100	L	1001100	l	1101100
CR	0001101	-	0101101	M	1001101	m	1101101
SO	0001110	.	0101110	N	1001110	n	1101110
SI	0001111	/	0101111	O	1001111	o	1101111
DLE	0010000	0	0110000	P	1010000	p	1110000
DC1	0010001	1	0110001	Q	1010001	q	1110001
DC2	0010010	2	0110010	R	1010010	r	1110010
DC3	0010011	3	0110011	S	1010011	s	1110011
DC4	0010100	4	0110100	T	1010100	t	1110100
NAK	0010101	5	0110101	U	1010101	u	1110101
SYN	0010110	6	0110110	V	1010110	v	1110110
ETB	0010111	7	0110111	W	1010111	w	1110111
CAN	0011000	8	0111000	X	1011000	x	1111000
EM	0011001	9	0111001	Y	1011001	y	1111001
SUB	0011010	:	0111010	Z	1011010	z	1111010
ESC	0011011	;	0111011	[	1011011	{	1111011
FS	0011100	<	0111100	\	1011100	|	1111100
GS	0011101	=	0111101	]	1011101	}	1111101
RS	0011110	>	0111110	^	1011110	~	1111110
US	0011111	?	0111111	_	1011111	del	1111111

Figure 3.2: ASCII codes

Representing numbers

Using ASCII, each character has a corresponding code, so that if for example the 'A' key on the keyboard is pressed, the code '01000001' will be sent to the CPU. If the key '1' is pressed, the code '00110001' will be sent to the CPU. To print the number '123', the codes for 1, 2 and 3 would be sent to the printer.

This is fine for input and output, but useless for arithmetic. There is no easy way of adding two numbers held in this way, and furthermore they occupy a great deal of space. Numbers which are to be used in calculations are therefore held in a different format, as **binary numbers**.

Before we look at the binary system, it is helpful to examine how our ordinary decimal or **denary** number system works. Consider for example the number '134'. These three digits represent one hundred, three tens and four ones.

i.e.

100	10	1	
1	3	4	This represents 100 + 30 + 4 = 134

As we move from right to left each digit is worth ten times as much as the previous one. We probably use a **base 10** number system because we have ten fingers, but essentially there is no reason why some other base such as 8 or 16 could not be used.

In the binary system, as we move from right to left each digit is worth twice as much as the previous one. Thus the binary number 10000110 can be set out under column headings as follows:

128	64	32	16	8	4	2	1	
1	0	0	0	0	1	1	0	This represents 128 + 4 + 2 = 134

Q2: Convert the following binary numbers to decimal:

0011   0110   1010   01000001   01000101

Q3: Convert the following numbers to binary:

5   7   1   26   68   137

Q4: What is the largest binary number that can be held in
(i) 8 bits?   (ii) 16 bits?   (iii) 24 bits?   (iv) 32 bits?

Obviously, using only one byte (8 bits) to hold a number places a severe restriction on the size of number the computer can hold. Therefore four or more consecutive bytes are commonly used to store numbers.

Memory addressing

The main memory of a computer can be thought of as a series of boxes, each containing 8 bits (1 byte), and each with its own unique address, counting from zero upwards. The memory capacity of a computer is measured in 1024-byte units called kilobytes, megabytes or gigabytes.

These measures can be abbreviated to Kb, Mb and Gb. These are all powers of 2; thus although 1Kb is often thought of as being 1,000 bytes, it is actually 1024 bytes.

You will find it useful to memorise certain powers of 2.

2^{10} bytes = 1024 = 1Kb

2^{20} bytes = 1024 x 1024 = 1Mb

2^{30} bytes = 1024 x 1024 x 1024 = 1Gb

Word size

The **word size** of a computer is the number of bits that the CPU can process simultaneously, as opposed to the bus size, which determines how many bits are transmitted together. Processors can have 8-, 16-, 32- or 64-bit word sizes (or even larger), and the word size will be one of the factors that determine the speed of the computer. The standard PCs have 32-bit processors. Recent processor architectures provide for a 64-bit word.

1-3

Exercises

1 (a) Show how the denary (decimal) numbers 13 and 32 would be represented as 8-bit binary integers. (2)

  (b) Given that the ASCII code for the character '1' is 00110001, show how the text string '1332' would be held in a 4-byte word in a computer's memory. (1)

New Question

2 (a) What will be the highest address in a computer with
   (i) 1K of memory?
   (ii) 16K of memory?

  (b) How many Mb are 2^{24} bytes?

  (c) How many Gb are 2^{32} bytes? (4)

New Question

3 Some personal computers are referred to as 32-bit machines. This means their word length is 32 bits.

  (a) What is a word in this context? (1)

  (b) State the different values for one bit. (1)

  (c) Give three different interpretations which can be associated with a pattern of bits in a 32-bit word. (3)

AQA CPT1 Qu 2 Jan 2002

Chapter 4 – Data Representation (Text and Numbers)

Input-process-output

The main purpose of using computers is to process data as quickly and efficiently as possible to produce useful information.

Computers read incoming data called input, process this data and display or print information called output.

Data: The raw facts and figures that a computer accepts as input and then processes to produce useful information.

A stream of data such as 44, 45, 66, 82, 77, 67 has no meaning until it is processed by the appropriate program and information produced. The numbers could represent the marks of 6 students, the number of computers sold by a manufacturer in the past 6 months (in thousands), the weekly hours of sunshine in the past 6 weeks.

Sources of data

Data can be collected from many sources, either directly or indirectly. Data that is collected for a specific purpose is said to be collected **directly**. For example, the times at which an employee clocks in and out may be collected by punching a time card, and this data is used in the calculation of the weekly pay packet. Similarly, when a library book is borrowed, data about the book and the borrower is collected by scanning the bar codes of the book and the borrower's library card. This data is used directly to produce information on where a particular book is.

On the other hand, information can be derived from data that was originally collected for a completely different purpose – in other words, collected **indirectly**. For example a credit card company collects data about each transaction or purchase made so that the customer can be billed at the end of the month. This is the direct collection of data. At a later date, the data may be used to build a profile of the customer – perhaps how often they use their credit card for holiday travel, for example. The company could sell a list of all well-travelled customers to a travel company who would use it in a direct mail advertising campaign. This is the **indirect** collection of data – use of the data for a purpose other than the one for which it was originally collected.

Q1: Think of several examples of data that is originally collected for one purpose, and then used for additional purposes.

Information: Any form of communication that provides understandable and useful knowledge to the recipient, such as a bar chart of examination grades achieved by a group of students.

Data can be seen as an encoded form of information. For example, an estate agent may collect information about the type of house a client is looking for. This information may be coded before being stored in a computer system: D for detached house, S for Semi-detached house, B for bungalow, LG for large garden, MG medium-sized garden, SG for small garden. The advantage of encoding information in such a way is that less storage space is needed and it is easy to specify search conditions. However, the user needs a list of valid codes and there may be a loss of precision of information. If all the houses the agent has for sale are coded in a similar manner, we may lose the precise size of the garden because the coding only groups the gardens into large, medium or small.

Character coding schemes

In Chapter 3 the ACSII coding scheme was described. This is a 7- or 8-bit code for representing characters and is used by almost all PCs.

Unicode is an international 16-bit coding scheme which can represent 65536 different characters. This is sufficient to represent all the characters in any language or script from ancient Egyptian hieroglyphics to Chinese, Russian, Greek, Japanese or Urdu, to name but a few.

The binary number system

You met binary numbers briefly in Chapter 3, so this is by way of a little recap.

A number such as 1, 25, 378 etc. can be represented in a computer in many different ways. It can be held as a number of characters so that, for example, the number 25 is coded in ASCII as 0011 0010 0011 0101 (refer to Figure 3.2 in Chapter 3). Alternatively, it can be held as a **pure binary integer**.

To translate 25 from decimal to binary, you can draw a table of powers of 2. Then find the largest power of 2 that is less than or equal to 25 (16 in this case). Subtract 16 from 25 and repeat. You end up with

128	64	32	16	8	4	2	1	
0	0	0	1	1	0	0	1	16+8+1 = 25

To translate from binary to decimal, perform the process backwards. Put each binary digit under the correct heading in the table. For example, to translate 01000101 into decimal, arrange the digits in the table as follows:

128	64	32	16	8	4	2	1	
0	1	0	0	0	1	0	1	64+4+1 = 69

The representation of negative numbers, numbers with decimal points and binary arithmetic will be covered in Section 4.

Q2: (i) Translate the number 227 into binary.
(ii) Translate the binary number 1011 0111 into denary (i.e. a decimal number).

Binary Coded Decimal (BCD)

In the BCD system each decimal digit is represented by its own 4-bit binary code.

Decimal	Binary
0	0000
1	0001
2	0010
3	0011
4	0100
5	0101
6	0110
7	0111
8	1000
9	1001

The number 3765 is coded as 0011 0111 0110 0101.

Q3: (i) Write down the BCD representation of 2906.

(ii) Translate the BCD number 0110 0111 1001 0011 into denary (i.e. a decimal number).

Advantages and disadvantages of BCD

The advantage of the BCD representation is the ease of conversion from BCD to decimal and vice versa. For example, when binary numbers have to be electronically decoded for a pocket calculator display, a number held in BCD format simply has to be split into groups of four bits and each group converted directly to the corresponding decimal digit.

When storing fractional numbers, a further advantage of the BCD representation is that since each decimal digit is encoded separately, using as many bits as necessary to represent the complete number exactly, no 'rounding' of numbers occurs. Hence BCD arithmetic is used in business applications where every significant digit has to be retained in a result.

A disadvantage of using BCD is that more bits are required to store a number than when using pure binary. Another disadvantage of BCD is that calculations with such numbers are more complex than with pure binary numbers. For example, try adding the BCD representations of 1 and 19:

We get   0000 0001

0001 1001
_____

0001 1010   The first digit, 1, is wrong and 1010 is an invalid code!

The problem arises because only the first ten out of sixteen combinations of four digits are used to encode the decimal symbols '0' to '9'. Therefore, whenever the sum of two binary digits is greater than 9, 6 has to be added to the result in order to skip over the six unused codes. Adding the binary representation for 6 to 1010:

0001   1010

0110
_____

0010   0000   i.e. 20 in BCD which is the correct answer.

Boolean values

So far we have seen how a given binary pattern could represent an ASCII character, a binary integer, or a number held in BCD. A Boolean variable (named after the English mathematician George Boole) is one that can only have one of two values, **true** or **false**, represented by 1 and 0, or 0 and –1. There are many occasions when it is useful to use one binary digit to show whether something is true or false. For example, a particular bit in memory can be set to show whether a disk drive is connected, another can be set if the 'Break' key is pressed, and yet another set if overflow occurs during an arithmetic operation. Single bits used in this way are called **flags**.

Exercises

1 (a) Data can be stored inside a computer system in several different representations. The number 25 is to be stored in a 16-bit word

What is the bit pattern if the number 25 is to be stored as

(i) a pure binary integer; (1)

(ii) a BCD (Binary Coded Decimal)? (1)

(b) The ASCII code for the character '3' is the decimal number 51.

(i) What is the ASCII code for the character '5'? (1)

(ii) If eight bits are used to store one character, what is the bit pattern when the string '25' is stored in a 16-bit word? (2)

AQA CPT1 Qu 4 Jan 2002

2 (a) Bit patterns can be interpreted in a number of different ways. A computer word contains the bit pattern 0101 1001. What is its decimal value if it represents:

(i) a pure binary integer; (1)

(ii) a BCD (Binary Coded Decimal)? (1)

(b) A binary pattern in a 16-bit word can represent different forms of information, such as pure binary or BCD, as above, or two ASCII characters.

Name **three** different forms of information, excluding those given above. (3)

AQA CPT1 Qu 9 Jan 2001

3 Members of the public can register with a video club after supplying name and address and proof of identity. Every registered member is issued with a membership card. Each time a member borrows a video, data about the video and the borrower are collected, by scanning the barcodes on the video box and on the membership card.

(a) Sources of data can be *direct* and *indirect*. Complete the table below with the correct type of source.

	Direct / Indirect
(i) The data collected above is used to record where a particular video is.	
(ii) The data collected above is used to build up a profile of the members for targeted advertising.	

(b) What is the difference between data and information? (2)

AQA CPT1 Qu 8 Jan 2003

1-4

Chapter 5 – Data Representation (Sound and Graphics)

Digital audio

Sound such as music or speech can be input via a microphone, to be processed by a computer. Since sound waves are continuously variable or **analogue** in nature, an **analogue to digital converter** is needed to transform the analogue input to a **digital** form, i.e. a binary pattern, so that it can be stored and processed. Undesirable sounds such as wrong notes or scratches on an old recording can be edited out before a new digital version is produced.

Sound in analogue form may be represented by wave forms. The height of these wave forms can be sampled at regularly spaced time intervals, with the height being represented by, say, a 16-bit code. The more frequently the samples are taken, the more faithfully the sound will be represented. (See Figure 5.1) Each sample represents the intensity of the sound pressure wave at that instant. Digital audio is typically created by taking 16-bit samples over a spectrum of 44.1KHz. Stereo sound doubles the number of samples taken, with 44,100 samples per second taking 32 bits each. This means that CD quality sound requires 1.4 million bits of data per second.

Sampling resolution: The number of bits used to store one sound sample.

The quality of sound produced using a sound sampler depends on the sampling rate and the sampling resolution.

Sampling rate: The frequency at which samples are taken.

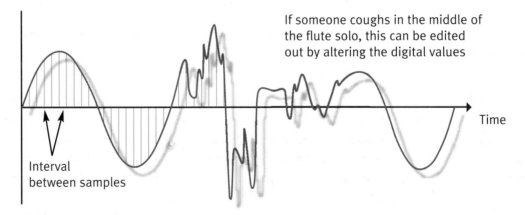

Figure 5.1: Converting sound from analogue to digital form

The sound wave can be recreated from the digital data by a digital-to-analogue (D-A) converter.

Sound Synthesis (Sound generation)

Sounds may be generated using either analogue or digital techniques. Digital sound generation is a recent development in which numbers representing sound waves are manipulated. There are several different methods. One such method uses sampled sounds as well as pure tones and arithmetic operations are carried out on the bit patterns representing the sounds.

Bit-mapped graphics

In a bit-mapped system for displaying text and graphics on a VDU, the screen is divided up into a grid, and each square on the grid is called a **pixel** (picture element). A low resolution screen may have 320 by 240 pixels, and a high resolution screen may have 1280 by 1024 pixels or more. A monochrome screen will need just one bit in memory to represent each pixel; if the bit is 1, the pixel is on, and if it is 0, the pixel is off. On a colour screen, each pixel may correspond to one byte in memory, giving a possible 256 colours for each pixel. Two bytes per pixel gives a possible 64K different colours. The memory used is additional to the RAM used for programs and data; it is supplied on a graphics 'card' specific to the type of screen.

If the screen were magnified you would be able to see the individual pixels. The more pixels to the square inch, the higher the resolution and the smoother the image.

Figure 5.2: An image on the screen is composed of thousands of pixels

Digital images

Pixel: The smallest resolvable rectangular area of an image.

A digital image is composed of pixels arranged in a rectangular array with a certain height and width. A bitmap is characterised by the width and height of the image in pixels and the number of bits per pixel, which determines the number of shades of grey, or colours it can represent. In a colour image, each pixel has its own colour, based on the level of the primary colours red, green and blue required to produce the colour. A 24-bit bitmap will use one byte for each of the red, green and blue intensities.

There are many formats used to store images in files, including BMP, GIF, TIFF and JPEG.

Images are usually taken from the real world via a digital camera or scanner, or they may be generated by computer.

Bit-mapped graphics become ragged when you re-size them. Programs that enable you to manipulate bit-mapped images are called Paint programs.

Bit-mapped images are sometimes called raster graphics.

1-5

Vector Graphics

Images are represented as mathematical formulae that define all the shapes in the image such as lines, polygons and text.

For example, a straight line is described by its features: start and end point co-ordinates, length, thickness, colour.

Vector graphics are more flexible than bit-mapped graphics because they look the same even when you scale them to different sizes. It is also easier to render an object. Almost all sophisticated graphics systems, including CAD systems and animation software, use vector graphics. Fonts represented with vector graphics are called scalable fonts or vector fonts. One very well known system is PostScript. Vector graphics often require less memory than bit-mapped images.

Programs that enable you to create and manipulate vector graphics are called Draw programs.

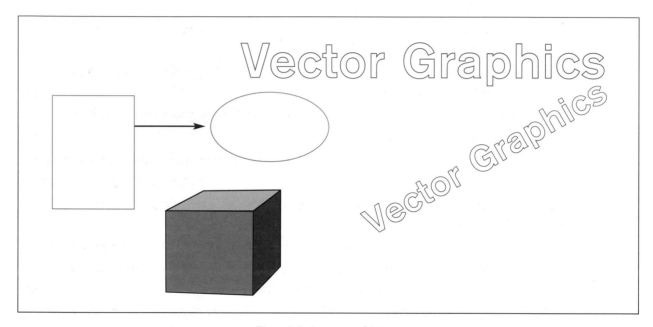

Figure 5.3: A vector graphic image

Note that most output devices such as display monitors and laser printers are raster devices (plotters use vector graphics). This means that all vector graphics must be translated into bitmaps before being output. The difference between vector graphics and raster graphics is that vector graphics are not translated into bitmaps until the last possible moment, after all sizes and resolutions have been specified. This results in a better quality image.

Exercises

1   State **four** different possible interpretations of a given bit pattern in a
    computer's memory.   (4)

New Question

2   Music is often recorded digitally. Describe briefly **two** advantages of this
    method of representing sound.   (2)

New Question

3   Bit patterns can be interpreted in a number of different ways. A computer
    word contains the bit pattern 0011 0110.

    (a)   What is its decimal value if it represents:

        (i) a pure binary integer   (1)

        (ii) a BCD (Binary Coded Decimal)?   (1)

    (b) Give one advantage of BCD over pure binary.   (1)

    (c) (i) The ASCII value for the character '2' is 50. What is the character stored
    in the computer word 0011 0100?   (2)

        (ii) Name **one** other standard coding system for coding information expressed
    in character or text-based form.   (1)

    (d) One method of storing graphics in a computer system is as vector graphics.

        (i) Name **one** other method.   (1)

        (ii) Describe how a black-and-white image would be stored using your method. (2)

AQA CPT1 Qu 7 May 2002

4   Computer systems store not just information representing numbers and characters,
    but also sounds and images.

    (a) A microphone converts sound into an electrical signal which may be recorded.

        (i) Explain how the electrical signal from the microphone is converted into
    a form which can be stored in a computer system   (3)

        (ii) What piece of hardware is required to convert the digitally recorded sound
    before it is amplified and played back through speakers?   (1)

    (b) Images can be stored as bit-mapped graphics or vector graphics.
    If vector graphics is used, what information will be stored to describe
    one straight line?   (2)

AQA CPT1 Qu 4 June 2003

5   Video RAM (VRAM) is separate memory on the graphics card, into which the
    processor writes screen data which are then read to the screen for display. A computer
    has a colour monitor and 1 Mb (Megabytes) of VRAM, and its screen display has been
    set to a *resolution of 1024x1024*.

    (a) Exactly how many bytes are 1Mb?   (1)

    (b) What is a pixel?   (1)

    (c) (i) What does a resolution of 1024 x 1024 mean?   (1)

        (ii) How many bytes would be available to represent each pixel in the above
    computer system?   (1)

        (iii) How many colours can this computer system display?   (1)

AQA CPT1 Qu 5 Jan 2002

1-5

Chapter 6 – Programming Concepts

The earliest computers

It is an astonishing fact that as we enter the 21st century, computers have been around for less than 60 years. Many of those who worked on the earliest computers are still alive to tell us of their experiences. If you ever get a chance to visit Bletchley Park, do not miss it – it is the location of the breaking of the Enigma code (used by the Germans to code all their most secret messages), with the aid of the first programmable computer, named Colossus, built for this purpose in 1943. A fascinating exhibition tells the story and Colossus has been reconstructed there.

Generations of programming language

Machine language – the first generation

Programming languages are often characterised by 'generation'. The first generation of computer language, known as machine code, executes directly without translation. Machine code is the actual pattern of 0s and 1s used in a computer's memory. The programming of Colossus and other early computers was laboriously done with toggle switches representing a pattern of binary codes for each instruction.

Machine language, however it is entered into a computer, is time-consuming, laborious and error-prone. Few programmers code in it today. A language suited to the particular application would be used instead.

Assembly code – the second generation

In the 1950s when computers were first used commercially, machine code gave way to **assembly code**, which allowed programmers to use mnemonics (abbreviations that represent the instructions in a more memorable way) and denary numbers (i.e. 0–9) instead of 0s and 1s. Thus ADD or ADX might be an instruction to add two numbers, SUB or SBX an instruction to subtract.

Programs written in assembly languages have to be translated into machine code before they can be executed, using a program called an **assembler**. There is more or less a one-to-one correspondence between each assembly code statement and its equivalent machine code statement, which means that programs can be written in the most efficient way possible, occupying as little space as possible and executing as fast as possible. For this reason assembly code is still used for applications where timing or storage space is critical. Assembly languages are called **low level** languages because they are close to machine code and the detail of the computer architecture.

Since different types of computer have different instruction sets, which depend on how the machine carries out the instructions, both machine code and assembly code are machine-dependent – each type of computer will have its own assembly language.

```
         LOAD    A, #0              \Load register A with 0
         LOAD    X, #8              \Load index register with 8
LOOP:    SUB     X, #1              \Subtract 1 from index register
         STORE   X, (&50000), A     \Store contents of A in location
                                    \50000 indexed by contents of X
         BNE     X, LOOP            \Branch if not zero to LOOP
         HALT                       \Stop execution
```

Figure 6.1: Part of an assembly code program

Imperative high level languages – the third generation

As computer use increased dramatically in the 1950s, the need grew to make it easier and faster to write error-free programs. Computer manufacturers and user groups started to develop so-called **high-level languages** such as Algol (standing for ALGOrithmic Language) and Fortran (standing for FORmula TRANslation). In the 1950s most of the people actually writing programs were scientists, mathematicians and engineers and so both these languages were created to be used in mathematical applications.

COBOL (COmmon Business Oriented Language) was invented by the redoubtable Admiral Grace Hopper in 1960 specifically for writing commercial and business, rather than scientific, programs. Whilst serving in the US Navy in 1947, Grace Hopper was investigating why one of the earliest computers was not working, and discovered a small dead moth in the machine. After removing it (and taping it in her logbook) the machine worked fine, and from then on computer errors were known as 'bugs'.

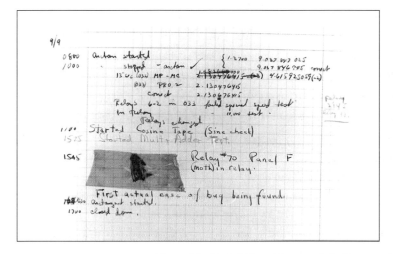

Figure 6.2: Admiral Grace Hopper and the first computer 'bug'

Other third generation languages followed: **BASIC** was created in the 1960s as a language for students to learn programming. Early versions of the language however did not contain the facilities to write well-structured programs that were easy to maintain and debug, although the language has since developed. In 1971 Nicklaus Wirth designed **Pascal** (named after the seventeenth century French mathematician) to teach structured programming to students.

High level languages are so-called because they are independent of the architecture of any particular computer; one statement written in a high level language is translated into several machine code instructions before it can be executed. The term **imperative** high level language refers to languages such as Pascal, BASIC, COBOL and Fortran – in contrast to **object-oriented** and **declarative** languages, which you will learn about in the second year of this course.

Imperative High Level Languages: The high-level language instructions are executed in a programmer-defined sequence.

Q1: Do you know the names of any other high-level languages? Why do you suppose there are so many of them?

Why use assembly code?

Assembly language, although it is laborious to write and hard to debug, is still used in some circumstances, for example:
- when there is a need for the program to execute as fast as possible;
- when the program must occupy as little space as possible;

Parts of an operating system, and device drivers that control the operation of devices such as a printer, mouse or CD-ROM may be written in assembly code. Programs in embedded systems like satellite decoders, encryption and decryption software, and routines that are called frequently from high-level programs may also be written in assembly code.

Types of program translator

There are three types of program used for translating the code that a programmer writes into a form (i.e. machine code) that the computer can execute. These are:
- assembler;
- compiler;
- interpreter.

Assembler

An assembler is a program that translates an assembly code program into machine code ready for the computer to execute it. Since each type of computer has its own assembly language, it also has its own assembler. The assembler itself could be written in assembly code or in a high level language such as C, which has special facilities useful for this type of programming.

Compiler

A compiler is a program that translates a high level language program into machine code. The Turbo Pascal compiler, for example, translates a program written in Turbo Pascal on a PC into object code, which can be run on a PC. The code written by the programmer is known as the **source code**, and the compiled code is known as the **object code**.

A compiler is a complex program which takes the source code and scans through it several times, each time performing different checks and building up tables of information needed to produce the final object code. When you write a short program, this process appears to happen almost instantaneously, but a long program of several thousand lines can take several minutes to compile.

Compiler: Translates the whole high level language source code into object code, which can then be executed without the presence of a compiler.

Interpreter

An interpreter also translates high-level source code. However the crucial difference between a compiler and an interpreter is **that an interpreter translates one line at a time and then executes it;** no object code is produced, and so the program has to be interpreted each time it is to be run. If the program performs a section of code 10,000 times, then that section of code is translated into machine code 10,000 times as each line is interpreted and then executed.

Interpreter: Analyses the source code statement by statement as execution proceeds, decoding each statement and calling routines to carry out each instruction.

Relative advantages of compilers and interpreters

A compiler has many advantages over an interpreter:

- the object code can be saved on disk and run whenever required without the need to recompile. However, if an error is discovered in the program, the whole program has to be recompiled.
- the object code executes faster than interpreted code.
- the object code produced by a compiler can be distributed or executed without having to have the compiler present.
- the object code is more secure, as it cannot be read without a great deal of 'reverse engineering'.

An interpreter has some advantages over a compiler:

- it is useful for program development as there is no need for lengthy recompilation each time an error is discovered.
- it is easier to partially test and debug programs.

Typically, a programmer might use an interpreter during program development. A program that is tested and ready for distribution would then be compiled and the saved object code would be distributed.

Features of Imperative High Level Languages

If you have chosen to do Computing rather than Information Technology, you will probably find learning to program is one of the most enjoyable parts of the course. The choice of programming language will be a matter for individual schools and colleges, and to some extent it does not matter which imperative high-level language you study. C, Basic and Pascal all have similar statements and structures.

Pascal was invented in the 1970s by Niklaus Wirth to teach structured programming. It is a good language to start with and you will find it easy to learn, say, Delphi (which is based on Pascal) or Visual Basic if you have studied Pascal.

You should have experience of using the following features in your chosen language (the example statements are given in Pascal).

Built-in data types

Integer	`var NoOfSpaces : Integer;`
Real	`var Average : Real;`
String	`var Surname : String;`
Character	`var FirstLetter : Char;`
Boolean	`var Found : Boolean;`

User-defined Types

| Records | ```
type TStudent = record
                    FirstName : String [15];
                    Surname : String [25];
                    DateOfBirth : TDateTime;
                end;
``` |
|---|---|
| Symbolic types | `type TSeason = (Spring, Summer, Autumn, Winter);` |
| Sub-range types | `type TCapitalLetter = 'A' .. 'Z'` |

Declarations

Type definitions	`type TSeason = (Spring, Summer, Autumn, Winter);`
Variable declarations	`var NoOfStars : Integer;`
| Array declarations | ```
var Total : array[1..150] of real;
var Sales : array[1..150, 1..5] of real;
``` |
| Constant definitions | `const Pi = 3.14;` |
| Procedure declarations | ```
procedure Adjust (var Spaces, Stars : Integer);
begin
    Spaces := Spaces — 1;
    Stars := Stars + 2;
end;
``` |
| Function declarations | ```
function Initial (S: String) : String;
begin
    S := LeftStr (S,1);
    Initial := Uppercase (S);
end;
``` |

Programming statements

Assignment	`Spaces := Spaces — 1;`
| Iteration | ```
for Count := 1 to 10
    do Writeln(Counter);
``` |
| Selection | ```
if Number = 0
    then Number := Number + 1
    else Number := Number — 1;
``` |
| Procedure calls | `Adjust (NoOfSpaces, NoOfStars);` |
| Function calls | `FirstLetter := Initial (Surname);` |

1-6

Advantages of using routines

Breaking down code into self-contained routines (for example, a procedure or function) aids understanding of code as statements are grouped together and given a name. This also makes testing easier as a routine can be tested in isolation before being added to a larger program. It helps trouble-shooting as a fault can be narrowed down to a particular routine. It minimises the number of statements as routines can be called from anywhere in the program any number of times. Parameters can be used to pass data within programs.

Procedures vs Functions

A function call must be part of an expression, as a value is associated with its name.
A procedure call is a statement on its own.

Exercises

1 Programming languages are subdivided into generations. An imperative high level language is a third generation language.

    (a) Name the language type for:

        (i)   first generation; (1)

        (ii) second generation. (1)

    (b) Name **one** specific example of a third generation programming language. (1)

AQA CPT1 Qu 3 January 2001

1-6

2 (a) Give **two** advantages of programming in third generation programming languages, rather than in the previous two generations. (2)

    (b) Third generation programming languages may be compiled or interpreted. Describe the process performed by

        (i)   a compiler (2)

        (ii) an interpreter. (2)

    (c) When would it be appropriate to use **each** of the following?

    In **each** case give the reason for your choice.

        (i)   a compiler (2)

        (ii) an interpreter. (2)

New Question

3 The structured approach when writing programs uses functions and procedures.

    (a) Give **two** reasons why procedures are used. (2)

    (b) What are parameters used for in the context of procedures and functions? (1)

AQA CPT1 Qu 6 May 2002

4 The following code is part of a high level language program:

```
CONST Max = 5;
VAR Tptr : INTEGER;
VAR Store : ARRAY[1..Max] OF CHAR;

PROCEDURE add (a: CHAR);
BEGIN
    IF Tptr < Max THEN
    BEGIN
       Tptr := Tptr + 1;
       Store[Tptr] := a;
    END;
END;

FUNCTION Take : CHAR;
VAR Ptr: INTEGER;
BEGIN
    IF Tptr>0 THEN
    BEGIN
       Take := Store[1];
       Tptr := Tptr-1;
       FOR Ptr := 1 TO Tptr DO store[Ptr] := store[Ptr+1]
    END;
END;
```

(a) Identify the following by copying **one** relevant statement from the above code.

(i)   constant definition (1)

(ii)   variable declaration (1)

(iii) local variable (1)

(iv)   global variable (1)

(v)   parameter (1)

(vi)   assignment statement (1)

(vii) selection statement (1)

(viii) iteration (1)

(b) Functions and procedures are both subroutines. What is a difference between a function and a procedure? (1)

AQA CPT1 Qu 7 January 2002

Chapter 7 – Program Design and Maintenance

Program design aims

Effort put into good program design can often save substantial maintenance and debugging costs later on. The aims of program design may be summarised as:

- reliability; the program must always do what it is supposed to do;
- maintainability; the program must be easy to change or modify if this becomes necessary;
- readability; the program must be easy for another programmer to read and understand;
- performance; the program must do its job fast and efficiently;
- storage saving; the program ideally must occupy as little memory as possible, especially if it is a very large program.

Top-down design

Top-down design is the technique of breaking down a problem into the major tasks to be performed; each of these tasks is then further broken down into separate subtasks, and so on until each subtask is sufficiently simple to be written as a self-contained **module** or procedure. The program then consists of a series of calls to these modules, which may themselves call other modules.

Structure charts

Before writing a program using procedures, it is useful to have some way of representing the **structure** of a program – how the modules all relate to form the whole solution – and a structure chart is one way of doing this. When a program is large and complex, it becomes especially important to plan out the solution before doing any coding, and a structure chart also serves a useful purpose as documentation when the program is complete.

The chart resembles a family tree, with the main program modules written **across** the top line.

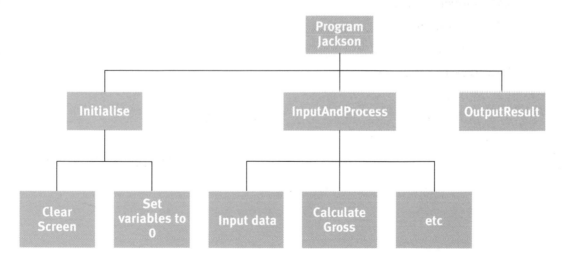

Figure 7.1: A structure chart

The building blocks of a structured program

Only three different 'building blocks' or **program constructs** are needed to write a structured program. These are

- **sequence** – in which one statement follows another and the program executes them in the sequence given
- **selection** – 'if..then..else' is an example of selection, where the next statement to be executed depends on the value of an expression
- **iteration** – a section of the program is repeated many times, as for example in the 'while..do' statement.

Notice the absence of the GO TO statement! Experience has shown that programs which are written without using GO TO statements are easier to follow, easier to debug and easier to maintain.

Programs that are written using **top-down** techniques, and using only the three constructs described, are called **structured programs**.

Representation of a loop

An asterisk in a box, with the condition written outside the box and the statements or modules within the loop written on the next level down, is used to indicate a section of code to be repeated.

```
e.g. while a<b do
        begin
            statement1
            statement2
            statement3
        end   {endwhile}
```

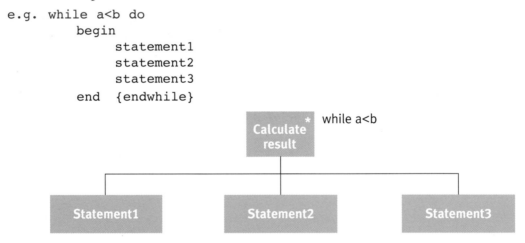

Figure 7.2: Iteration

Representation of selection

Selection is represented by a small circle in each of the boxes representing the alternative paths:

```
if (answer='Y') or (answer='y') then
        statement 1
else
        statement 2
```

Figure 7.3: Selection

1-7

The structure chart can also be used to show what parameters will be needed to pass data between procedures. This is the data interface.

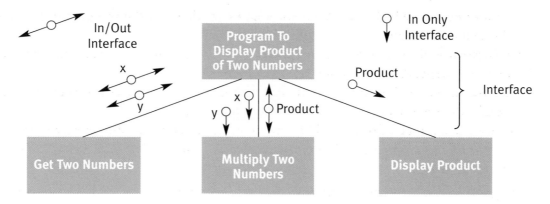

Figure 7.4: Structure Chart showing the data interface

Structure charts, in addition to interfaces may have control information placed on them. (A hierarchy chart is a chart without interface and control information).

Example:

Draw a structure chart and code a program to input a number of sales transaction records each of which contains a salesperson's number (between 1 and 3) and a sales amount in £. Accumulate the total sales for each salesperson and the total overall sales, and output these figures at the end of the program.

The structure chart can be drawn as follows:

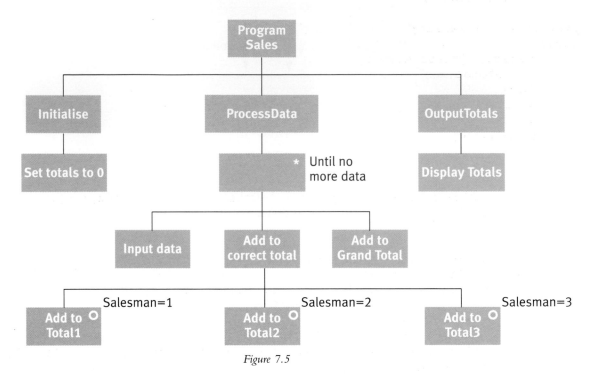

Figure 7.5

A guideline for drawing structure charts is that you should not put boxes representing loops (i.e. boxes containing asterisks) on the same level as other types of boxes. This is why in the diagram above, the box containing the asterisk appears **below** the 'ProcessData' box.

The same guideline applies to boxes containing circles representing selection; **all** the boxes on the same level must be 'selection' boxes if any of them are.

Q1: Compare the structure chart above with the coding on the next page. What details of the procedure **ProcessData** have been omitted from the structure chart? Do you think the omissions matter?

```pascal
program Sales;
{program to accumulate sales totals for three salesmen}

uses crt;    {calls in Turbo Pascal's library routines}

var
    GrandTotal, Total1, Total2, Total3, Amount: real;
    Salesman: Integer;

procedure Initialise;
begin
     Clrscr; {clear screen}
     GrandTotal:=0;
     Total1:=0;
     Total2:=0;
     Total3:=0;
end; {procedure}

procedure ProcessData;
begin
     write('Please enter salesperson''s number (0 to finish): ');
     readln(Salesman);
     while Salesman<>0 do
        begin
           write('Enter sales amount: ');
           readln(Amount);
           if (salesman=1) then Total1:=Total1+amount;
           if (salesman=2) then Total2:=Total2+amount;
           if (salesman=3) then Total3:=Total3+amount;
           GrandTotal:=GrandTotal + Amount;
           write('Please enter next salesperson''s number (0 to finish): ');
           readln(Salesman)
        end
     {endwhile}
end;  {procedure}

procedure OutputTotals;
begin
     writeln;
     writeln('Total for salesperson 1: ',Total1:8:2);
     writeln('Total for salesperson 2: ',Total2:8:2);
     writeln('Total for salesperson 3: ',Total3:8:2);
     writeln('Grand Total of all sales: ',GrandTotal:8:2)
end;  {procedure}



{***** MAIN PROGRAM ******}

begin
     Initialise;
     ProcessData;
     OutputTotals
end.
```

Pseudocode

Structure diagrams are one way of developing a solution to a problem, and they are useful in implementing a top-down approach. If, however, we try to write down all the details of every module in a structure diagram, it becomes unwieldy. It is most useful in specifying the structure of a program down to the module level.

Pseudocode provides a means of expressing algorithms without worrying about the syntax of a particular language. (An **algorithm** is a sequence of instructions for solving a problem.)

Typical pseudocode constructs include the following:

```
If .. Then .. Else .. EndIf
Case .. Of .. EndCase
For .. To .. EndFor
Repeat .. Until ..
While .. Do .. EndWhile
Procedure .. EndProc
Function .. EndFun
```

There are no hard and fast rules as to how pseudocode statements should be written; an assignment statement to assign the value 10 to X, for example, could be written in any of the following ways:

```
Assign 10 to X
X ← 10
X:=10;
Put 10 in X
```

Example:

Write pseudocode for an algorithm to find the maximum, minimum and average of a set of marks.

```
Procedure FindMaxMark
begin
    set max no. of marks and total to zero
    set min to 100
    read the first mark
    while not end of data
      if mark > max then set max = mark
      endif
      if mark < min then set min = mark
      endif
      add mark to total
      add 1 to no. of marks
      read the next mark
    endwhile
    calculate average
    print results
end procedure
```

Note that

- keywords such as **begin**, **end**, **while**, **endwhile**, **if**, and **endif** mark the limits of procedures, loops and conditional statements;
- the actual statements of the algorithm can be written in ordinary English;
- the indentation is important – it gives a visual picture of the extent of loops and conditional statements.

As stated above, there are no absolute rules for writing pseudocode; for example both versions of the **repeat** construct shown below would be quite acceptable:

```
repeat until end of data
       statements
       .....
       .....
       .....
end repeat

repeat
       statements
       .....
       .....
       .....
until end of data
```

Modular programming

Any programs that you write for this course are likely to be relatively short; however, in industry and commerce most problems will require thousands, if not tens of thousands, of lines of code to solve. Windows 2000, at 35 million lines of code, is the biggest program ever written. The importance of splitting up the problem into a series of self-contained modules then becomes obvious. A module should not exceed 100 or so lines, and preferably be short enough to fit on a single page; some modules may be only a few lines.

Advantages of modular programming

1 Some modules will be standard procedures used again and again in different programs or parts of the same program; for example, a routine to display a standard opening screen.

2 A module is small enough to be understandable as a unit of code. It is therefore easier to understand and debug, especially if its purpose is clearly defined and documented.

3 Program **maintenance** becomes easier because the affected modules can be quickly identified and changed.

4 In a very large project, several programmers may be working on a single program. Using a modular approach, each programmer can be given a specific set of modules to work on. This enables the whole program to be finished sooner.

5 More experienced programmers can be given the more complex modules to write, and the junior programmers can work on the simpler modules.

6 Modules can be tested independently, thereby shortening the time taken to get the whole program working.

7 If a programmer leaves part way through a project, it is easier for someone else to take over a set of self-contained modules.

8 A large project becomes easier to monitor and control.

1-7

Exercises

1 (a) Programmers are encouraged to adopt a structured approach to writing programs. One reason is so that programmers can write code which can be more easily understood by another programmer.

Explain **two** other reasons. (4)

(b) Give **three** features of an imperative high level programming language which allow programmers to write "easy-to-understand" code. (3)

(c) Distinguish between a compiler and an interpreter. (2)

AQA CPT1 Qu 4 May 2001

2 The following pseudocode represents a program that reads 5 numbers entered by a user and outputs the sum.

```
Program Add
Table[5] : Array of Real
Sum : Real
Call Procedure Read5Numbers(Table)
Call Procedure CalculateSum(Table, Sum)
Call Procedure Display(Sum)
```

(a) (i) Name a parameter used in the above program. (1)

(ii) Explain how this parameter is used. (1)

(b) Draw a structure chart to represent the above program. (2)

New Question

Chapter 8 – Dry-run Exercises

Trace tables

When a program is not working correctly (perhaps producing a wrong answer, or getting into an infinite loop), it is useful to trace through the program manually, writing down the values of the variables as they change. The variable names can be written as column headings and their values underneath the headings to form a trace table. Being able to trace manually through the steps of a program is an essential skill in program debugging.

Example:

Use a trace table to show the values of the variables **StudentMark**, **TotalMark**, **NoOfMarks** and **Average** when the program **MarkAvg** is run (see below). You may assume that the user enters the marks 7, 5, 9, -1.

```
Program MarkAvg(input,output);
   {program to calculate average of a set of students' marks}
   var
      StudentMark, TotalMark, NoOfMarks: integer;
      Average:real;

   Procedure Initialise;
   begin
        NoOfMarks := 0;
        TotalMark := 0;
   end; {end of procedure}


Procedure InputAndProcess;
begin
     write('Please enter the first mark, -1 to end: ');
     readln(StudentMark);
     while StudentMark <> -1 do
     begin
        TotalMark := TotalMark+StudentMark;
        NoOfMarks := NoOfMarks + 1;
        write('Please enter the next mark, -1 to end: ');
        readln(StudentMark)
     end; {endwhile}
end;      {end of procedure}

Procedure OutputResult;
begin
     Average := TotalMark / NoOfMarks;
     writeln('Average mark is ',Average:5:2);
     writeln('Total number of students: ',NoOfMarks:3)
end; {end of procedure}

{******   MAIN PROGRAM  - EXECUTION STARTS HERE   *******}
begin
    Initialise;
    InputAndProcess;
    OutputResult
end.
```

Answer:

Take a look at the program and write down the variable names across the page. The order is not particularly important; in the example below, they have been written in the order in which they will first be encountered. Then start at the first instruction in the main program and trace the instructions in the order that the computer will execute them.

NoOfMarks	TotalMark	StudentMark	Average
0	0	7	?
1	7	5	
2	12	9	
3	21	-1	7

Q1: The following extract from a program is intended to calculate the sum of the squares of a series of numbers entered by the user. The end of data entry is signalled by the dummy value –1. Use a trace table to find out why the program is not giving the right answer when the user enters the values 2, 5, 3, 1, –1.

The first couple of lines of the trace table have been filled in for you; Notice that a column has been allocated for the condition n <> –1, and this can only take the values True or False.

What output would you expect the program to produce if it was working correctly?

```
n:=0;
total:=0;
while n<>-1 do
begin
    write ('Please enter a number');
    readln(n);
    total:=total+n*n;
end; {while}
writeln('Total=',n:8:2);
```

n	n*n	total	n<>-1
0	0	0	True
2	4	4	True

Exercises

1   Use a trace table to show the values of var1, n and the condition n < 5 when the following statements are executed:

```
var1 ← 3
n ← 0
while n < 5 do
   begin
      var1 ← var1 + n
      n ← n + 1
   end;
```

var1	n	n < 5

(5)

New Question

2   The operators DIV and MOD perform integer arithmetic.

x DIV y calculates how many times y divides into x, for example 7 DIV 3 = 2.

x MOD y calculates the remainder that results after the division, for example 7 MOD 3 = 1.

(a)   The following algorithm uses an array Result. Dry run this algorithm by completing the trace table below.

```
x ← 5
Index ← 0
REPEAT
    y ← x MOD 2
    x ← x DIV 2
    Index ← Index + 1
    Result[Index] ← y
UNTIL x=0
```

y	x	Index	Result		
			[3]	[2]	[1]
-	5	0	-	-	-
1	2	1	-	-	1

(6)

(b)   What is the purpose of this algorithm?   (1)

AQA CPT1 Qu 8 May 2002

1-8

3 (a) A unique numerical code, occupying a single byte, is generated for each key pressed on a computer's keyboard. What is meant by a byte?   (1)

  (b) In one coding system, the character digits 0 to 9 are assigned the decimal number codes 48 to 57 and the letters A to Z the decimal number codes 65 to 90.

     Which keys produce the following codes?

     (i) 0100 0001   (1)

     (ii) 0011 1001   (1)

  (c) A number is entered at the keyboard as a sequence of character digits. This sequence is processed to convert the code representation into its decimal integer value using the following algorithm:

$$Number \leftarrow 0$$

While more character digits Do

    get next character digit

    and store its ASCII code in the variable Code

    $Number \leftarrow Number * 10 + Code - 48$

EndWhile

Complete the trace table for the sequence 7321.

Code	Number
-	0
55	7

(6)

AQA CPT1 Qu 3 May 2001

4   The algorithm below re-arranges numbers stored in a one-dimensional array called **List**.

Ptr is an integer variable used as an index (subscript) which identifies elements within **List**.

Temp is a variable, which is used as a temporary store for numbers from **List**.

```
Ptr ← 1
While Ptr < 10 Do
    If List [Ptr] > List [Ptr+1] Then
        Temp ← List [Ptr]
        List [Ptr] ← List [Ptr+1]
        List [Ptr+1] ← Temp
    Endif
    Ptr ← Ptr+1
Endwhile
```

(a)   Dry-run the algorithm by completing the table below.

It is only necessary to show those numbers which change at a particular step.

Ptr	Temp	List									
		[1]	[2]	[3]	[4]	[5]	[6]	[7]	[8]	[9]	[10]
		43	25	37	81	18	70	64	96	52	4

1-8

(7)

(b)   What will happen when **Ptr**=10?   (1)

(c)   If the whole algorithm is now applied to this rearranged list, what will be the values of:

(i)   List[1]

(ii)   List[9]

(iii) List[10] ?   (3)

AQA CPT1 Qu 10 Jan 2003

Chapter 9 – Queues and Stacks

Introduction to data structures

All data processing on a computer involves the manipulation of data. This data can be organised in the computer's memory in different ways according to how it is to be processed, and the different methods of organising data are known as **data structures**.

Computer languages such as Pascal have built-in **elementary data types** (such as *integer*, *real*, *Boolean* and *char*) and some built-in **structured** or **composite** data types (data structures) such as *record*, *array* and *string*. These composite data types are made up of a number of elements of a specified type such as *integer* or *real*.

Some data structures such as queues, stacks and binary trees are not built into the language and have to be constructed by the programmer. These are known as Abstract Data Types (ADT). In this module it is only necessary to recognize the different data structures and use them in simple ways. In the second year of the course you will learn how to implement them.

Queues

A queue is a First In First Out (FIFO) data structure. New elements may only be added to the end of a queue, and elements may only be retrieved from the front of a queue. The sequence of data items in a queue is determined, therefore, by the order in which they are inserted. The size of the queue depends on the number of items in it, just like a queue at the cinema or supermarket checkout.

Queues are used in a variety of applications.

• Output waiting to be printed is commonly stored in a queue on disk. In a room full of networked computers, several people may send work to be printed at more or less the same time. By putting the output into a queue on disk, the output is printed on a first come, first served basis as soon as the printer is free.

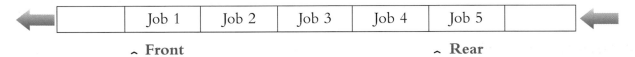

    ⌃ Front   **⌃ Rear**

Pointers mark the front and rear of the queue.

> **Q1:** What will the queue look like when 4 jobs have been printed and 2 new jobs, Job 6 and Job 7, have joined the queue? Remember to mark in the pointers Front and Rear.

• Characters typed at a keyboard are held in a queue in a keyboard buffer.
• Jobs waiting to be run by the computer may be held in a queue.
• Queues are also useful in simulation problems. A simulation program is one, which attempts to model a real-life situation so as to learn something about it. An example is a program that simulates customers arriving at random times at the check-outs in a supermarket store, and taking random times to pass through the checkout. With the aid of a simulation program, the optimum number of check-out counters can be established.

Stacks

A stack is a particular kind of sequence that may only be accessed at one end, known as the top of the stack (like plates on a pile in a cafeteria).

Only two operations can be carried out on a stack. **Adding** a new item involves placing it on top of the stack (**pushing** or stacking the item). **Removing** an item involves the removal of the item that was most recently added (**popping** the stack). The stack is a **LIFO** structure – **Last In, First Out**.

Note that items do not move up and down as the stack is pushed and popped. Instead, the position of the top of the stack changes. A pointer called a stack pointer indicates the position of the top of the stack:

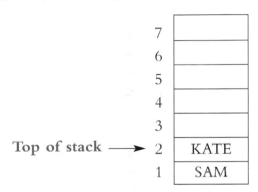

1-9

> **Q2:** Show the state of the stack and stack pointer after each of the following operations:
> - (i) Initialise the stack
> - (ii) Add ELAINE
> - (iii) Add HOWARD
> - (iv) Remove one item
> - (v) Add MICHAEL
> - (vi) Add TAMARA

Implementation of a stack

A stack can be represented in memory by an array and two additional integer variables, one holding the size of the array (i.e. the maximum size of the stack) and one holding the pointer to the top of the stack (**Top**). **Top** will initially be set to 0, representing an empty stack.

Applications of stacks

Stacks are very important data structures in computing. They are used in calculations, translating from one computer language to another, and transferring control from one part of a program to another.

Using a stack to reverse the elements of a queue

The elements of a queue can be reversed by pushing them one by one on to the stack, and then popping them one by one and replacing them in the queue. For example:

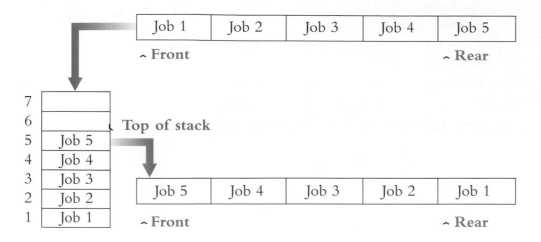

Overflow and Underflow

A queue or a stack may have a maximum size. An attempt to add a new element to a queue or stack which is already full will result in an **overflow** error. An attempt to remove an item from an empty queue or stack will result in an **underflow** error.

Exercises

1 With the aid of a clearly labelled diagram which includes a stack pointer, describe how a previously empty stack would hold these names arriving in the given sequence:

Shane, Eithne, Greta, Petroc, Abdul

Show what the stack would then contain if three of these names were popped (retrieved) from it, and two more names (**Simon** and **Jasmine**) were pushed (added). (4)

New Question

2 With the aid of a clearly labelled diagram which includes front and rear pointers, describe how a previously empty queue would hold these names arriving in the given sequence:

Phil, Trevor, Anna, Laura, Gary

Show what the queue would then contain if two of these names were retrieved from it, and one more name (**Sue**) was added. (4)

New Question

3 (a) An example of an iteration in Pascal is:

FOR x := 1 TO 10 DO writeln ('Hello');

In a high level programming language you are familiar with, using the correct syntax, give an example of:

(i) declaration; (2)

(ii) assignment; (1)

(iii) selection. (2)

(b) A one-dimensional array q contains the following characters:

q

D	[5]
K	[4]
C	[3]
T	[2]
M	[1]

(i) Dry run the following algorithm, recording your results in the diagram.

```
FOR pointer ← 1 to 5
    s[pointer]← q[pointer]
END FOR
pointer1 ← 1
pointer2 ← 5
REPEAT
    q[pointer1]← s[pointer2]
    pointer1 ← pointer1 + 1
    pointer2 ← pointer2 – 1
UNTIL pointer2 = 0
```

q

D	[5]
K	[4]
C	[3]
T	[2]
M	[1]

s

D	[5]
K	[4]
C	[3]
T	[2]
M	[1]

q

M	[5]
T	[4]
C	[3]
K	[2]
D	[1]

(10)

(ii) What is the purpose of the above algorithm? (1)

AQA CPT1 Qu 10 January 2001

4   A stack is an abstract data type that is often known as a LIFO data type. A stack with a single element 7 may be drawn as follows:

(a)   What is meant by LIFO?   (1)

(b)   A stack has two operations, **Push** and **Pop**. **Push x** adds item **x** to the stack. **Pop** removes one item from the stack. A number of operations are performed, **in sequence**, on the stack drawn above. Using the stack diagrams below show the effect of this sequence of operations.

(i) Push 8   (1)

(ii) Push 3   (1)

(iii) Pop   (1)

(iv) Push 4   (1)

(c)   Give **one** example of the use of a stack.   (1)

New Question

Chapter 10 – Binary Trees

Introduction

A binary tree is a data structure consisting of a root node and zero, one or two subtrees as shown in the diagram below.

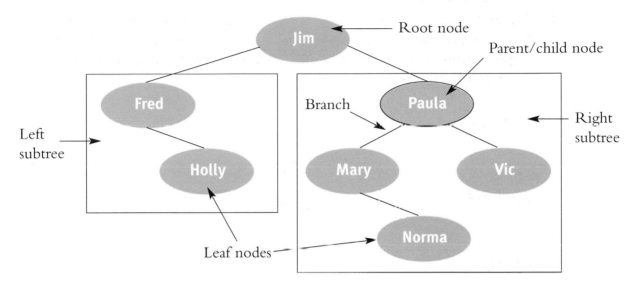

Figure 10.1: A binary tree

Note that:

- Lines connecting the nodes are called **branches** and every node except the root is joined to just one node at the higher level (its parent).
- Nodes that have no children are called **leaf nodes**.
- Some nodes may be both **parent** and **child** nodes. For example **Paula** is the child of Jim and the parent of **Mary** and **Vic**.

An ordered binary tree

A **search tree** is a particular application of a binary tree, such that a list of items held in the tree can be searched easily and quickly, new items easily added, and the whole tree printed out in sequence (alphabetic or numeric).

1-10

Constructing a binary tree

We could, for example, store a list of names (and, say, telephone numbers or other data as required) in a binary tree. Take the following list of names:

Long, Charlesworth, Illman, Hawthorne, Todd, Youngman, Jones, Ravage.

In order to create a binary tree that can be quickly searched for a given name, we follow the rules:

- Place the first item in the root.
- Take each subsequent item in turn.
- Start at the root each time. If the item is less than the root, branch to the left and if it is greater than the root, branch to the right.
- Apply the rule at each node encountered.

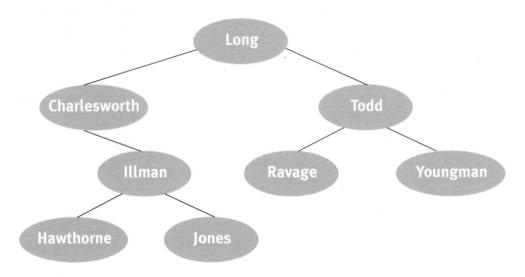

Figure 10.2: Items in an ordered binary tree

Exercises

1 A binary search tree is a data structure where items of data are held such that they can be searched for quickly and easily.

The following data items are to be entered into a binary search tree in the order given:

London, Paris, Rome, Berlin, Amsterdam, Lisbon, Madrid.

(a) Draw a diagram to show how these values will be stored.   (4)

(b) Circle the root node in your diagram.   (1)

(c) If Madrid is being searched for in this binary tree, list the data items which have to be accessed.   (1)

AQA CPT1 Qu 8 May 2001

2 (a) The series of characters J, F, H, U, S, X, T are to be entered into a binary search tree in the order given. Draw a diagram to show how these values will be stored.   (4)

   (b) The following data are held in arrays Data, L and R:

Data

'J'	'F'	'H'	'U'	'S'	'X'	'T'
[1]	[2]	[3]	[4]	[5]	[6]	[7]

L

2	0	0	5	0	0	0
[1]	[2]	[3]	[4]	[5]	[6]	[7]

R

4	3	0	6	7	0	0
[1]	[2]	[3]	[4]	[5]	[6]	[7]

Using the arrays above, dry-run the following pseudo-code by completing the trace table:

```
Item  ←  "T"
Ptr  ←  1
WHILE Data[Ptr] < > Item DO
    PRINT Data[Ptr]
    IF Data[Ptr] > Item
        THEN Ptr  ←  L[Ptr]
        ELSE Ptr  ←  R[Ptr]
    ENDIF
ENDWHILE
PRINT Data[Ptr]
```

Trace Table:

Item	Ptr	Printed Output
'T'	1	'J'

(6)

AQA CPT1 Qu 10 Jan 2002

Chapter 11 – Inside the Computer

Introduction

A computer system is composed of both internal and external components. In this chapter we'll look in more detail at the computer's **internal components** and how programs and data are stored.

The internal components are contained in the **Central Processing Unit** (CPU). The terminology here is vague and often ambiguous: the term CPU is sometimes used to mean the actual processor unit which carries out the fetching, decoding and executing of instructions. Other times it is used in a broader sense as the unit which houses the components shown in Figure 11.1:

- The processor;
- Main memory;
- I/O controllers, some of which may be input only, some output only, some both input and output;
- Buses.

The **external components** are also known as **peripherals** and include input, output and storage devices such as keyboard, mouse, printer and disk drives. The processor receives and transmits data from and to the processor through a part of an I/O controller called an **I/O port**.

The components of a simple computer system are shown in the diagram below:

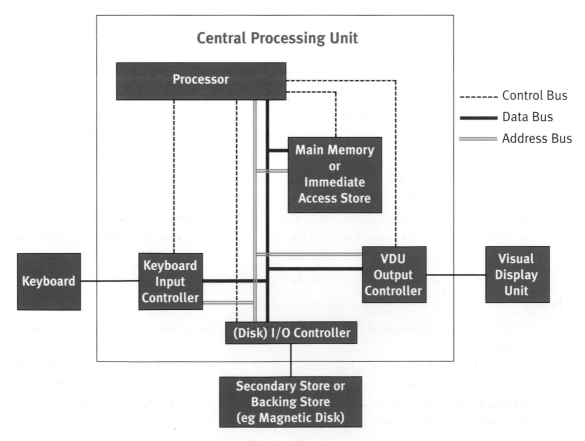

Figure 11.1: The internal and external components of a computer

Memory and the stored program concept

Computers as we know them were first built in the 1940s, and two of the early pioneers were Alan Turing and John von Neumann. Each of them separately came up with the concept of a machine that would hold in a single store (main memory) both the instructions (program) and the data on which the instructions were to be carried out. Virtually all computers today are built on this principle, and so the general structure as shown in Figure 11.2 is sometimes referred to as the **von Neumann machine**.

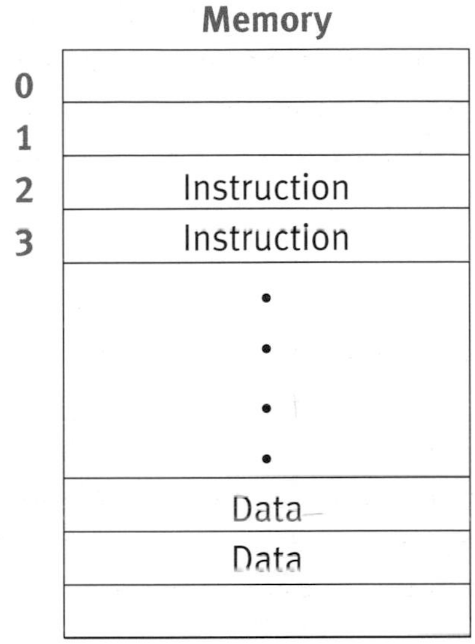

Figure 11.2: The stored program concept

The Processor

The processor contains the **control unit**, the **arithmetic/logic unit (ALU) and registers**.

The control unit coordinates and controls all the operations carried out by the computer. It operates by repeating three operations:

- **Fetch** – cause the next instruction to be fetched from main memory;
- **Decode** – produces signals which control the other parts of the computer such as the ALU;
- **Execute** – cause the instruction to be executed;

The ALU can perform two sorts of operations on data. **Arithmetic** operations include addition, subtraction, multiplication and division. **Logical** operations consist of comparing one data item with another to determine whether the first data item is smaller than, equal to or greater than the second data item.

Registers are special memory cells that operate at very high speed.

Buses

A bus is a set of parallel wires connecting two or more components of the computer.

The CPU is connected to main memory by three separate **buses**. When the CPU wishes to access a particular main memory location, it sends this address to memory on the **address bus**. The data in that location is then returned to the CPU on the **data bus**. Control signals are sent along the **control bus**.

In Figure 11.3, you can see that data, address and control buses connect the processor, memory and I/O controllers. These are all **system buses**. Each bus is a shared transmission medium, so that only one device can transmit along a bus at any one time.

Data and control signals travel in both directions between the processor, memory and I/O controllers. Addresses, on the other hand, travel only one way along the address bus: the processor sends the address of an instruction, or of data to be stored or retrieved, **to** memory or **to** an I/O controller (see figure below.)

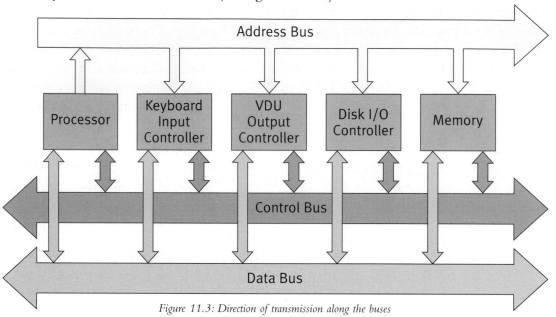

Figure 11.3: Direction of transmission along the buses

Control bus

The control bus is a bi-directional bus meaning that signals can be carried in both directions. The data and address buses are **shared** by all components of the system. Control lines must therefore be provided to ensure that **access to and use of the data and address buses** by the different components of the system does not lead to conflict. The purpose of the control bus is to transmit command, timing and specific status information between system components. Timing signals indicate the validity of data and address information. Command signals specify operations to be performed. Specific status signals indicate the state of a data transfer request, or the status of a request by a component to gain control of the system bus.

Typical control lines include:

- Memory Write: causes data on the data bus to be written into the addressed location.
- Memory Read: causes data from the addressed location to be placed on the data bus.
- I/O Write: causes data on the data bus to be output to the addressed I/O port.
- I/O Read: causes data from the addressed I/O port to be placed on the data bus.
- Transfer ACK: indicates that data have been accepted from or placed on the data bus.
- Bus Request: indicates that a component needs to gain control of the system bus.
- Bus Grant: indicates that a requesting component has been granted control of the system bus.
- Interrupt request: indicates that an interrupt is pending.
- Interrupt ACK: acknowledges that the pending interrupt has been recognised.
- Clock: used to synchronise operations.
- Reset: initialises all components.

1-11

Data bus

The data bus, typically consisting of 8, 16, 32 or 64 separate lines provides a bi-directional path for moving data and instructions between system components. **The width of the data bus is a key factor in determining overall system performance**. For example, if the data bus is 8 bits wide, and each instruction is 16 bits long, then the processor must access the main memory twice just to fetch the instruction.

Address bus

When the processor wishes to read a word (say 8, 16 or 32 bits) of data from memory, it first puts the address of the desired word on the address bus. **The width of the address bus determines the maximum possible memory capacity of the system**. For example, if the address bus consisted of only 8 lines, then the maximum address it could transmit would be (in binary) 11111111 or 255 - giving a maximum memory capacity of 256 (including address 0). A more realistic minimum bus width would be 20 lines, giving a memory capacity of 220, i.e. 1Mb.

The address bus is also used to address I/O ports during input/output operations.

No of address lines, m	Maximum no of addressable cells	Maximum no of addressable cells expressed as a power of two, 2^m
1	2	2^1
2	4	2^2
3	8	2^3
4	16	2^4
8	256	2^8
16	65536	2^{16}
20	1048576	2^{20}
24	16777216	2^{24}

*Table 11.4: Relationship between number of address lines **m** and maximum number of addressable memory cells*

I/O Controllers

Peripheral devices cannot be connected directly to the processor. Each peripheral operates in a different way and it would not be sensible to design processors to directly control every possible peripheral. Otherwise, the invention of a new type of peripheral would require the processor to be redesigned. Instead, the processor controls and communicates with a peripheral device through an **I/O or device controller**. I/O controllers are available which can operate both input and output transfers of bits, e.g. floppy disk controller. Other controllers operate in one direction only, either as an input controller, e.g. keyboard controller or as output controller, e.g. VDU controller.

The controller is an electronic circuit board consisting of three parts:
• an interface that allows connection of the controller to the system or I/O bus;
• a set of data, command and status registers;
• an interface that enables connection of the controller to the cable connecting the device to the computer.

An interface is a standardised form of connection defining such things as signals, number of connecting pins/sockets and voltage levels that appear at the interface. An example is an RS232 interface, which enables serial transmission of data between a computer and a serially connected printer. The printer also contains an RS232 interface so that both ends of the connection are compatible with each other.

Exercises

1 Some of the internal components of a computer system are processor, main memory, control bus, address bus, data bus, keyboard controller, VDU controller, disk controller.

The diagram below shows how these are connected.

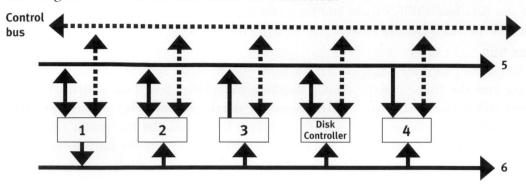

(a) Give the correct name for each of the components as labelled in the diagram above. (6)

(b) If the data bus consists of 8 lines what is the largest denary value which could be transferred in one go? (1)

(c) Computer systems built using the von Neumann architecture use the stored program concept.

   (i) Where is a program stored while it is being executed? (1)

   (ii) Where is the data stored? (1)

AQA CPT1 Qu 4 May 2002

2 Some of the components of a computer system are processor, main memory, address bus, data bus, control bus, I/O port and secondary storage.

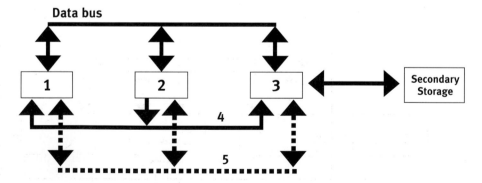

The diagram above shows how these components are connected.

(a) Name each of the following components 1 to 5 (5)

(b) (i) What is the function of the following components:

   processor;

   main memory;

   secondary storage? (3)

   (ii) Give **two** examples of a signal carried by the control bus. (2)

   (iii) Apart from data, what else is carried on the data bus? (1)

AQA CPT1 Qu 4 Jan 2003

3 Some of the components of a computer system are:

    Peripherals:

        keyboard   1

        monitor   2

    I/O Ports:

        VDU controller   3

        keyboard controller 4

    Memory

        main memory   5

        secondary storage 6

    System Bus:

        Data Bus   7

        Address Bus   8

1-11

(a) In the diagram below, identify each component by writing its number, given in the list above, in the appropriate circle.

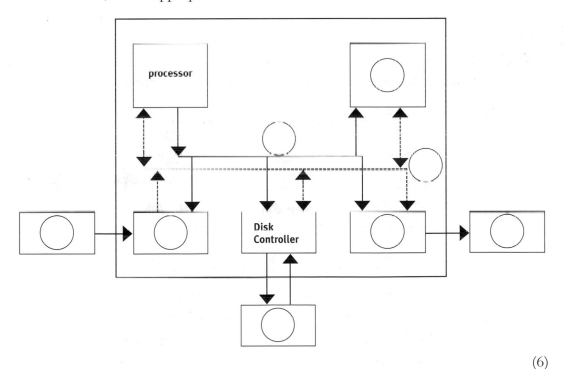

(6)

(b) The above computer system uses the *stored program concept*.

    Explain this term.   (2)

AQA CPT1 Qu 3 June 2003

Chapter 12 – Communication Methods

Principle of electronic data communication

Data communication involves sending and receiving data from one computer or data processing device to another. Applications using e-mail, supermarket EPOS (electronic point of sale) terminals, cash dispensers, facsimile, and video conferencing are all examples of this.

Data communication also takes place between the CPU and its peripheral devices; for example, data to be printed has to be sent to the printer, or in the case of a computer controlling a robot, signals have to be sent to tell the robot what to do.

Serial and parallel data communication

Data can be sent in one of two ways: serial or parallel.

Serial data transmission: Bits are sent via an interface one bit at a time over a single wire from the source to the destination.

Very high data transfer rates can be achieved – for example using fibre-optic cable data transfer rates of 64 Gbits per second can be achieved, which is much faster than parallel transmission in some systems.

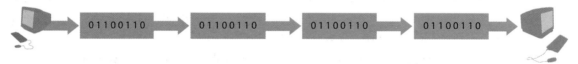

Figure 12.1: Serial transmission

Parallel data transmission: Several bits are sent simultaneously over a number of parallel wires.

This method is used inside the computer (using the various computer **buses**) and for very short distances of up to a few metres. A parallel port, for example, can send 8, 16 or 32 bits simultaneously down separate lines. A printer is often connected to a PC via a parallel port if the printer is sitting right next to the computer.

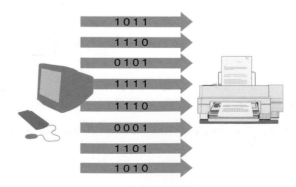

Figure 12.2: Parallel transmission

Parallel transmission will transmit data more quickly than serial transmission. However, because each individual wire has slightly different properties, there is a possibility that bits could travel at slightly different speeds over each of the wires. This produces a problem known as **skew**. So parallel transmission is really only reliable over short distances.

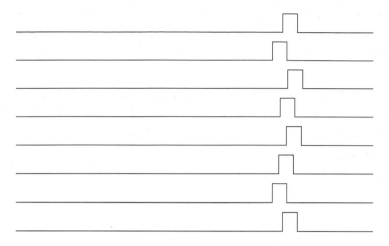

Figure 12.3: Skew developing in parallel wires

Transmission rate

The speed at which data is transmitted serially is measured in bits per second **(bit rate)**.

Baud rate: The rate at which the signal changes.

In baseband mode of operation bit rate is equivalent to **baud rate**. However with higher bandwidths more than one bit can be coded into a signal and the bit rate will be higher than the baud rate (also called symbol rate).

bit rate of channel = (baud rate) x (number of bits per signal)

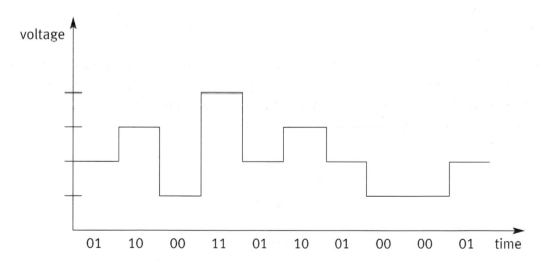

Figure 12.4: One Signal encoding 2 bits: Bit rate is twice the baud rate

1-12

Signalling Methods

The principal signalling methods are baseband, broadband and carrierband. In baseband signalling the voltage levels representing 0 and 1 occupy the full bandwidth of the medium. The data in the broadband and carrierband methods are placed onto the medium using a modulated carrier. In carrierband transmission the signal transmitted occupies the whole bandwidth. In broadband transmission multiple channels exist, with each channel having its own frequency range. Each channel can transmit a separate data stream. The greater the bandwidth, the more data can be transmitted per unit time.

Bandwidth: The range of frequencies that a medium can correctly transmit.

Parity

Computers use either even or odd parity. In an even parity machine, the total number of 'on' bits in every byte (including the parity bit) must be an even number. When data is transmitted, the parity bit is set at the transmitting end and parity is checked at the receiving end, and if the wrong number of bits are 'on', an error has occurred. In the diagram below the parity bit is the most significant bit (MSB).

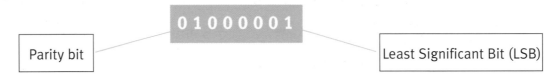

Figure 12.5: Parity bit in even parity system

Q1: The ASCII codes for P and Q are 1010000 and 1010001 respectively. In an even parity transmission system, what will be the value of the parity bit for the characters P and Q?

Asynchronous data transmission

Asynchronous transmission: one character at a time is sent, with each character being preceded by a start bit and followed by one or two stop bits.

The start bit alerts the receiving device and synchronises the clock inside the receiver ready to receive the character. The baud rate at the receiving end has to be set up to be the same as the sender's baud rate or the signal will not be received correctly.

A parity bit is also usually included as a check against incorrect transmission. Thus for each character being sent, a total of 10 bits is transmitted, including the parity bit, a start bit and a stop bit. The start bit may be a 0 or a 1, the stop bit is then a 1 or a 0 (always different). A series of electrical pulses is sent down the line as illustrated in Figure 12.6:

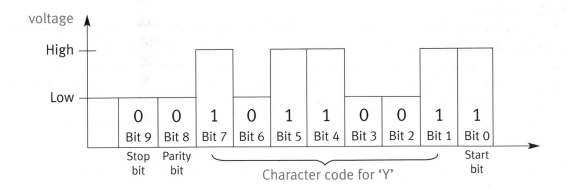

Figure 12.6: Asynchronous transmission

This type of transmission is usually used by PCs, and is fast and economical for relatively small amounts of data.

Handshaking

Handshaking is the exchange of signals between devices to establish their readiness to send or receive data, for example between a computer and printer. It is one method of ensuring that both the sender and receiver are ready before transmission begins. The 'conversation' between two devices is along the lines of the following:

Device 1:   "Are you ready to receive some data?"

Device 2:   "Yes, go ahead."

Device 1:   *(sends data)*

Device 2:   "Message received."

Protocol

Protocol: a set of rules relating to communication between devices.

In order to allow equipment from different suppliers to be networked, a standardised set of rules **(protocols)** has been devised covering standards for physical connections, cabling, mode of transmission, speed, data format, error detection and correction. Any equipment which uses the same communication protocol can be linked together.

Exercises

1. One method of sending data to a printer is by using parallel transmission.

   (a) What is meant by parallel transmission? (1)

   (b) Parallel transmission should **not** be used over long distances.

      (i) Why not? (1)

      (ii) How should data be transmitted over long distances? (1)

      AQA CPT1Qu 9 May 2002

2. Bit patterns can be interpreted in a number of different ways.

   (a) A computer word contains the bit pattern 0001 0111.

      What is its decimal value if it represents

      (i) a pure binary integer; (1)

      (ii) a BCD (Binary Coded Decimal)? (1)

   (b) A computer system uses **odd** parity. The most significant bit (MSB) is used as a parity bit. The ASCII value for the character '!' is decimal number 33.

      (i) What would be the 8-bit binary pattern to represent the character '!'? (2)

      (ii) Asynchronous data transmission is used if one character is sent at a time. One start bit marks the beginning of a character and one stop bit marks the end of a character.

      What would be the bit pattern if the character '!' above is sent using asynchronous data transmission? (1)

      AQA CPT1 Qu 2 Jan 2003

3. Baud rate and bit rate tell us about the speed of data transmission.

   (a) What exactly do bit rate and baud rate measure? (2)

   (b) What is the relationship between bit rate and bandwidth? (1)

   New Question

4. A stand-alone computer and printer use *handshaking* as they communicate with each other. Explain the term *handshaking* in this context. (2)

   New Question

5. (a) What is serial transmission?

   (b) Explain the difference between serial and parallel data transmission.

   (c) Under what circumstances would it be appropriate to use parallel transmission? (3)

   New Question

1-12

Chapter 13 – Local Area Networks

Communications networks

A Local Area Network (LAN) is a method of connecting computers together in a small geographical area, for example confined to one building or site.

Computers and peripheral devices are linked via a direct physical connection (cable) or a wireless connection. A LAN can be connected to other LANs, or to a Wide Area Network (WAN).

Network Adapter

To communicate on a network a computer needs a network adapter or network interface card. The network adapter converts data from the computer into a form that can be transmitted over the network and converts data received from the network into a form that can be stored in the computer.

Advantages of networks

A network has several **advantages** over a collection of stand-alone microcomputers:

- It allows the sharing of resources such as disk storage, printers, image scanners, modems and central servers;
- It allows sharing of information held on disk drives accessible by all users;
- It is easier to back up data held on a file server than on many individual machines;
- It is easier to store application programs on one computer and make them available to all users rather than having copies individually installed on each computer;
- It allows electronic mail to be sent between users;
- It is easier to set up new users and equipment;
- It allows the connection of different types of computer, which can communicate with each other.

Disadvantages of networks

The main **disadvantages** of networks are:

- Users become dependent on them; if for example the network file server develops a fault, then many users will be unable to run application programs. (On many sites, a back-up file server can be switched into action if the main server fails).
- If the network stops operating then it may not be possible to access various hardware and software resources.
- The efficiency of a network is very dependent on the skill of the system manager. A badly managed network may operate less efficiently than stand-alone machines.
- It is difficult to make the system secure from hackers.
- As traffic increases on the network the performance degrades unless it is properly designed.

1-13

Network topologies

The **topology** of a network is its physical layout – the way in which the computers and other units (commonly referred to as **nodes**) are connected. Common topologies include **star**, **bus** and **ring**, discussed below.

Star network

Each node in a star network is connected to a central **host computer** that controls the network. This is a common topology for a wide area network in large companies, which have a mainframe computer at the Head Office, and computer facilities (perhaps linked together in a LAN) at each branch. It has the advantage that each node is independent of the others so a fault at one branch will not affect the other branches. On the other hand if the main computer goes down, all users are affected.

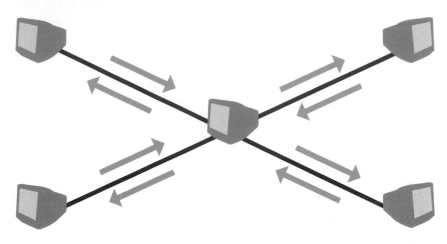

Figure 13.1: A star network

Advantages of a star network

- If one cable fails, only one station is affected.
- Therefore, it is simple to isolate faults.
- Consistent performance even when the network is being heavily used.
- No problems with 'collisions' of data since each station has its own cable to the server.
- The system is more secure as messages are sent directly to the central computer and cannot be intercepted by other stations.
- Easy to add new stations without disrupting the network.
- Different stations can transmit at different speeds.

Disadvantage of star network

- May be costly to install because of the length of cable required. The cabling can be a substantial part of the overall cost of installing a network.

A variation of the star topology is the **distributed star** topology. A number of stations are linked to connection boxes which are then linked together to form a 'string of stars'.

Bus network

This is a common topology for a LAN, with all the devices on the network sharing a single cable. Data is transmitted in all directions from any PC to any other. This system works well if the channels are not too heavily loaded. On the other hand if sixteen students sit down at sixteen computers all at once and all try to load software from the network's hard disk, the whole system may grind to a halt!

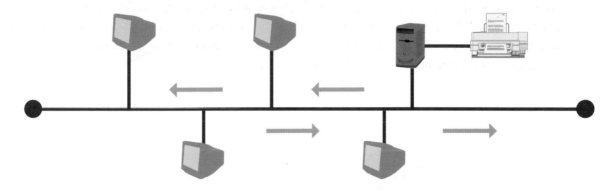

Figure 13.2: A bus network

Advantages of a bus network

• Easy and inexpensive to install as it requires the least amount of cable.

• Easy to add more stations without disrupting the network.

Disadvantage of bus network

• The whole network goes down if the main cable fails at any point.
• Cable failure is difficult to isolate.
• Network performance degrades under a heavy load.
Example of a bus network: Ethernet.

1-13

Ring network

In a ring network, computers are connected together and there is no central controlling computer. Each computer may communicate with any other computer in the ring, with messages being specificallyaddressed to the destination computer. Messages are passed around the ring in one direction only.

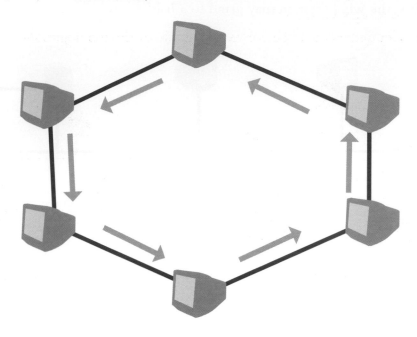

Figure 13.3: A ring network

Advantages of a ring network

• There is no dependence on a central computer or file server, and each node controls transmission to and from itself.

• Transmission of messages around the ring is relatively simple, with messages travelling in one direction only.

• Very high transmission rates are possible.

Disadvantages of a ring network

• If one node in the ring breaks down, transmission between any of the devices in the ring is disrupted.

• If any node fails the whole network may fail.

Example of a ring network: Token Ring.

1-13

Exercises

1   Acme Design, a small graphic design firm, has several stand-alone computers which staff use for their design work. They would like to use a LAN (Local Area Network) to share printers, scanners and plotters.

(a)   What extra hardware is needed for each stand-alone computer to be connected to a LAN via cables?   (1)

(b)   Computers could be connected in one of the topologies shown below.

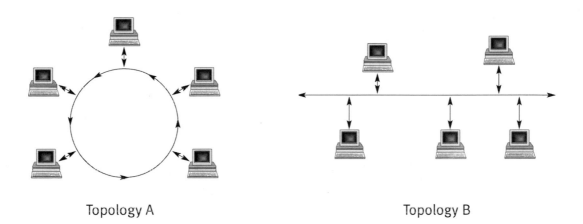

Topology A   Topology B

(i)   Name these network topologies.   (2)

(ii) Give **one** advantage of topology A over topology B.   (1)

(iii) Give **one** advantage of topology B over topology A.   (1)

(c) (i)   What is a protocol?   (1)

(ii) Why is a protocol needed?   (1)

AQA CPT1 Qu 3 Jan 2003

2   A school has several stand-alone computers which pupils use for word-processing coursework and accessing the library catalogue, stored in a database. A copy of the database is stored on each computer.

(a)   The teacher in charge of these computers thinks it would be beneficial to network these computers.

(i)   State **two** advantages for the pupils of a Local Area Network (LAN).   (2)

(ii) What extra hardware is needed on each stand-alone computer to connect it to a LAN via cables?   (1)

(b)   The computers could be connected in a topology such as a bus or a star network.

State **one** advantage of a bus network over a star network and one advantage of a star network over a bus network.   (2)

New Question

Chapter 14 – Wide Area Networks

Wide Area Network (WAN)

A WAN connects geographically remote computers or networks; for example computers in different sites, towns or continents.

The connection between computers in a WAN may be any of several alternatives, described below.

Communications links

Communication may take place over a combination of connections:

• The public telephone network;

• Dedicated leased lines;

• Radio waves;

• Fibre optic cable through which pulses of light, rather than electricity, are sent in digital form;

• Microwave – similar to radio waves. Microwave stations cannot be much more than 30 miles apart because of the earth's curvature as microwaves travel in straight lines. Mobile telephones use microwave radio links.

• Communications satellite, using one of the hundreds of satellites now in geosynchronous orbit about 22,000 miles above the earth. (Geosynchronous orbit means that they are rotating at the same speed as the Earth, and are therefore stationary relative to Earth.)

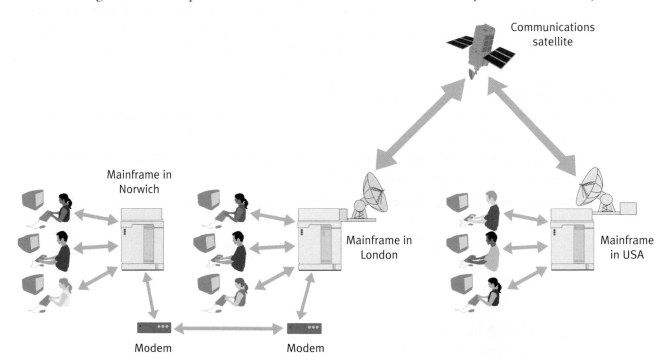

Figure 14.1: Satellite transmission

Modems

When data is sent over long distances, a cable no longer suffices and data must be transmitted by some other means such as a telephone line. Telephone lines were originally designed for speech, which is transmitted in analogue or waveform. In order for digital data to be sent over a telephone line, it must first be converted to analogue form and then converted back to digital at the other end. This is achieved by means of a modem (MOdulator DEModulator) at either end of the line.

Figure 14.2: A modem converts digital signals to analogue and vice versa.

ISDN lines

The amount of data that can be sent over a line depends on the bandwidth, which is the range of frequencies that the line can carry. The greater the **bandwidth**, the greater the rate at which data can be sent, as several messages can be transmitted simultaneously.

A network that is capable of sending voice, video and computer data is called an **Integrated Services Digital Network (ISDN)**, and this requires a high bandwidth.

Data compression

Data compression is frequently used when transmitting large quantities of data, thereby reducing the number of blocks transmitted and hence the cost. One method works by replacing repeated bytes by one copy of the byte plus a count of the repetitions.

Factors affecting rate of data transmission

- The speed of the modem. Different modems provide different data transmission rates, varying typically between 9K bps (bits per second) to 56K bps.
- The nature of the transmission line. A digital line such as an ISDN line has a much higher transmission speed than an analogue line.
- The type of cable used. Twisted pair cable has a transfer rate of about 1000 Mbps, whereas fibre optic cable is about 100 times as fast.
- The type of transmission, synchronous or asynchronous.

1-14

The Internet

The Internet is a world-wide collection of computers using the same protocol (TCP/IP).

The Internet is the largest wide area network in the world. In fact it is not a single network, but a collection of thousands of computer networks throughout the world. These linked networks are of two types:

• LAN (Local Area Network), covering, for example, an office block or University campus;

• WAN (Wide Area Network), connecting computers over a wide geographical area, even over several countries.

All LANs and some WANs are owned by individual organisations. Some WANs act as **service providers**, and members of the public or businesses can join these networks in return for a monthly charge.

There is no central authority or governing body running the Internet: it started with an initial 4 computers in 1969 and grew over the next ten years to connect 200 computers in military and research establishments in the US. Today there are more than 4 million host computers, any of which could be holding the information you are looking for, and as many as 50 million people connected, any of whom could be future customers, friends or problem-solvers.

1-14

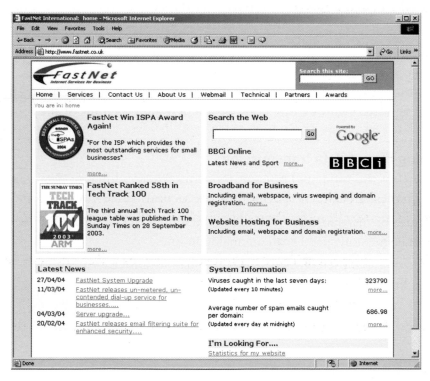

Figure 14.3: An Internet Service Provider

Dial-up Networking

In dial-up networking the connection to a WAN is made using the existing telephone network and a modem or ISDN adaptor. Whenever data transmission is required, the computer dials the number to set up a connection. The connection is dropped when no longer in use.

Dial-up networking: using a telephone line to connect to a network as required.

Leased Line Networking

With leased line networking the local nodes are permanently connected to the WAN. No time is wasted making a connection when data transmission is required. These lines usually have a higher bandwidth than dial-up lines and therefore can transmit more data per unit time. Data transmission is more reliable because no switches are being operated. The line is more secure as it is not shared with other organisations. Leased lines are more expensive than dial-up lines, however, the cost per bit may be lower than for dial-up networking if the data volumes transmitted are high.

Leased-line networking: A dedicated line connecting geographically remote computer systems is permanently on.

Uniform Resource Locator (URL)

A URL is the standard address used to find a page, Web server or other device on the Web or the Internet.

A typical address or URL is

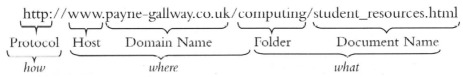

The first part of the address specifies the protocol used for connection to the server. http stands for Hypertext Transfer Protocol, which is used for Web sites. Other kinds of addresses include:

https://   'Hypertext Transfer Protocol, secure' or a Web site with security features. Credit card numbers should be safer here.

ftp://   'File Transfer Protocol' – an FTP site.

Localhost://   Information from a local Web server – typically on a user's own computer.

Domain names

The next part of the URL specifies the name of the server on which the Web resource is held. This name, called the domain name, is a string of identifiers separated by full-stops (called 'dot' when you are reading out an address).

Domain names provide a system of easy-to-remember Internet addresses, which can be translated by the Domain Name System (DNS) into the numeric addresses (Internet Protocol (IP) addresses) used by the network.

DNS is a distributed database of information that is used to translate domain names, which are easy for humans to remember and use, into IP addresses, which are what computers need to find each other on the Internet. The domain name system defines how domain names are structured. Domain names are allocated and registered in this format. The domain name system is based on a tree structure called the domain name space. The top-level domains were assigned by organisation and by country and are shown by the suffix attached to Internet domain names. There are a limited number of predefined suffixes, and each one represents a top-level domain. Current top-level domains include:

.com - commercial businesses; this is the most common top level domain

.gov -   U.S. government agencies

.edu –   U.S. Educational institutions such as universities

.mil –   U.S. Military

.net -   Network organisations

UK-specific codes include

.ac   an academic institution

.co   a company that trades in a single country

.gov   a government department or other related facility

.org   Organisations (mostly non-profit)

.tm   a trade-marked business name

.ltd   a UK Limited company

.sch   a school

A 2-character country code may follow (the country where the host computer is located) – there are hundreds of these including

au   Australia

es   Spain

sg   Singapore

uk   UK

Q1: Suppose you wanted to log on to the IBM Web site but did not know the address. What would you try first?

Q2: What address would you try for the AQA (Assessment and Qualifications Alliance?)

IP addresses

Every Web site has a unique address known as its IP address. Currently IP addresses are 32-bit (4-byte) binary numbers (IPv4). These addresses are written as a set of four numbers, each in the range 0-255, separated by full-stops, like 177.234.143.186 for example. However, as nobody can remember or work out addresses like these, the domain name system (DNS) server maps the domain names onto the IP addresses.

IP address: Numerical address stored in 4 bytes, used to identify an individual computer.

IPv6 is just beginning to come into use to solve the problem of the shortage of IP addresses (16 byte addresses instead of 4 bytes).

Intranets

An Intranet is an organisation-wide network using the same protocol as the internet, making it possible to share documents, databases and applications. Information on intranets is accessed through browsers. Many schools have Intranets, and selected information is downloaded from the Internet for students to access. This saves wasting time browsing aimlessly through thousands of files and also enables unsuitable material to be screened out.

Intranet: local area network providing Internet facilities within an organisation using Internet protocol.

1-14

Exercises

1   What type of application software is required to access a web site?   (1)

New Question

2   What is an Intranet? Give **two** advantages to a company of setting up an Intranet.   (3)

New Question

3   An example of a Uniform Resource Locator (URL)
    is **http://www.bbc.co.uk/history**.

(a)   What part of the above URL constitutes the domain name?   (1)

(b)   Using the URL, explain what each part can tell us.

(i)   http

(ii) www

(iii) bbc

(iv) co

(v)   uk

(vi) history   (6)

(c)   The IP address of the above site is 212.58.224.32.

(i)   What is the relationship between the IP address and the domain name?   (1)

(ii) If each group of digits is stored in one byte, what is the range of
      possible IP addresses?   (2)

AQA CPT1 Qu 6 June 2000

4 (a) A college uses a LAN (Local Area Network) to share software and printers between its students. Describe a LAN. (2)

(b) The diagram below shows the current topology.

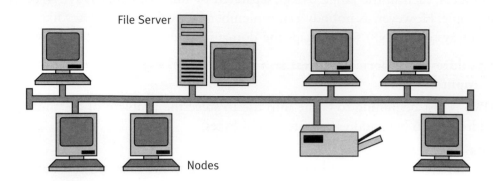

(i)   Name this topology (1)

(ii) Give **one** advantage of this topology. (1)

(iii) Give **one** disadvantage of this topology. (1)

(c) The college decides to link to a WAN (Wide Area Network). When accessing a website, the connection can be made through either leased line networking or dial-up networking. What is meant by:

(i)   leased line networking; (1)

(ii) dial-up networking? (1)

(d) Give **one** reason for the college selecting leased line networking. (1)

(e) Give **one** reason for the college selecting dial-up networking. (1)

AQA CPT1 Qu 8 Jan 2001

1-14

Module 2

Principles of Hardware, Software and Applications

In this section:

Chapter 15	General Purpose Packages	76
Chapter 16	Spreadsheets	80
Chapter 17	Records and Files	89
Chapter 18	Serial and Sequential Files	93
Chapter 19	Direct Access Files	100
Chapter 20	File Security Methods	105
Chapter 21	Data Processing Integrity Methods	110
Chapter 22	Entity-Relationship Modelling	116
Chapter 23	Database Concepts	119
Chapter 24	Operating Systems	128
Chapter 25	Hardware Devices	135
Chapter 26	Computer Crime and the Law	150
Chapter 27	Data Protection and Health and Safety	155
Chapter 28	Information Processing Applications	161

2

Chapter 15 – General Purpose Packages

Introduction

In your exam or assessment, you may be asked to write about the 'features' of various common software packages. There is no substitute for practical experience, so if at all possible you should use each of these packages yourself and make notes on their capabilities. You are expected to have basic skills in using a spreadsheet and a database, and these packages are discussed in Chapters 16 and 22-23 respectively.

General purpose packages can be used for a variety of tasks. They can usually be customized or tailored to perform specific tasks by creating templates, macros and customised menus and toolbars. They have features such as help systems and wizards that guide the user through the steps of a complex task.

Word processing software

Word processing software is used to write letters, reports, books and articles, and any other document that in the past would have been typed on a typewriter. As the user keys in the text, it appears on the screen and is held in the computer's memory. The user can easily edit the text, correct spelling mistakes, change margins and so on before printing out the final version. The document can also be saved on disk for future amendment or use. Until the instruction is given to save, however, the document held in main memory will be lost if for example there is a power cut. Main memory is a **volatile** storage medium, and users are well advised to save their work frequently.

Below is a summary of some of the things you can do in a word processing package such as MS Word.

- type, correct, delete and move text; copy and paste, cut and paste;
- change font size, set italics, bold and underline, subscripts and superscripts;
- align text (left, right, centre or fully justified), set tabs and margins;
- find and replace text;
- insert graphics and diagrams, import graphics or charts from other packages such as a spreadsheet;
- check spelling and grammar;
- set up templates with type styles for different types of document;
- work in tables or columns;
- add headers and footers to each page, with or without page numbers;
- create indexes and tables of contents;
- type equations with mathematical symbols;
- perform a mail merge to send personalised letters to people selected from a list held in a database.

Desktop publishing

Desktop publishing is an extension of word processing. Desktop publishing packages such as Adobe PageMaker or QuarkXPress allow easier control over page layout for many types of document such as flyers, newspapers, magazines and books. Graphics, scanned photographic images and text can be easily combined and laid out exactly as required.

Using templates and wizards you can select a style suitable for a newsletter, poster, web page, advertisement, theatre programme, business card, invitation, calendar or any of hundreds of types of publication. To create a web site, for example, Microsoft Publisher has a Web Site Wizard which enables you to easily add graphics, animation and hyperlinks to other pages or Internet sites. any of hundreds of types of publication. To create a web site, for example, Microsoft Publisher has a Web Site Wizard which enables you to easily add graphics, animation and hyperlinks to other pages or Internet sites.

A typical desktop publishing system includes a desktop computer, a laser printer and software.

Figure 15.1: Documents produced using a Desktop publishing package

Electronic mail (e-mail)

E-mail systems allow you to send memos, letters and files containing data of all types from your computer to any other computer with an e-mail address and a modem, simply by typing the recipient's name and pressing the 'Send' button.

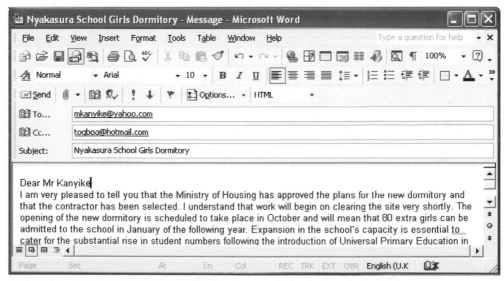

Figure 15.2: Creating an e-mail letter

Advantages of e-mail

E-mail has many advantages over ordinary mail. For example:

- a message can be sent anywhere in the world for the price of a local call;

- it is quicker to type and send because it is less formal – you do not need to type the recipient's address, find and address an envelope, affix the correct postage and go out to post the letter;

- the same message can be sent simultaneously to a group of people;

- the message will arrive in at most a few hours, and can be picked up the next time the recipient looks at their e-mail;

- it is very easy to send a reply to an e-mail as soon as it is received, using a 'reply' button, or forward it to someone else with your comments;

- files, such as graphics, video or software, can be sent as attachments.

Q1: What are some advantages of e-mail over using the telephone?

Disadvantages of e-mail

Viruses and spam e-mails are two of the biggest disadvantages of using e-mail. In 2004 the 'MyDoom' virus became the fastest-spreading virus of all time, replicating itself exponentially to spread millions of copies of itself worldwide. It sends more and more infected messages to every single address found on the hard drive, and although the virus is easy to spot, and a virus checker will disable it automatically, it is infuriating for users to have to sift through dozens or even hundreds of spurious e-mails every day.

A massive 62% of all the e-mail in the world is now spam. Some experts think that spam will bring e-mail to an end by overloading the entire e-mail system by sending out millions of generic, unfilterable messages in a loop, round the clock, for ever. Then we would all have to stop using e-mail.

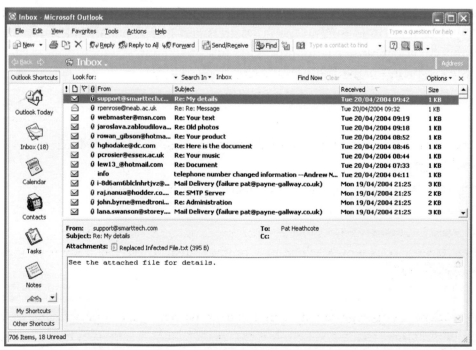

Figure 15.3: Only one of these e-mails does not contain a virus!

Presentation software

Using presentation software such as PowerPoint, professional-looking presentations can quickly and easily be designed. As well as showing text, clip art or scanned pictures and various types of chart, transition effects, sound and animation can easily be added. A transition effect determines how each new screen will appear – it could open like a curtain or blind, come in from left or right, etc. The presentation can then be delivered on a large screen attached to a computer, or by making sheets to be shown using an overhead projector. (Of course in this type of presentation, you can't use sound, animation or transition effects.) Alternatively, the presentation can be automated so that it moves continuously through the slides at a preset rate. This type of presentation is often used in shopping malls and tourist information centres.

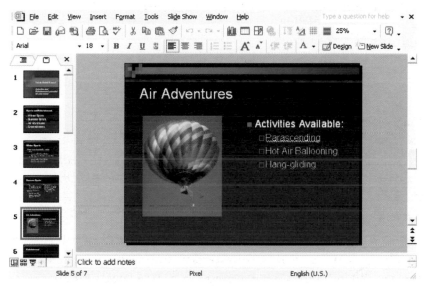

Figure 15.4: Creating a PowerPoint presentation

Exercises

1 A Mathematics teacher using a word-processing package to write a text book needs different features from a school librarian writing reminder letters to pupils who have overdue library books.

State **three** features needed by the Mathematics teacher.

State **three** features needed by the librarian. (6)

New Question

2 Name the most suitable type of application package to help produce a school magazine. (1)

State three features that make this package useful for the task. (3)

New Question

3 Some teachers now communicate with pupils' parents using e-mail.
State **three** reasons why teachers may prefer e-mail to writing a letter or making a telephone call. (3)

New Question

4 The student union representative in a college wishes to use a presentation package for a presentation she is giving about the year's planned activities. Describe **three** design features she should bear in mind when writing the presentation. (3)

New Question

Chapter 16 – Spreadsheets

Spreadsheet software is used by people who work with numbers: accountants, bank and building society employees, engineers and financial planners. The user enters the data and the formulae to be used in manipulating the data, and the program calculates the results. If any numbers are changed, the software automatically recalculates the results. One of the most useful features of a spreadsheet is its ability to perform **'What If'** calculations: "What if we produce 30% more widgets and wages increase by 10% – how much will we have to charge in order to show a profit?" Spreadsheets are therefore often used in **planning and budgeting,** but are also widely used by anyone working with figures – for example, keeping a set of students' marks.

Spreadsheet features

Using spreadsheet facilities a user can:

- format cells, rows and columns, specifying for example, the alignment of text, number of decimal places, height and width of cell;

- merge cells;

- enter formulae referencing other cells;

- copy cell contents to other locations, with automatic adjustment of formulae from say B9 to C9, D9 etc.

- insert, move or delete rows and columns;

- use functions such as sum, average, round, trunc, max, min in formulae;

- use a lookup table;

- determine the effect of several different hypothetical changes of data – this facility is termed a 'what-if' calculation;

- create scenarios to examine the effects of changing a number of variables;

- create a simple database and sort or query the data to produce a report of, say, all females earning over £20,000 for a list of employees;

- write macros to automate common procedures;

- create templates – spreadsheets with formats and formulae already entered, into which new figures may be inserted;

- create 'multi-dimensional' spreadsheets using several sheets, and copy data from one sheet to another;

- create many different types of charts and graphs (see Figure 16.6).

Worked Example (using MS Excel)

Set up a spreadsheet as follows:

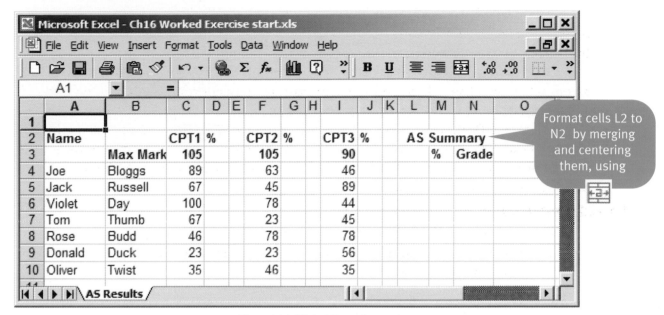

Figure 16.1: Worked Example part 1

Now insert formulae as follows:

Column L: Add the marks gained for each of the three modules.

Type **=C3+F3+I3** into cell L3 and copy it into cells L4 to L10 by filling down.

In cell L10 you should have the formula **=C10+F10+I10**.

Column D: Calculate the marks gained as a percentage of the maximum marks (the number in cell C3). If you precede a column or a row name with $ that makes the reference absolute. This means it will always refer to that specific row/column when you copy the formula into another cell. For example, $C$3 is an **absolute cell reference** of cell C3 and when used in a formula will not change when filled down or across.

In cell D4 enter **=TRUNC(C4/$C$3*100)**

Then fill down to the last row.

In D10 you should have **=TRUNC(C10/$C$3*100)**

Note that the absolute cell reference $C$3 does not change as the formula is copied down. However, the **relative cell reference** C4 changes with each row, and becomes C10 in row 10. TRUNC is a function that returns an integer value as a result, as we are not interested in fractional percentages here. You could have formatted the cells to display zero decimal places instead.

Columns G, J and M: Now complete the formulae in a similar manner to column D.

Columns E, H, K and N will display the grade, which will be looked up from a lookup table.

Set up the grade table as shown below:

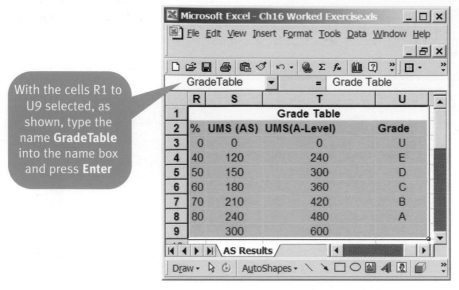

Figure 16.2: Grade Look up Table

In cell E4 type **=VLOOKUP(D4,GradeTable,4)**

You can fill this formula down to row 10.

Complete equivalent formulae for columns H, K and N.

Explanation of function VLOOKUP(LookupValue, TableArray, ColIndexNum, RangeLookup):

LookupValue is the value to be found in the first column of the array.

TableArray is the table in which data is looked up. (Note the values in the first column must be in ascending order). Use a reference to a range or a range name.

ColIndexNum is the column number in *TableArray* from which the matching value must be returned.

RangeLookup is a logical value that specifies whether you want VLOOKUP to find an exact match or an approximate match. If TRUE is omitted, an approximate match is returned. In other words, if an exact match is not found, the next largest value that is less than **lookup_value** is returned. If FALSE is omitted, VLOOKUP will find an exact match. If one is not found, the error value **#N/A** is returned.

Column O will display the message **Retake** if the AS grade was **U**.

In cell O4 enter the formula **=IF(N4="U","Retake","")**.

Fill this formula down to cell O10.

Use of the Formula Palette to help in the use of a new function:

When you create a formula that contains a function, the Formula Palette helps you enter worksheet functions. As you enter a function into the formula, the Formula Palette displays the name of the function, each of its arguments, a description of the function and each argument, the current result of the function, and the current result of the entire formula.

To display the Formula Palette, click **Edit Formula** in the formula bar.

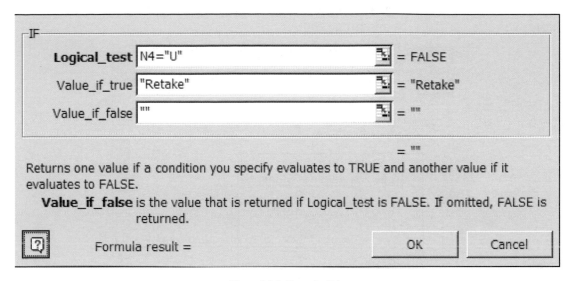

Figure 16.3: Formula Palette

Your spreadsheet should now look like this:

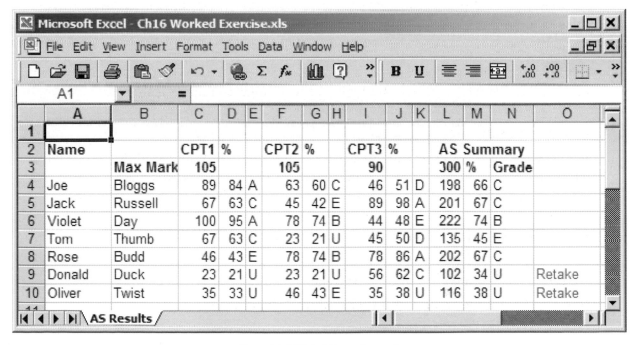

Figure 16.4: Worked Example part 2

Set up a Grade Distribution table (Figure 16.5 below), which counts the number of each AS grade and displays the summary.

Use the COUNTIF function as shown in the formula bar for cell T13. Enter similar formulae into cells T14 to T18. COUNTIF will return the number of occurrences of the second argument found in the range given in the first argument.

Cell T19 adds up the number of students at each grade in that column. Use the formula **=SUM(T13:T18)**.

Note we refer to T13:T18 as a range.

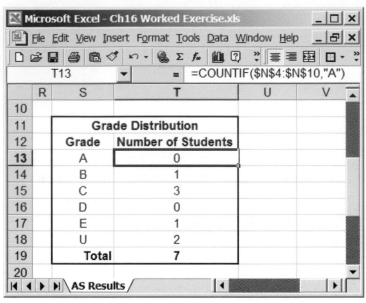

Figure 16.5: Grade Distribution table

Now use the Chart Wizard to make a simple bar chart. Select the chart type *Column*. Use the data range S11:T18 and fill in the appropriate labels for heading, x–axis and y–axis to achieve the following:

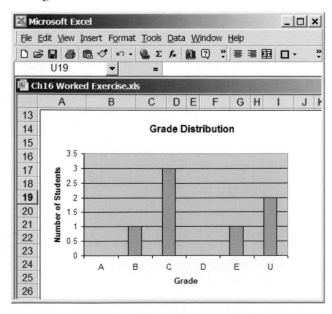

Figure 16.6: A chart created from the Grade Distribution table

You can record macros and assign them to buttons, so frequently performed actions can be executed at the click of a button. Record two macros *SortBySurname* and *SortByGrade* using the following technique:

Use the **Tools, Macro, Record New Macro** menu option. Give your macro a name. As soon as the Record Macro window closes, all your actions are recorded.

Select the range A4:O10 and choose the menu option **Tools, Sort...**

Choose the relevant columns to order by and then stop the recorder.

From the Forms toolbar you can use the button tool to place two buttons on your form and assign one of your macros to each button.

Test that your buttons work as expected.

2-16

You should practise your spreadsheet skills. You could implement the spreadsheets given in the Exercises on the next few pages.

Exercises

1 The following is an extract from a spreadsheet that shows how many supermarket loyalty points a customer would earn by spending different amounts of money on supermarket goods. The supermarket is currently operating a bonus scheme which adds a fixed percentage of points to the points earned. The fixed percentage used is 10%.

	B	C	D	E	F	G
1	Bonus %	10		Pounds Spent	Points Earned Without Bonus	Points Earned With Bonus
2	Points earned per pound if £10.00 or less spent	2				
3	Points earned per pound when more than £10 but not more than £30.00 spent	3				
4	Points earned per pound if more than £30.00 spent	4				
5				5	10	11
6				15	45	50
7				30	90	99
8				60	240	264
9				90	360	396
				:	:	:
				:	:	:
20				240	960	1056
21				270	1080	1188
22				300	1200	1320

(a) The formula in G5 is F5*(1 + $C$1/100) where $ denotes absolute cell referencing. What is the formula in cell G8? (3)

(b) The value in cell G6 is calculated from 45 x (1 + 10/100) which equals 49.5. However, the value displayed in cell G6 is 50. How might this happen? (1)

(c) Write the formula that was entered in F5 and copied to cells F6 to F22. Your formula should perform an automatic recalculation if the value in C2, or the value in C3, or the value in C4, is changed. (6)

AQA CPT2 Qu 8 May 2002

2 (a) The following is an extract from a spreadsheet which calculates Value Added Tax (VAT) on goods sold by mail-order catalogue. In column E the digit 1 means that VAT is charged at the rate stored in cell I2; the digit 0 means VAT is zero.

	C	D	E	F	G	H	I
1	Catalogue No	Price excluding VAT	VAT rating	VAT	Price including VAT	Postage	VAT rate %
2						£10.00	17.5
3							
4	30	53	1	9.28	62.28	£4.00	
5	45		1				
6	61		0				
:	:		:				
:	:		:				
520	746		1				
521	768		0				
522	777		1				

2-16

(i) When this spreadsheet was being developed the formula I2 x D4 x E4/100 was placed in F4. Why will this formula not work as desired without further editing when copied down into any of the cells in column F below F4? How should it be changed? (2)

(ii) The value in cell F4 is calculated from 17.5 x 53 x 1/100 which equals 9.275 to three decimal places. However, the value displayed in cell F4 is 9.28. Why might this happen? (1)

(b) Postage is in one of two bands: £2 if the price excluding VAT is less than £10.00, £4 otherwise. Write the formula for cell H4. The postage band boundary price is held in cell H2. Your formula should perform an automatic recalculation if the value in H2 is changed. (3)

AQA CPT2 Qu 7 January 2002

3 (a) One common business application package is the spreadsheet.

Give two different reasons why a spreadsheet package is particularly useful as a decision making tool. (2)

A spreadsheet is used to record examination scores and grades as follows:

	A	B	C	D
1	**Surname**	**Percentage**	**Grade**	
2				
3	Bloggs	65	P	
4	Boon	39		
5	Deedes	70		
6				
7				40
8				70

(b) The formula in C3, IF($B3<$D$7, "F", IF($B3<$D$8, "P", "M")) is copied to cells C4 to C5. The symbol $ indicates absolute addressing.

(i) Write the format of the formula in Cell C4. (1)

(ii) After the formula is copied, what is displayed in the cells C4 and C5? (2)

(c) The value in cell D7 is changed to 30. What effect, if any, will this change have on any other cell? (1)

AQA CPT2 Qu 7 June 2003

4 The part of a spreadsheet given below holds a table of product details.

	A	B	C	D
1			Mark up	1.2
2				
3	Product	Part Number	Cost Price	Selling Price
4	Bar Code Reader 1000	BCR123	105	
5	CD ROM Drive 12 speed	CD1286	210	
6	Colour Scanner 24/600	CS24600	450	
7	Hard Disk 1.2 Gb external	HD12	300	
8	Ink Jet printer 100	IP100	120	
9	Keyboard II	KB185	43	
10	LaserWriter 4040	LW4040	675	
11	Monitor 15" Colour	M1536	185	
12	Midi Interface	M1267	56	
13	Mouse plus	MP34	20	
14	Performance Computer 456	PC456	645	
15				

The formula in cell D4 is: =C4 * $D$1 (where the d1 is an absolute reference to cell D1). This formula is to be replicated down the column.

(a) (i) Briefly describe how to replicate the formula in D4 down the column to row 14. (2)

(ii) Why is it necessary to have the cell D1 as an absolute reference? (1)

(b) A different part of the spreadsheet obtains the selling price for any given part number from this table using a lookup function. State the parameters needed by such a lookup function. (3)

NEAB CP04 Qu 8 1998

Chapter 17 – Records and Files

Hierarchy of data

An effective information system provides users with timely, accurate and relevant information. This information is stored in computer files, which need to be suitably organised and properly maintained so that users can easily access the information they need.

We'll look at the way that data is represented and structured in a computer, starting with the very lowest level.

BIT   All data is stored in a computer's memory or storage devices in the form of binary digits or **bits**. A bit can be either 'ON' or 'OFF' representing 1 or 0.

BYTE   Bits are grouped together, with a group of 8 bits forming a **byte**. One byte can represent one character or, in different contexts, other data such as a sound, part of a picture, etc.

There are different codes used for representing characters, one of the most common being ASCII (American Standard Code for Information Interchange). Using 8 bits it is possible to represent 256 (2^8) different characters.

FIELD   Characters are grouped together to form **fields**. Data held about a person, for example, may be split into many fields including ID Number, Surname, Initials, Title, Street, Village, Town, County, Postcode, Date of Birth, Credit Limit and so on.

RECORD   All the information about one person or item is held in a **record**.

ID Number:	432768
Surname:	King
Initials:	DF
Title:	Mr
Street:	2 Burghley Crescent
Town:	Ipswich
County:	Suffolk
Post code:	IP3 5WT
Date of Birth:	14/8/78
Credit Limit:	£250

FILE   A **file** is defined as a collection of records. A stock file will contain a record for each item of stock, a payroll file a record for each employee and so on.

DATABASE   A **database** may consist of many different files, linked in such a way that information can be retrieved from several files simultaneously. There are many different ways of organising data in a database, and many different database software products for use on all types of computer from micros to mainframes.

2-17

Text and non-text files

The term **file** can be used in a broader sense to mean a data structure which could hold, for example:

- a source code program written in a high-level language;
- a binary file containing executable code;
- a bitmapped graphics file;
- a word processed letter;
- an ASCII text file.

Text file: a file containing characters organised on a line-by-line basis.
Examples of text files: HTML document, program source code, or a basic text editor file such as a MS Notepad file.

Non-text file: content of file cannot be displayed sensibly in a text editor because it contains binary codes of nonprintable characters.
Examples: pictures, executable files.

For the rest of this chapter, the word **file** will be used in the sense of a **collection of records** such as a file of employees containing one record for each employee.

Record: a set of related data fields.

File: a collection of records.

Primary key

Each individual record in a file needs to be given a unique identifier, and this is termed the **primary key**. It needs to be carefully chosen so that there is no possibility of two people or items having the same primary key; **Surname**, for example, is no use as an identifier. The primary key sometimes consists of more than one field: for example several stores in a national chain may each have a store number, and each store may have Departments 1, 2, 3 etc. To identify a particular department in a particular store, the primary key would be composed of both **Store number** and **Department number**.

Primary key: a unique field of a record used to identify the record.

Q1: What would be a suitable primary key for: a book in a bookshop?
a book in a library?
a hospital patient?
a car owned by a car-hire firm?

Secondary (alternate) key

Other fields in a record may be defined as **secondary keys**, also known as **alternate** keys. These fields are not unique to each record, but may be used to quickly locate a group of records. For example, the field **Department** may be defined as a secondary key on an Employee file.

Secondary (alternate) key: a field that may not be unique, but may be used to locate a group of records.

Fixed and variable length records

In some circumstances records in a file may not all be the same length. **Variable length records** may be used when either:

- the number of characters in any field varies between records;

- records have a varying number of fields.

A variable length record has to have some way of showing where each field ends, and where the record ends, in order that it can be processed. There are two ways of doing this:

- use a special end-of-field character at the end of each field, and an end-of-record marker at the end of the record, as shown below. (* is used as the end-of-field marker, and # is used as the end-of-record marker in this example.)

```
SH12345*laser printer*HP laserjet2100*750.00*999.99*7#
MH452*colour flatbed scanner*Microtek Scanmaker II*150.00*289.00*3#
```

- use a character count at the beginning of each field, and an end-of-record marker. In the implementation shown below, the byte holding the count is included in the number of characters for the field, and a real number is assumed to occupy 4 bytes, an integer 2 bytes. (You could also have a character count for the entire record instead of the end-of-record marker.)

```
8SH1234514laser printer15HP Laserjet21005270.005399.9937#
6MH45223colour flatbed scanner22Microtek Scanmaker II5150.005289.0033#
```

2-17

Advantages and disadvantages of variable length records

The advantages of variable length records are:

- less space is wasted on the storage medium;

- it enables as many fields as necessary to be held on a particular record, for example a field for each subject taken by an A Level student;

- no truncation of data occurs;

- it may reduce the time taken to read a file because the records are more tightly packed.

The disadvantages are:

- the processing required to separate out the fields is more complex;

- records cannot be updated in situ;

- it is harder to estimate file sizes accurately when a new system is being designed.

Estimating file size

In a file of fixed length records, you can estimate the file size by multiplying the number of bytes in each record by the number of records. You need to know how many bytes are in each field, and you need to add a few extra bytes for each **block** of records. Data is physically held on disk or tape in blocks of say 512 bytes. If the record length is 80 bytes, there will be a maximum of 6 records per block. Therefore 1000 records would occupy 1000/6 blocks, each of $\frac{1}{2}$Kb. Therefore the file will occupy 167/2 Kb, i.e. approximately 84Kb.

If the records are 102 bytes long, 5 records would probably not fit into a block of 512 bytes because a few bytes are required in each block for information about record size etc. However if you were asked to estimate file size in an exam question, this would be made very clear.

Q2: Estimate the number of bytes used by a file of 800 records each of 120 bytes. You can assume that 4 records fit into each block of 512 bytes.

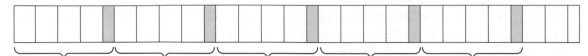

Each block contains 4 records of 120 bytes with some space left over

Exercises

1 A file of 80 records has the following record structure.

ProductID, ProductDescription, QuantityInStock

ProductID is a four-byte integer, ProductDescription is a fifty-six byte fixed length string,

QuantityInStock is a four-byte integer.

(a) What is the size of this file in bytes? Show your working.   (2)

(b) Suggest a suitable primary key for this file. Justify your choice.   (2)

(c) On closer examination, it is found that 30% of the file storage space is wasted.

   (i) Explain why this may occur with the current record structure.   (1)

   (ii) How could the record structure be changed whilst retaining three-fields per record so that this problem is overcome?   (1)

   (iii) Give **one** disadvantage of the restructured solution.   (1)

AQA CPT2 Qu 2 May 2002

2 Distinguish between the terms **primary key** and **secondary key** as applied to files and give an example of each from within an employee master file.   (4)

New Question

3 In a Pascal program the record structure of a file is declared in the following way:

```
type
  TStudent = record
    FirstName: String[15];
    Surname: String[25];
    DepositPaid: Currency;
    DateOfBirth: TDateTime;
  end; {of TStudent}
var StudentFile : File of TStudent;
```

Pascal uses 8 bytes to store the data types **Currency** and **TdateTime**.

If **StudentFile** is to hold 300 records, how many bytes will the file take up?   (3)

New Question

2-17

Chapter 18 – Serial and Sequential Files

Master and transaction files

In the last chapter a **file** was defined as a collection of **records**. Most large companies have hundreds or even thousands of files that store data pertaining to the business. Some of the files will be **transaction files** and some will be **master files.**

Transaction files contain details of all transactions that have occurred in the last period. A period may be the time that has elapsed since business started that day, or it may be a day, a week, a month or more. For example a sales transaction file may contain details of all sales made that day. Once the data has been processed it can be discarded (although the files may be kept as backup copies for a while).

Transaction file: a collection of records used in batch processing to update a master file.

Master files are permanent files kept up-to-date by applying the transactions that occur during the operation of the business. They contain generally two basic types of data:

- Data of a more or less permanent nature such as, on a payroll file, name, address, rate of pay etc.
- Data which will change every time transactions are applied to the file – for example, gross pay to date, tax paid to date, etc.

Master file: permanent file of data, which is a principal source of information for a job.

2-18

> **Q1:** A file of student records is to be kept holding student number, personal details such as name and address, course number and course grade (A–F).
> Design a record structure for the file, under the following headings:
>
> **Field description   Field length   Field type (character or numeric)**

File organisation

Files stored on magnetic media can be organised in a number of ways, just as in a manual system. There are advantages and disadvantages to each type of file organisation, and the method chosen will depend on several factors such as:

- how the file is to be used;
- how many records are processed each time the file is updated;
- whether individual records need to be quickly accessible.

Types of file organisation

- serial;
- sequential;
- indexed sequential; *(Note: not required for the AQA syllabus)*
- direct access (random).

Serial file organisation

The records on a serial file are not in any particular sequence, and so this type of organisation would not be used for a master file as there would be no way to find a particular record except by reading through the whole file, starting at the beginning, until the right record was located. Serial files are used as temporary files to store transaction data. Records are stored in the order in which they are received, with new records added to the end of the file.

Serial file: a collection of records stored one after another, in no particular sequence.

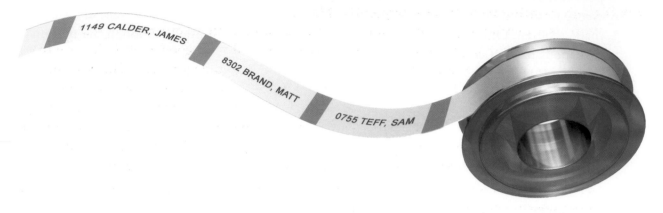

Figure 18.1: A serial file

Sequential file organisation

As with serial organisation, records are stored one after the other, but in a sequential file the records are sorted into **key sequence**. Files that are stored on tape are **always** either serial or sequential, as it is impossible to write records to a tape in any way except one after the other. From the computer's point of view there is essentially no difference between a serial and a sequential file. In both cases, in order to find a particular record, each record must be read, starting from the beginning of the file, until the required record is located. However, when the whole file has to be processed (for example a payroll file prior to payday) sequential processing is fast and efficient.

Sequential file: collection of records stored one after another, in key sequence.

Figure 18.2: A sequential file

2-18

Adding and deleting records on a serial file

Deleting a record is more complex. It is easy to understand the problem if you imagine the file is held on magnetic tape, and understand that in any particular program run you can **either** read from the tape **or** write to the tape. To find the record to be deleted, the computer has to read the tape from the beginning; but once it has found it, it cannot back up and 'wipe' just that portion of the tape occupied by the record, leaving a blank space. The technique therefore is to create a brand new tape, copying over all the records up to the one to be deleted, leaving that one off the new tape, and then copying over all the rest of the records.

Adding and deleting records on a sequential file

With a **sequential** file, all the records on the tape (or disk) are in order, perhaps of employee number, so just adding a new record on the end is no good at all. Of course the records could then be sorted but sorting is a very time-consuming process. The best and 'correct' way is to make a new copy of the file, copying over all records until the new one can be written in its proper place, and then copying over the rest of the records. It's exactly as if you had just made a list on a nice clean sheet of paper of all the students in the class in order of surname, and then discovered you had left out Carter, A.N. The only way to end up with a perfect list is to copy it out again, remembering to include Carter this time.

Deleting a record is exactly the same as for serial organisation. The file is copied to a new disk or tape, leaving out the record to be deleted.

2-18

Algorithms to add a new record to:

Serial File	Sequential File
Open file	Open old file for reading
Append record to	Open new file for writing
end of file	Starting from beginning of old file
	Repeat
	Read next record (call it current record)
	If current record key > new record key
	then write new record to new file
	EndIf
	Write current record to new file
	Until new record inserted or End Of File (old)
	If new record not yet inserted,
	Then write new record to new file
	EndIf
	If not End Of File (old) then
	Repeat
	Read next record (call it current record)
	Write current record to new file
	Until End Of File (old)
	Endif

Algorithm to delete a record from a Serial or Sequential File:

> Open old file for reading
> Open new file for writing
> Starting from beginning of old file
> Repeat
> > Read next record (call it current record)
> > If current record key <> key of record to be deleted
> > > then write record to the new file
> >
> > EndIf
>
> Until End Of File

The role of various files in a computer system

All data processing systems except the most trivial will need to store data in files. These files can be categorised as:

- master files,
- transaction files (sometimes called **movement** files) **or**
- reference files.

Master and transaction files were defined at the beginning of this chapter. A **reference file** is a file that contains data used by a program during processing. For example, in a payroll system:

- the **master file** contains details on each employee
- the **transaction file** contains details of the hours worked, holiday and sick days etc. last period
- the **reference file** contains data on tax bands, union rates, etc.

> **Q2:** In an electricity billing system, briefly outline the contents of the customer master file, the transaction file and a reference file.

> **Q3:** Why not hold the data in the reference file either on the customer master file or within the program which calculates the customers' bills?

Operations on files

The following operations are commonly carried out on files:

- Interrogating/referencing
- Updating.

Interrogating or referencing files

When a file is interrogated or referenced it is first searched to find a record with a particular **key**, and that record is then displayed on a screen, printed out or used in further processing, without itself being altered in any way.

How the record is located will depend entirely on how the file is organised.

Algorithms to search for a record with a particular key:

Serial File	Sequential File
Open file	Open file
Start from beginning of file	Start from beginning of file
Repeat	Repeat
Read next record	Read next record
Test for a match	Test for match
Until End Of File OR match made	Until record matches wanted record OR key of this record > key of wanted record (i.e. record does not exist)

Note the difference between the two algorithms. Which one will take longer to find out that the record searched for does not exist?

Q4: A bicycle shop selling bicycles and spare parts has a computerised stock control system so that the salespersons can see whether any item is in stock via a terminal in the shop. What file organisation would you recommend for the master file of all stock items? Justify your answer.

2-18

Updating files

A master file is **updated** when one or more records are altered, by applying a transaction, or a file of transactions, to it. First of all the correct record has to be located and read into memory, then updated in memory, and written back to the master file.

Once again, the method of doing this will depend on the file organisation.

If the master file is sequentially organised, it is impossible to read a record into memory, update it and then write it back to the same location.

The method used to update a sequential file was developed when virtually all master files were stored on magnetic tape (or even on punched cards or paper tape!). Although disks are often used nowadays to store sequential files, the same method is still used because it is very efficient under certain circumstances.

The method is called **'updating by copying'** and it requires the transaction file to be sorted in the same order as the master file, so that the updating can be done in one pass.

The steps are as follows:

1 A record is read from the master file into main memory

2 A record is read from the transaction file into main memory

3 The record keys from each file are compared. If no updating is required to the master file record currently in main memory (the master key is less than the transaction key) the master record is copied from main memory to a **new master file** on a different tape or area of disk, and another master file record is read into main memory, overwriting the previous one. This step is then repeated.

4 If there **is** a transaction for the master record currently in main memory, the record is updated. It will be retained in main memory in case there are any more transactions that apply to it. Steps 2-4 are then repeated.

Algorithm to update a sequential master file:

```
Open master file for reading
Open transaction file for reading
Open new master file for writing
Repeat
    Read next transaction record
    While master record key < transaction record key
        Write master record to new master file
            Read next master record
    EndWhile
    Update record
Until End Of File (transaction)
While Not End Of File (master)
    Read next master record
    Write master record to new master file
EndWhile
```

After a sequential file has been updated, two versions or **generations** of the master file exist; the **old master file**, still in the same state it was in prior to the update, and the **new master file** just created. The next time the file is updated, a third version of the master file will be created, and so on.

It is obviously not necessary to keep dozens of out-of-date master files, and the general practice is to keep three generations, called **grandfather**, **father** and **son** for obvious reasons, and then reuse the tapes or disk space for the next update that takes place.

The following diagram illustrates the process.

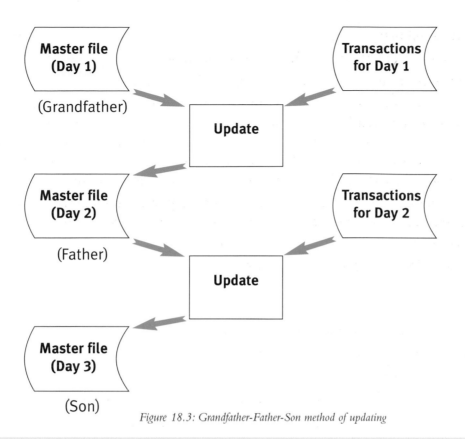

Figure 18.3: Grandfather-Father-Son method of updating

2-18

Q5: How would you **change** a record on a sequential file held on magnetic tape? (e.g. if you had got Carter's initials wrong?)

Exercises

1 A stock master file is updated by a transaction file using sequential file access. A purpose of the stock master file is to ensure that the levels of stock will meet demand.

  (a) (i) Give **four** essential fields for the stock master file. (4)

      (ii) Give **three** essential fields for the transaction file. (3)

  (b) Why should the transaction file be sorted, and in what order, prior to updating the master file? (2)

AQA CPT2 Qu 8 January 2001

2 A new copy of a sequentially organised master file is made whenever records are added.

  (a) A program is written to add a single record to this master file. List the processing steps for this program that generate an amended copy of the master file. (5)

  (b) When many records need to be inserted, these records are stored in a transaction file. The program is modified so that it reads the transaction records from the transaction file.

      (i) What file organisation should be used for this transaction file? (1)

      (ii) In what order should the transaction records be stored in the transaction file? Justify your answer. (2)

AQA CPT2 Qu 9 May 2002

Chapter 19 – Direct Access Files

Direct access files

A direct access file (also called a **hash**, **random** or **relative** file) has records that are stored and retrieved according to either their disk address or their relative position within the file. This means that the program which stores and retrieves the records has first to specify the address of the record in the file.

This is done by means of an **algorithm** or formula, which transforms the record key into an address at which the record is stored. In the simplest case, record number 1 will be stored in block 1, record number 2 in block 2 and so on. This is called **relative** file addressing, because each record is stored at a location given by its key, relative to the start of the file.

More often, however, record keys do not lend themselves to such simple treatment. If for example we have about 1000 records to store, and each record key is 5 digits long, it would be a waste of space to allow 99999 blocks in which to store records. Therefore, a **hashing algorithm** is used to translate the key into an address.

Direct access file: a collection of records, where each record is stored at a disk address, calculated from the record's primary key.

One hashing method is the division/remainder method. Using this method, the key of the record is divided by the total number of addresses on the file, and the remainder is taken as the address of the record.

For example, the address of record number 75481 would be calculated as follows:

$75481/1000 = 75$ remainder 481.   Address = 481.

> **Q1:** Using this hashing algorithm, calculate the addresses of records with keys 00067, 00500, 35648.

Synonyms

This method of file organization presents a problem: however cunning the hashing algorithm, synonyms are bound to occur, when two record keys generate the same address. This is also known as a collision. One method of resolving synonyms is to place the record that caused the collision into the next available free space. When the highest address is reached, the next record can be stored at address 0 (known as wrap round). Another technique is to have a separate overflow area and leave a tag in the original location to indicate where to look next.

Properties of a good hashing algorithm

A hashing algorithm needs to be chosen so that it gives a good spread of records. This will partly depend on the properties of the record keys. Sometimes, to obtain a better spread of record addresses, a prime number close to the number of records to be stored on the file is chosen and the key of the record is divided by this number to obtain the remainder. For example, on the file of 1000 records discussed above, you could try dividing the keys by the prime number 997 instead of 1000 before taking the remainder. Hashing algorithms are also known as randomizing functions.

The algorithm should be chosen so that:

• It can generate any of the available addresses on the file;
• It is fast to calculate;
• It minimises 'collisions' (synonyms).

Adding new records to a direct access file

To add a new record to a direct access file, its address first has to be calculated by applying the hashing algorithm. If that address is already full, the record can be put in the next available free space.

Example:

Assume we have a file of 1000 records and use wrap round with the hashing algorithm described earlier: **(address = key MOD 1000)**. Records with the following keys, added in the given order, will be stored as follows:

12345	⟶	stored at address 345
17998	⟶	stored at address 998
56998	⟶	stored at address 999 because 998 is already full
35345	⟶	stored at address 346 because 345 is already full
88000	⟶	stored at address 000
54999	⟶	stored at address 001 because 999 and 000 are already full

When searching for a record, the search has to continue until either the record is found or a blank space is encountered.

Adding new records to a direct access file

This poses a problem for deleting records. If the record 17998 in the example above, were subsequently deleted, 56998 would not be found as its proper address 998 would be empty. The way round this problem is to leave the deleted record in place, and to set a flag labelling it as deleted. In other words, although *logically* deleted, the record is still *physically* present. A '**flag**' is simply an extra variable, e.g. a Boolean variable, stored with each record as an extra field. When the file is initialised and contains no records, the flag in each address can be set to 0, meaning that the record position is empty. When a record is written to an address, the flag is set to 1. When the record is deleted, the only change made to the record is to set the flag back to 0. When looking for a particular record, if the record key is found but it has a flag of 0, it is considered to be logically 'not there'. It's as though it's been crossed out, so it is to be ignored, but we can still see that there was a record there at one time. This means the space can be reused if a new record with a key hashing to this address is to be added to the file but, because the space is not actually empty, the search for a record that may have overflowed to the next address will still continue until either the record is found or an empty space is encountered.

Updating by overlay

If the file to be updated is indexed sequential or random, it is possible to access a record directly, read it into memory, update it, and write it back to its original location. This is called **updating by overlay**, **updating in place** or **updating in situ** if you are a Latin speaker. It is possible to do this because, unlike in sequential file processing, the record is accessed by means of its address on the file and so can be written back to the same address.

File maintenance

File maintenance is similar to file updating, but refers to the updating of the more permanent fields on each record such as in a stock file, for example, the description of the item, price, location in warehouse, etc. It also involves adding new records to the file and deleting records for items that are no longer held.

Once again, depending on the file organisation, either the grandfather–father–son technique will be used, or, if the file is direct access, **updating by overlay** may be used.

File access methods

How a file is **organised** determines how it can be **accessed**:

- a sequential file can only be accessed sequentially;
- a direct access file would normally only be accessed directly (it *could* be accessed serially but the records would not be in any particular sequence so this would be unusual);

Criteria for use of sequential and direct access files

The choice of file organization (or more likely today, database design) is one of the most important decisions made by the system designer. A number of questions needs to be answered, including:

- Must the user have immediate access to the data, with a response time of no more than a few seconds?
- Must the information be completely up to date, or will last night's or last week's information be sufficient?
- Can requests for information be batched, sequenced and processed all together?
- Are reports needed in a particular sequence?
- What is the most suitable storage medium for the volume of data involved?
- What will happen if the information on the files is lost or destroyed?

In addition two further factors need to be considered; **hit rate** and **volatility**.

Hit rate

Hit rate measures the proportion of records being accessed on any one run. It is calculated by dividing the number of records accessed by the total number of records on the file, and expressed as a percentage.

For example, on a payroll run if 190 out of 200 employees were to be paid, the hit rate would be 95%. In a system for processing car insurance renewals in weekly batches, the hit rate would be about 2% if renewals were spread more or less evenly through the year.

Sequential updating is inefficient with a low hit rate; direct access would be better.

Use of serial files

Serial files are normally only used as transaction files, recording data in the order in which events take place; for example, sales in a shop, customers taking cash from a cash machine, orders arriving at a mail order company. The transactions may be batched and the master files updated at a later time, or alternatively in a real-time system, the files may be updated straight away but the transaction file is kept for record-keeping purposes. It will also be used in the event of a disaster like a disk head crash, to restore the master file from the previous night's backup.

Use of sequential files

Sequential files are used as master files for high hit rate applications such as payroll. The main bulk of processing time is taken up with the weekly or monthly payroll, when every employee's record needs to be accessed and the year-to-date fields brought up to date, and sequential organisation is fast and efficient. It is not efficient when only a few records need to be accessed; for example if an employee changes address and the record needs to be updated, since the entire file has to be read and copied over to a new master file. However as this happens relatively infrequently it still makes sense to use a sequential file organisation.

Use of direct access files

Direct access files are used in situations where extremely fast access to individual records is required. To find a record, the hashing algorithm is applied to the record key and the record address immediately found, so no time is wasted looking up various levels of index. In a network system, user ids and passwords could be stored on a direct access file; the user id would be the key field from which the address is calculated, and the record would hold the password (encrypted for security reasons) and other information on access rights. Direct access file organisation might also be used in an airline booking system, where thousands of bookings are made every day for each airline from terminals all over the country. A fast response time to the desired record is crucial here. Note that direct access file organisation is not suitable if reports are going to be needed in key sequence, as the records are scattered 'at random' around the file.

Generating a direct access file from a sequential file

If the records in a sequential file need to be accessed quickly, it may be necessary to convert the file into a direct access file. A new file is generated using the following algorithm:

Algorithm

Generate new file with sufficient empty records

Work from beginning of sequential file

Repeat

      Read next record

      Hash the primary key to generate address

      Insert record at this position in new file

Until End Of File

2-19

Exercises

1   A *text file* of words is read by a program which creates a *non-text serial file*.

   (a) What is meant by:

      (i) a text file; (1)

      (ii) a non-text file; (1)

      (iii) a serial file? (1)

   (b) The serial file is processed by a program which removes duplicate words and writes the results to a *sequential file* with a *variable length record structure*.

      What is meant by:

      (i) a sequential file; (1)

      (ii) a variable length record structure? (1)

   (c) State **one** advantage and **one** disadvantage of variable length records over fixed length records. (2)

   (d) A program is written which searches the sequential file for a match with a given word that might be recorded in the file. List the steps for this process. (3)

(e) For a very large sequential file looking up words can be quite slow. It is suggested that look up time can be reduced by searching a different file in which the words have been stored according to a hashing algorithm.

List the steps to generate this new file from the sequential file (do not describe the details of any particular hashing algorithm). (4)

AQA CPT2 Qu 8 May 2001

2 The construction of an electronic English-French dictionary is trialled by creating a simpler version using one hundred English-French word pairs stored line-by-line in a text file, file A.

(a) (i) What is a text file? (1)

(ii) Name the most suitable type of software for a typist to use to create the contents of file A. (1)

(iii) What hardware could have been used to enter the word pairs, printed on paper, **directly** into the computer system? (1)

(b) A computer program reads word pairs, one line at a time, from file A.

It stores each word pair in a sequentially organised file of records, file B, by English word.

(i) State **two** characteristics of a sequentially organised file. (2)

(ii) Give the field names for **two** essential fields of file B. (2)

(c) File B is read sequentially and its records are stored in file C, on a direct access medium, by applying the following hashing function to each English word in file B.

(Sum of ASCII codes of all letters in the English word) Mod 150

For example, applying the hashing function to the word BAD using ASCII codes

A = 65, B = 66, D = 68 produces

$(66 + 65 + 68)$ Mod 150 = 49

(Mod gives the remainder after integer division)

File C consists of one hundred and fifty initially empty records.

(i) What use is made of the number produced by the hashing function when storing each word-pair record in file C? (1)

(ii) Why is Mod 150 used? (1)

(iii) Give **two** properties that this hashing function should have. (2)

(d) Using only file C, list the main steps that a computer program must follow to display on a VDU the French equivalent of an English word entered at the keyboard. Your solution must take account of the case when the English-French word pair is **not** present in file C. (5)

AQA CPT2 Qu 8 January 2003

2-19

Chapter 20 – File Security Methods

Threats to information systems

Computer-based information systems are vulnerable to crime and abuse, natural disaster and human error. In this chapter we'll look at some of the ways that an organisation can protect the **security** of data from theft or destruction.

Data security

Maintaining data security means keeping data safe from the various hazards to which it may be subjected. These include:

- natural hazards such as fire, floods, hurricanes or earthquakes;

- deliberate corruption or destruction of data by malicious or terrorist acts;

- illegal access to data by 'hackers';

- accidental destruction of data by hardware failure or program or operator error.

Data Security: Protection against loss, corruption of, or unauthorised access to data.

Q1: Suggest measures to minimize the danger of loss of data from natural hazards.

Keeping data secure from fraudulent use or malicious damage

Data may be at risk not only from outside 'hackers' but from employees within the company. Organisations are often exposed to the possibility of fraud, deliberate corruption of data by disgruntled employees or theft of software or data which may fall into the hands of competitors. Measures to counteract these risks include the following:

- careful vetting of prospective employees;

- immediate removal of employees who have been sacked or who hand in their resignation, and cancellation of all passwords and authorisations;

- 'separation of duties'; i.e. trying to ensure that it would take the collusion of two or more employees to be able to defraud the company. The functions of data preparation, computer operations and other jobs should be separate, with no overlap of responsibility;

- prevention of unauthorised access by employees and others to secure areas such as computer operations rooms, by means of machine-readable cards or badges or other types of locks;

- the use of passwords to gain access to the computer system from terminals;

- educating staff to be aware of possible breaches of security, and to be alert in preventing them or reporting them. This can include politely challenging strangers with a "May I help you?" approach, not leaving output lying around, machines logged on, or doors unlocked;

- appointing a security manager and using special software which can monitor all terminal activity. Such software can enable the security manager to see, either with or without users' knowledge, everything being typed on any screen in a network. It will also record statistics such as number of logins at each terminal, hours of login time, number of times particular programs or databases were accessed and so on. It will even log the security manager's activities!

Password protection

Most password schemes use tables to store the current password for each authorised user. These tables will be stored on disk and will be backed up along with other vital system files, and in addition may be printed out in a dump of system files. For this reason password lists should not be stored in plain form but should be **encrypted**, and held in an irreversibly transformed state.

User IDs and passwords

Each user in an organisation who is permitted to access a company computer system is issued with a user id and a password, which will normally give them a certain level of access rights set by the systems manager. Common rules issued by companies regarding passwords include the following:

- Passwords must be at least 6 characters;
- Password display must be automatically suppressed on screen or printed output;
- Files containing passwords must be encrypted;
- All users must ensure that their password is kept confidential, not written down, not made up of easily-guessed words and is changed regularly, at least every 3 months.

Q2: Describe several ways by which a password may become known to an unauthorised person.

Q3: If the encrypted passwords cannot be decoded, how will the system be able to compare a password entered by the user with the coded password held in the password table?

Q4: What happens if the user forgets his password?

When a user types a password at a keyboard, the password is usually concealed in some way, for example by not echoing it on the screen. However, it can still be observed by wire-tapping. Passwords can be protected during transmission by encrypting them, but this is costly.

Communications security

Telecommunications systems are vulnerable to hackers who discover a user id and password and can gain entry to a networked computer system from their own computer. One way of preventing this is to use a call-back procedure so that when a remote user logs in, the computer automatically calls them back at a pre-arranged telephone number to verify their access request before allowing them to log on.

Data encryption can also be used to 'scramble' highly sensitive or confidential data before transmission.

Data encryption

Data on a network is vulnerable to wire-tapping when it is being transmitted over a network, and one method of preventing confidential data from being read by unauthorised hackers is to **encrypt** it, making it incomprehensible to anyone who does not hold the 'key' to decode it.

Figure 20.1: Data encryption

There are many ways of encrypting data, often based on either **transposition** (where characters are switched around) or substitution (where characters are replaced by other characters).

In a **transposition** cipher, the message could be written in a grid row by row and transmitted column by column. The sentence 'Here is the exam paper' could be written in a 5 x 5 grid:

```
H E R E *
I S * T H
E * E X A
M * P A P
E R * * *
```

And transmitted as HIEMEES**RR*EP*ETHXA**HAP*

Q5: Using the same grid, decode the message ITT*O*E*HRWDNIYA*OS*NITT*

Using a substitution cipher, a 'key' that is known to both sender and receiver is used to code the message. A very simple example is to substitute each letter with the next one in the alphabet.

In practice, since the key must be difficult to break, a much more sophisticated algorithm must be used, with frequent changes of key. (See also discussion of strong and weak encryption in Chapter 27.)

Cryptography serves three purposes:

- it helps to identify authentic users;
- it prevents alteration of the message;
- it prevents unauthorised users from reading the message.

Access rights

Even authorised users do not normally have the right to see all the data held on a company computer system – they can see only the data that they need to do their job. In a hospital, for example, receptionists may have the right to view and change some patient details such as name, address and appointments but may not access the patient's medical records. In a stock control system, salesmen may be permitted to view the price, description and quantity in stock of a particular item, but not to change any of the details held.

Access rights to a particular set of data could typically be set to Read-Only, Read/Write, or No Access. This ensures that users within a company can only gain access to data which they are permitted to see, and can only change or delete data on the database if they are authorised to do so.

Likewise, the computer can also be programmed to allow access to particular data only from certain terminals, and only at certain times of day. The terminal in the database administrator's office may be the only terminal from which changes to the structure of a database may be made. An 'access directory' specifying each user's access rights is shown in Figure 20.2.

Access Profile: User ID 26885

Data	Access right	Terminal number	Permitted time	Security level
Customer Number	Read only	04,05	0830-1800	7
Credit Limit	Read/Write	04	0830-1800	10
Payment	Read/Write	04,05	0830-1700	7
Credit Rating	No Access			12

Figure 20.2: A security access table as part of a database

Biometric security measures

Passwords are only effective if people use them properly: if obvious passwords are used, or people tell them to their friends or write them down on a piece of paper blue-tacked to the computer, they are useless. *Biometric* methods of identifying an authorised user include fingerprint recognition techniques, voice recognition and face recognition. One such system uses an infra-red scanner to capture the unique pattern of blood vessels under the skin, and can even differentiate between identical twins by comparing the scan with the one on disk stored for each person.

Case study: National Identity cards

In April 2004 the Government conducted its first trial of a national Identity card using 10,000 volunteers. It has been claimed that a national ID card will help to fight financial services fraud, such as the rising problem of identity theft, credit card fraud and money laundering, all of which have been linked to the funding of terrorism.

The ID cards need to be fraud-proof, and that is likely to mean using some kind of "biometric" form of identification, such as a fingerprint or iris scanning. There is, however, some doubt about the quality of biometric identification – it has been rejected for the new generation of chip and pin credit and debit cards because no system was found to be reliable enough. But, even if a reliable biometric system is developed, it raises a question about how the card will be verified. For example, if iris scanning were adopted as an identifier, then a bank or shop would need some kind of iris scanning device to check that the card details matched the customer's eye. Are customers really going to queue to get their eyes scanned?

Disaster planning

No matter what precautions are taken against fire, flood, power surges, and deliberate or accidental destruction of data, the possibility always exists that data will be destroyed. A simple disk head crash can destroy a disk pack in a fraction of a second. System designers must provide a reasonable backup facility that does not degrade the performance of the system and does not cost too much.

The cost of lack of planning for computer failure can be ruinous. IBM estimates that 70% of organisations that experience a failure (caused by fire, flood, power failure, malice etc) cease operating within 18 months. The main consequence of a computer failure is loss of business, but other problems include loss of credibility, cashflow interruptions, poorer service to customers and loss of production.

Periodic backups

The most common technique used to ensure that data is not lost is to make **periodic backups**, by copying files regularly and keeping them in a safe place. This scheme has several weaknesses:

- All updates to a file since the last backup may be lost;
- The system may need to be shut down during backup operations;
- Backups of large files can be extremely time-consuming;
- When a failure occurs, recovery from the backup can be even more time-consuming.

A **benefit** of periodic backups is that files which may have become fragmented by additions and deletions can be reorganised to occupy contiguous space, usually resulting in much faster access time.

An important feature of all backup systems is the safe storage of the backup copies: it is usually necessary to store one backup copy in a fire-proof safe in the building, and another copy off-site.

2-20

Recovery procedures

A contingency plan needs to be developed to allow rapid recovery from major disruptions. In addition to file back-up procedures, it is necessary to:

• identify alternative compatible equipment and security facilities, or implement a service agreement which provides replacement equipment when needed. This may also include putting up temporary office space;

• have provision for alternative communication links.

Exercises

1 (a) What is meant by data security? (1)

(b) Name one technique for ensuring the security of data. (1)

New Question

2 A school stores confidential pupil data in an on-line information retrieval system to which teachers, office staff and management have authorised access.

(a) (i) Name **two** precautions that should be taken to minimise unauthorised access by pupils.

(ii) Describe how unauthorised access could be detected. (1)

(b) Why might teachers have different access privileges to office staff? (1)

(c) Explain how the data should be protected from corruption. (1)

(d) Every authorised user of the on-line system is given a user ID and a password. Describe **three** ways in which the use of passwords can be made as secure as possible. (3)

(e) What safeguards should the school use to protect from threats to its data from

(i) Power failure of the on-line system; (1)

(ii) Fire; (1)

(iii) Viruses; (1)

(iv) Theft. (1)

New Question

2-20

Chapter 21 – Data Processing Integrity Methods

Data integrity

This refers to the **accuracy** of the data. The data held in a computer system may become incorrect or corrupted in many different ways and at many stages during data processing.

- **Errors on input**. Data that is keyed in may be wrongly transcribed. A batch of transaction data could go astray, or be keyed in twice by mistake.

- **Errors in operating procedure**. An update program could for example be run twice in error and quantities on a master file would then be updated twice.

- **Program errors**. These could lead to corruption of files; a new system may have errors in it that will not surface for some time, or errors may be introduced during program maintenance.

- **Viruses**. Files can be corrupted or deleted if a disk becomes infected with a virus.

- **Transmission errors**. Interference or noise in a communications link may cause bits to be wrongly received.

Data integrity: the accuracy or validity of data.

Standard clerical procedures

To protect against input and operating procedure errors, standard procedures may be documented and followed for both input and output.

Input

- Data entry must be limited to authorised personnel only.

- In large volume data entry, data may be verified (keyed in twice by different operators) to guard against keying errors.

- Data control totals must be used wherever possible to verify the completeness and accuracy of the data, and to guard against duplicate or illegal entry.

Output

- All output should be inspected for reasonableness and any inconsistencies investigated.

- Printed output containing sensitive information should be shredded after use.

Data entry methods

Methods of 'direct data capture' which cut out the need to key in data from input documents are likely to have advantages in terms of speed, accuracy and cost, and so are becoming more and more common. However, we are a long way off from escaping the chore of filling in forms of one sort or another, a large number of which will then have to be keyed into a computer system.

> **Q1:** Name (a) some applications which use direct data entry, eliminating the need for keying in data and
>
> (b) applications which require data to be keyed in.

Types of input error

Figure 21.1 shows an example of an order form filled in by customers of a mail order company.

ORDERED BY						
MR/MRS/MISS/MS					CUSTOMER NO	
SURNAME					POST TO:	
ADDRESS					MANSION HOUSE, MAIN STREET	
					BANSTEAD	
					LAKE DISTRICT	
POSTCODE					LA31 8TR	
DAYTIME TEL NO						

PAGE NO	CODE	COLOUR	SIZE	QTY	DESCRIPTION	PRICE
					GOODS TOTAL	
					P&P	
					TOTAL PAYABLE	

CARD NO   VALID FROM   EXPIRY DATE

Figure 21.1: A Mail Order form

The information from this form will be keyed in to the computer and then processed to produce a set of documents including a delivery note and invoice for the customer, as well as updating stock and sales records. There are several possible sources of error before the data is processed:

- the customer could make a mistake, entering the wrong product codes, adding up the total cost wrongly, forgetting to enter their address or card expiry date, etc.

- the person keying in the data could make a **transcription** error, keying in the wrong product code or quantity, misreading the customer's name, adding an extra couple of 0's to the total price by keeping a finger down too long, and so on;

- a form could be blown into the bin by a sudden draught as a fan starts up or someone flounces out, slamming the door – or the operator might decide the writing was so bad it simply wasn't worth the effort of struggling with it, and bin it;

- a bored keypunch operator, chatting to a colleague, could enter the same form twice without realising it;

- a faulty connection between hardware components such as the processor and the disk drive could mean that some characters are wrongly transmitted.

Now clearly a mail order company would not stay in business very long if this was how the operation worked! So what can be done to minimise the possibility of error?

Batch processing

In a batch processing system, documents such as the sales orders described above are collected into batches of typically 50 documents. A **data control clerk** has the responsibility of:

- counting the documents;
- checking each one visually to see that the customer has entered essential details such as their name and address, and card details if that is the payment method;
- calculating a **control total** of some crucial field such as Total Payable, for the entire batch of 50 documents;
- calculating **hash totals** of other fields such as size or quantity (see below):
- filling in a batch header document which will show, for example:

  - batch number
  - date received
  - hash total
  - number of documents in batch
  - control total

- logging the batch in a book kept for this purpose.

A **hash total** is a sum of values calculated purely for validation purposes. For example, if the sizes of all garments ordered on a batch of forms (12,10, 12, 34, 36, etc.) are added together and the total entered on the batch header and keyed in, the computer will be able to perform the same calculation and if the figures don't match, then the batch must have an error in it somewhere.

Control totals and hash totals have a similar purpose; the data from the batch header is keyed in as well as the contents of all the documents in the batch, and the computer performs the same summing calculations that the data entry clerk made manually. If there is any discrepancy, then an error is reported and the batch is rechecked. The difference between the two types of total is only that a hash total has no meaning, whereas a control total (e.g. number of documents in the batch) does.

Validation checks

As the data is being keyed in, a computer program controlling the input can perform various validation checks on the data. For example:

1. **Presence check**. Certain fields such as customer number, item code, quantity etc. must be present. The data control clerk may have visually checked this but the program can perform a second check. Also, if this is a new customer, a number could be automatically assigned.

2. **Format check** (also called **picture check**). For example the code perhaps has a pattern of 2 letters followed by 4 numbers. The quantity and price must be numeric. In a MS Access database this is set up using an **Input Mask**.

3. **Range check**. The expiry date of a card must have a month number between 1 and 12, and the date must be later than today's date.

4. **Uniqueness check**. If the field is used as an identifier, it must be unique.

5. **Type check**. Only entries of a certain data type are accepted, such as only digits in a number field.

6. **File lookup check**. If the customer has filled in their customer number, the computer can look this up on the customer file and display the name and address. The data entry operator can check that it tallies.

7 **Check digit check**. (see below).

8 **Batch header checks**. The total number of records in the batch should be calculated by the computer and compared with the figure on the batch header. The control totals and hash totals are also calculated and compared.

Check digits

Code numbers such as a customer number, employee number or product number are often lengthy and prone to error when being keyed in. One way of preventing these errors occurring is to add an extra digit to the end of a code number, which has been calculated from the digits of the code number. In this way the code number with its extra check digit is self-checking.

Check digit: an extra digit added to the end of a code number, which has been calculated from the digits of the code number.

The best-known method of calculating check digits is the modulus-11 system, which traps over 99% of all errors. The most common errors are a single incorrect digit being entered or a transposition error (two digits swapped). The calculation of a check digit is shown below.

1 Each digit of the code number is assigned a 'weight'. The right hand (least significant) digit is given a weight of 2, the next digit to the left 3 and so on.

2 Each digit is multiplied by its weight and the products added together.

3 The sum of the products is divided by 11 and the remainder obtained.

4 The remainder is subtracted from 11.

5 The result is divided again by 11 and the remainder is the check digit. The only exception is:

• If the remainder is 10, we 'borrow' the Roman numeral 'X' and use this as a check digit.

Example:

To calculate the check digit for the number 1587:

Original code number	1	5	8	7
Weights	5	4	3	2
Multiply digit by its weight	5	20	24	14
Add products together	$5 + 20 + 24 + 14 = 63$			
Divide by 11	5 remainder 8			
Subtract remainder from 11	$11 - 8 = 3$			
Divide by 11 again	0 remainder 3			

Check digit = 3. The complete code number is 15873.

To check that a code number is valid, it is not necessary to recalculate the check digit completely. If the check digit itself is assigned a weight of 1, and the products of the digits (including the check digit) and their respective weights are calculated, their sum will be divisible by 11 if the check digit is correct.

Q2: All books have an ISBN number which has a modulus-11 check digit. Try checking whether the ISBN number 1-85805-170-3 is valid. (Ignore the hyphens). Check whether the ISBN 0-582-27544-X is valid.

Verification

Verification is the process of entering data twice, with the second entry being compared with the first to ensure that it is accurate. It is common in batch processing for a second data entry operator to key in a batch of data to verify it. You have probably come across another example of verification when setting a password; you are asked to key the password in a second time to ensure that you didn't make a keying error the first time, as it is not echoed on the screen.

Detecting transmission errors

In order to guard against the possibility of data being wrongly transmitted between the various hardware components of a computer, a **parity bit** is added to each character. In an even parity machine, the total number of 'On' bits in every byte (including the parity bit) must be an even number. When data is moved from one location to another, the parity bits are checked at both the sending and receiving end and, if the wrong number of bits are 'On', an error message is displayed.

Thus a character code of 1101010 will have a parity bit of 0 appended to it, and a character code of 1101110 will have a parity bit of 1 appended.

(See Chapter 12, Figure 12.5.)

Data is transmitted over a transmission line between computers in **blocks** of say 256 bytes. A **checksum** may be calculated by adding together the numeric value of all the bytes in a block, and this sum is transmitted with the data, to be checked again at the receiving end.

Protection against viruses

Steps can be taken which minimise the risk of suffering damage from viruses. These include:

- making sure that all purchased software comes in sealed, tamper-proof packaging;

- not permitting floppy disks containing software or data to be removed from or brought into the office. (This is a sackable offence in some companies.)

- using anti-virus software to check all floppy disks before use.

Accuracy vs validity of data

Validation can only check that data is sensible. To be accurate, data must also be correct when entered and up-to-date. Validation cannot ensure that data entered represents the correct values, so it is possible for data to be valid but not accurate.

Exercises

1   Data integrity is paramount when processing data using computer systems.

    (a)   What is meant by data integrity?   (1)

    (b)   Outline two ways in which data integrity may be compromised.   (2)

    (c)   Name two methods for ensuring the integrity of data.   (2)

New Question

2   When data is first entered into the system it is validated and verified.

    (a)   What is validation?   (1)

    (b)   What is verification?   (1)

New Question

3   The last digit of an ISBN (International Standard Book Number) is a check digit. For example, the check digit of the ISBN 1-904467-29-6 is 6.

    (a)   How is the check digit arrived at?   (1)

    (b)   What is its purpose?   (1)

New Question

4   The following data records are going to be entered as batch number 127 by keyboard operator 1 (initials AK) and again by keyboard operator 2 (initials BL).

EmployeeID	WeekNo	HoursWorked
003	5	35
005	5	30
007	5	25
011	5	35
023	5	20
030	4	35
101	4	23
205	5	17

    (a)   Complete the batch header document for the above records:

Batch Number		Date received	11/02/2004
Number of documents in batch		Control Total	
Operator Initials		Hash Total	
Verifier Initials		Date completed	

(6)

    (b)   What is the purpose of the batch header?   (1)

    (c)   How is the information on the batch header used by the system?   (2)

New Question

2-21

Chapter 22 – Entity-Relationship Modelling

The conceptual data model

When a systems analyst sits down to design a new system, one crucial task is to identify and state what **data** needs to be held. From the statement of data requirements a **conceptual data model** is produced. This describes how the data elements in the system are to be grouped. Three terms are used in building a picture of the data requirements: entity, attribute and relationship.

An entity is an object, person, event or thing of interest to an organisation about which data is to be recorded.

Example: Customer, Employee, Stock Item, Supplier.

An attribute is a property or characteristic of an entity.

Example: Attributes associated with a Customer include Customer ID, Surname, Initials, Title, Address.

A relationship is a link or association between two entities.

Example: Dentist and Patient; one dentist has many patients, but each patient only has one dentist.

Types of relationship

There are only three different 'degrees' of relationship between two attributes. A relationship may be:

- **One-to-one**   Examples of such a relationship include the relationship between Husband and Wife, or between Householder and Main Residence.
- **One-to-many**   Examples include the relationship between Mother and Children, between Customer and Order, between Borrower and Library Book
- **Many-to-many** Examples include the relationship between Student and Course, between Stock Item and Supplier, between Film and Film Star.

Entity-relationship diagrams

An entity-relationship diagram is a diagrammatic way of representing the relationships between the entities in a database. To show the relationship between two entities, both the **degree** and the **name** of the relationship need to be specified. E.g. In the first relationship shown below, the **degree** is *One-to-one*, the **name** of the relationship is *Drives*:

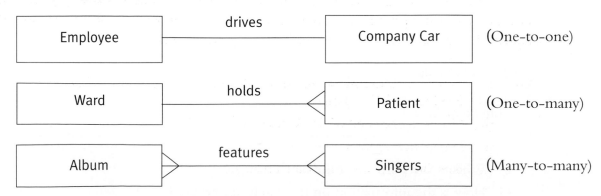

Figure 22.1: Entity-relationships

Sometimes it can be tricky to establish the degree of the relationship. For example, several employees may use the same company car at different times. A single employee may change the company car that he uses. The relationship will depend upon whether the data held refers to the current situation, or is a historical record. The assumption has been made above that the database is to record the current car driven by an employee.

Example:

The data requirements for a hospital in-patient system are defined as follows:
A hospital is organised into a number of wards. Each ward has a ward number and a name recorded, along with a number of beds in that ward. Each ward is staffed by nurses. Nurses have their staff number and name recorded, and are assigned to a single ward.

Each patient in the hospital has a patient identification number, and their name, address and date of birth are recorded. Each patient is under the care of a single consultant and is assigned to a single ward. Each consultant is responsible for a number of patients. Consultants have their staff number, name and specialism recorded.

State four entities for the hospital in-patient system and suggest an identifier for each of these entities.

Draw an entity-relationship diagram to show the relationship between the entities.

Answer:

Entity	Identifier
Ward	WardID
Nurse	StaffID
Patient	PatientID
Consultant	StaffID

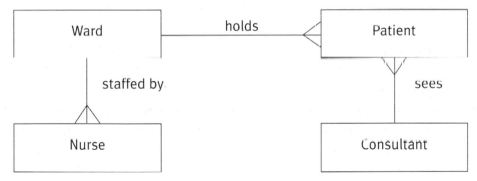

Note that a one-to-many relationship does not necessarily imply that **every** ward, for example, has many patients, merely that is possible that at least one ward has more than one patient. It is possible that some wards have no patients at all.

Q1: Draw entity-relationship diagrams to illustrate the relationships between
(a) Product and Component
(b) Home-owner and Main Residence
(c) Pet-owner and Pet
(d) Racehorse-owner and Racehorse

Once again there may be some argument about these relationships. Can a pet have more than one owner? For the purposes of a vet's database, probably not. A racehorse, on the other hand, is such a valuable animal that it is quite common for several people to have 'shares' in the horse.

When you are designing a database, it can often be quite hard to decide what is an entity and what is an attribute. Is **pet** an attribute of **owner**, or is **owner** an attribute of **pet**? Or is neither the case, since both are entities in their own right? The latter statement is probably the correct interpretation of the real world situation.

> **Q2:** In a database system used by a car dealer, Car is one entity, and it has a primary key RegistrationNumber. Is Manufacturer an attribute of car, or is it an entity?

Exercises

1. A library plans to set up a database to keep track of its members, stock and loans. For members, the fields MemberID, Surname and Address are to be stored. For stock, the fields ISBN, AcquisitionNo, Title and Author are to be stored. For loans the MemberID of the member borrowing the book, and the AcquisitionNo of the book are stored together with the date the book is due to be returned. When the book is returned the loan record is deleted.

   (a) State an identifier (primary key) for each of the entities Member, Stock and Loan. (3)

   (b) Draw an entity-relationship diagram showing the relationships between the entities. (3)

   New Question

2. A college wants to set up a database for its student, course and course enrolment data. The data to be stored for the student are StudentID, FirstName, Surname, DateOfBirth, Address. The fields required for the course are CourseID, CourseDescription. When a student enrols on a course the StudentID and the CourseID are to be stored.

   (a) State an identifier for each of the entities Student, Course and CourseEnrolment.   (3)

   (b) Draw an entity-relationship diagram showing the relationships between the entities. (3)

   New Question

3. An exam board wants to set up a database for all its exam modules, candidates and results. For the purpose of this exercise, assume that each candidate can enter each module once only. The data to be stored for the candidate are CandidateNumber, FirstName, Surname, DateOfBirth. The data to be stored for the exams are ModuleCode, Subject. When a candidate takes an exam, the following details are recorded: CandidateNumber, ModuleCode, UMS (Unified Mark Scheme).

   (a) State an identifier for each of the entities Candidate, ExamModule and Result.   (3)

   (b) Draw an entity-relationship diagram showing the relationships between the entities. (3)

   New Question

4. A company selling office furniture wants to set up a database to keep track of its customers, stock and orders. The data recorded for customers are CustomerID, Name, Address. The data to be stored for the stock are StockID, Description, UnitPrice. For each order the CustomerID, OrderID and OrderDate are recorded. For each item ordered, the StockID and NumberOf ItemsOrdered are recorded. One order form may include several order lines for different items, but the same item would not appear more than once on the same order form.

   (a) State an identifier for each of the entities Customer, Order, OrderLine, StockItem   (4)

   (b) Draw an entity-relationship diagram showing the relationships between the entities. (4)

   New Question

2-22

Chapter 23 – Database Concepts

Information is vital to organizations. Often one of the most valuable resources in a business is its accumulated information. The problem is the storage, retrieval and manipulation of all this information.

Traditional file approach

In the early days of computerised data processing, an organisation's data was duplicated in separate files for the use of individual departments. For example the Personnel Department would hold details on name, address, qualifications etc. of each employee, while the Payroll Department would hold details of name, address and salary of each employee. Each department had its own set of application programs to process the data in these files. This led to:

- **duplicated data**, meaning wasted space;

- **inconsistency problems**, where for example an address was updated on one file but not on another; e.g. Mr Johnstone moves house and passes his new address to Personnel who update their file. Unfortunately no-one tells the Payroll Department and his next payslip is sent to the old address.

- **the data was not shareable**; if one department needed data that was held by another, it was awkward to obtain it.

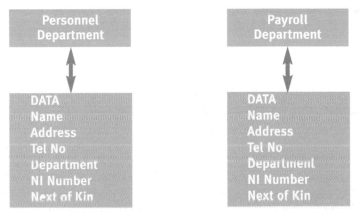

Figure 23.1 Traditional File Processing System

The database approach

In an attempt to solve the above problems, the data from the various departments was centralised in a common pool so that **all applications had access to the same set of data**. For example all the details about stock held by a garden centre would be held in a database which was accessible by all applications using the data. The Sales department would update quantities in stock, the Marketing department would use the data to produce a catalogue, the Reorder system would use it to decide what stock to reorder.

Although this solved problems of duplication and inconsistency, it introduced two major new problems:

- **Unproductive maintenance**; if one department needed some change to the number or length of fields in a record on one of the common files, every department had to change its application programs to take this change into account, even if the field was not one used by that department. In other words, the programs were still dependent on the record structure, and all departments were affected by even minor changes in another department.

- **Problems of security**; even confidential or commercially sensitive data was accessible by every application, because the data was centrally held.

A **database**, therefore, is defined as a collection of non-redundant data sharable between different application systems. The software used to control access to the data is known as a Data Base Management System (DBMS).

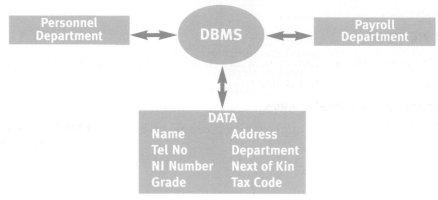

Figure 23.2 Database approach

Validation of input data

Almost every field in a database can be put through some type of **validation** to ensure that data entry is valid (see Chapter 21). There are several types of validation check that may be specified, for example:

- Presence check – must data be entered in this field?

- Range check – is there a low/high limit? (e.g. the date must be greater than or equal to today's date in a theatre booking file, the price of a new car from a particular manufacturer must be between £6,000 and £30,000 in a car sales database.)

- Format check – must the data be in a particular format? (e.g. a National Insurance number must be 2 letters followed by 6 digits and a letter.)

- Is there a list of valid values? (e.g. Gender must be either M or F.)

Relational database design

In a relational database, data is held in tables (also called relations) and the tables are linked by means of common attributes.

Relational database: a collection of tables in which relationships are modelled by shared attributes.

Conceptually then, one row of a table holds one record. Each column in the table represents one attribute.

e.g. A table holding data about an entity *Book* may have the following rows and columns:

Accession Number	DeweyCode	Title	Author	DatePublished
88	121.9	Let's Cook!	Chan, C	1992
123	345.440	Electricity	Glendenning, V	1995
300	345.440	Riders	Cooper, J	1995
657	200.00	Greek in 3 weeks	Stavros, G	1990
777	001.602	I.T. in Society	Laudon, K	1995
etc				

Figure 23.3: A table in a relational database

Standard Notation

There is a standard notation for describing a table in a relational database. For example, to describe the table shown above, you would write

Book (**AccessionNumber**, DeweyCode, Title, Author, DatePublished)

Note that:

The entity name is shown outside the brackets;

The primary key (unique identifier) is underlined;

The attributes are shown in brackets, separated by commas, names written in 'camel caps' and without spaces.

Primary and secondary (alternate) keys

Each entity in a database must have a unique key known as the **primary key**. The primary key in the above table is AccessionNumber. In a database holding data about students, the primary key in a table about students could be a unique student number.

Primary key: An attribute that will identify a particular instance of an entity uniquely.

In order that a record with a particular primary key can be quickly located in a database, an **index** of primary keys will be automatically maintained by the database software, giving the position of each record according to its primary key

If a database table often needs to be searched on a different attribute, for example, title or author, these can be defined as **secondary keys** (also known as **alternate** keys) so that the table will also be indexed on these attributes.

Secondary or alternate key: An attribute that will identify a particular instance of an entity, but not necessarily uniquely.

Indexing

A database table can have indexes on as many attributes as you choose. An index is, in effect, a list of numerical values, which gives the order of the records when they are sorted on a particular attribute. An index on the Title attribute in the table shown in Figure 23.3, assuming it had only 5 records, would have entries 2, 4, 5, 1, 3. The DBMS constructs and maintains all the indexes automatically. Indexing imposes a logical order on the rows in a table without changing the physical order. There are advantages and disadvantages to having multiple indexes:

• in large tables they speed up queries considerably;

• when a report is required in the sequence of the indexed attribute, they avoid having to sort the database;

• on the negative side, they slow down data entry and editing, because the indexes have to be updated each time a record is added or deleted.

Primary index: an ordered list of primary key values.
A table has only one primary index but may have many secondary indexes.

Secondary index: an ordered list of secondary key values.

Linking database tables

Tables may be linked through the use of a common attribute. This attribute must be a primary key of one of the tables, and is known as a foreign key in the second table.

Foreign key: an attribute in one table, which is the primary key in another table.

Linking tables in one-to-many relationships

In a library database, two entities named **Borrower** and **Book** have been identified. There is a one-to-many relationship between these two entities, because one borrower may borrow several books, but the same book cannot be taken out by many borrowers simultaneously. The relationship can be represented by the following E-R diagram:

Figure 23.4: E-R Diagram

The Borrower and Book tables can be described using standard notation as follows:

Borrower (**BorrowerID**, Name, Address)

Book (**AccessionNumber**, DeweyCode, Title, Author, DatePublished)

The relationship is made through shared attributes. In order to link the two entities, the primary key BorrowerID needs to be added to the Book table as a *foreign key*. So the tables can now be described as

Borrower (**BorrowerID**, Name, Address)

Book (**AccessionNumber**, DeweyCode, Title, Author, DatePublished, *BorrowerID*)

Note that a foreign key is shown in italics.

Note that the foreign key is always the primary key of the table at the 'one' end of the E-R diagram and is added to the table at the 'many' end of the E-R diagram.

Linking tables in a many-to-many relationship

Tables that make up a relational database cannot represent many-to-many relationships. A many-to-many relationship can be removed by creating a link entity. The link entity's identifier (primary key) will often be made up of the original entities' identifiers.

Figure 23.5: Many-to-many relationship

To resolve this many-to-many relationship, a link entity, Enrolment, can be introduced:

Figure 23.6: Link entity introduced

Using the standard table notation, the tables can be described as follows:

Student (**StudentID**, Surname, DateOfBirth)

Course (**CourseID**, CourseName, Level)

Enrolment (**StudentID**, CourseID)

Querying a database

Information can be obtained from a database using **Query by Example (QBE)**.

Using this method the user may:

- combine, into one table, information from two or more related tables;
- select which attributes are to be shown in the 'Answer' table;
- specify search criteria;
- save the query so that it can be executed whenever required;
- save the results of the query (the 'Answer' table).

The figure below shows a **query by example** window in the MS Access database.

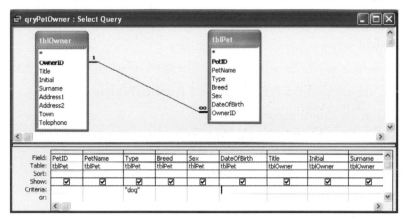

Figure 23.7: Query by Example

The above query is applied to the following tables:

Customer ID	Title	Initials	Surname	KnownAs
1234	Mr	F	Bloggs	Mr Bloggs
45673	Dr	K	Smith	Mr Smith
67821	Mrs	D	French	Mrs French

Figure 23.8: Customer Table

Order ID	Date	Customer ID	Paid	Order Total
4012	10/3/2004	1234	No	£45.60
4034	11/3/2004	45673	Yes	£38.90
4067	12/3/2004	67821	No	£74.35

Figure 23.9: Order Table

The query writes to an answer table the Customer ID, Surname and Order ID of unpaid orders. (The answer table is a new table created automatically when the query is run for the first time.)

Customer ID	Surname	Order ID
12345	Bloggs	4012
67821	French	4067

Figure 23.10: Answer Table

Exercises

1 A publisher uses a relational database to record details of articles it publishes in a monthly magazine.

Two relations (tables) **MagazineEdition** and **MagazineArticle** are used for this database.

MagazineEdition (MagazineEditionId, Month, Year)

MagazineArticle (ArticleId, ArticleType, ArticleTitle, Content, AuthorName, MagazineEditionId)

Each Article is assigned a unique ArticleId.

(a) What is a relational database? (1)

(b) State a suitable primary key for the MagazineEdition relation.
Justify your choice. (2)

(c) (i) Explain what is meant by foreign key. (2)

(ii) Name the attribute which is the foreign key in the relation MagazineArticle. (1)

(d) Indexes are created on **ArticleId** and **AuthorName** attributes.

(i) Why is an index used? (1)

(ii) Which of the two attribute indexes is a secondary index? (1)

(e) The following shows a sample of the MagazineEdition table and a sample of the MagazineArticle table.

MagazineEdition table

MagazineEditionId	Month	Year
:	:	:
240	December	1999
241	January	2000
242	February	2000
243	March	2000
:	:	:

MagazineArticle table

ArticleId	ArticleType	ArticleTitle	Content	AuthorName	MagazineEditionId
1	Business	....	....	Bloggs	89
2	Management	....	....	Smith	89
3	Business	....	....	Bloggs	89
4	Quality Control	....	....	Jones	89
5	Investments	....	....	Bloggs	90
:	:	:	:	:	:
1201	Recruitment	....	....	Jones	253
1202	Accounting	....	....	Smith	254
:	:	:	:	:	:

The following shows a Query By Example (QBE) applied to the MagazineEdition and MagazineArticle tables.

QBE

MagazineEditionId	AuthorName	ArticleType
	Bloggs	Business

(i) What will be the minimum number of records returned by this QBE? (1)

(ii) Complete the following QBE to extract the author names and article titles of all articles of the article type "Management" appearing in magazines published in the year 1999 or before.

(4)

AQA CPT2 Qu 10 May 2002

2 A charity uses a relational database to keep track of donors and their donations. Donations are given weekly, monthly and annually (donation type).

Two relations (tables) are used for this database.

Donors and **Donations**

Donor (DonorId, Name, Address, DonationType)

Donation (DonationId, AmountGiven, DateDonationGiven, DonorId)

Each donation is assigned a unique DonationId.

(a) What is a relational database? (1)

(b) Select a suitable primary key for the Donor relation. Justify your choice. (2)

(c) (i) Explain what is meant by the term foreign key. (2)

(ii) Name the attribute which is the foreign key in the relation Donation. (1)

(iii) Select a suitable primary key for the relation Donation. (1)

(d) Indexes are created on **DonorId** and **DonationType** attributes.

(i) Why is an index used? (1)

(ii) Which of the two attribute indexes is a secondary index? (1)

(e) The following are samples of the Donor table and the Donation table.

Donor table

DonorId	Name	Address	DonationType
:	:	:	:
:	:	:	:
567	Jones	....	Weekly
868	Smith	....	Monthly
919	Adams	....	Weekly
920	Gregory	....	Annually
:	:	:	:
:	:	:	:

Donation table

DonationId	Amount Given	DateDonation Given	DonorId
1	5	10/7/2000	567
2	7	10/7/2000	919
3	200	17/7/2000	920
4	7	17/7/2000	919
5	5	17/7/2000	567
:	:	:	:
:	:	:	:
12021	20	10/7/2000	868
12022	200	17/7/2000	920

The following shows a Query By Example (QBE) applied to the Donor and Donation tables.

QBE

DonorId	Name	Amount Given	Donation Type	Date Donation Given
			Weekly	10/7/2000

(i) How many records will be returned by this QBE? (1)

(ii) Using the result of the QBE, calculate the total amount given (1)

AQA CPT2 Qu January 2001

3 A newspaper publisher uses a relational database to record details of advertisements placed by businesses and members of the general public.

Two relations (tables) **Customer** and **Advertisement** are used for this database.

Customer (CustomerId, Name, Address, CustomerType)

Advertisement (AdvertId, Content, DateAdvertPlaced, NoOfNights, Classification, CustomerId)

Each advertisement is assigned a unique AdvertId.

(a) What is a relational database? (1)

(b) State a suitable primary key for the Customer relation. Justify your choice. (2)

(c) (i)   Explain what is meant by foreign key. (2)

(ii) Name the attribute which is the foreign key in the relation Advertisement. (1)

(iii) State a suitable primary key for the relation Advertisement. (1)

(d) Indexes are created on **CustomerId** and **Name** attributes.

(i) Why is an index used? (1)

(ii) Which of the two attribute indexes is a secondary index? (1)

(e) The following shows a sample of the Customer table and of the Advertisement table.

Customer table

CustomerId	Name	Address	Customer Type
:	:	:	:
:	:	:	:
920	Jones	......	Business
868	Smith	.....	Non-Business
919	Adams	.....	Non-Business
655	Gregory	.....	Business
:	:	:	:
:	:	:	:

Advertisement table

AdvertId	Content	DateAdvertPlaced	NoOfNights	Classification	CustomerId
1	Lawn Mower for Sale	10/7/2000	3	General Sales	567
2	Child's bicycle...	10/7/2000	2	General Sales	868
3	Ford Mondeo, T reg	11/7/2000	5	Cars for Sale	920
4	Ford Fiesta, T reg	12/7/2000	5	Cars for Sale	655
5	Electrician, no job too small	12/7/2000	10	Electricians	800
: :	: :	: :	: :	: :	: :
12021	Fiat Uno, P reg....	1/12/2000	3	Cars for Sale	868
12022	Study desk for sale	11/12/2000	2	General Sales	919

The following shows a Query By Example **(QBE)** applied to the Customer and Advertisement tables.

QBE

CustomerId	Name	CustomerType	Classification	DateAdvertPlaced
		Business	Cars for Sale	

(i)   What will be the minimum number of records returned by this QBE?   (1)

(ii)   Complete the following **QBE** to extract the names and addresses of all non-business customers placing an advert after 12/7/2000.

(4)

AQA CPT2 Qu 9 May 2001

Chapter 24 – Operating Systems

What is an operating system?

Computers require two types of software: **applications software** such as word processing, spreadsheet or graphics packages, and **systems software** to perform tasks needed to run the computer system. The operating system is systems software to control and monitor the running of application programs, and to allow users to communicate with the computer.

The operating system consists of a number of programs that are typically 'bundled' with the hardware; in other words, when you buy a new PC, for example, you will also be supplied with a CD containing the latest version of the Windows operating system. This then has to be installed by running a special installation program supplied on the CD, which will copy the operating system to your hard disk and customise it to your particular hardware configuration.

Each time you switch on your PC, the operating system kernel (the part you need in memory at all times) will be copied from the hard disk into memory, which takes a few minutes.

Operating system: software that handles the interface to the hardware and manages resources.

2-23

Functions of an operating system

Obviously the operating system (OS) for a standalone microcomputer system will be very much simpler than that of a supercomputer which is controlling hundreds of terminals and running many different kinds of job simultaneously. Nevertheless, all operating systems perform certain basic functions, including:

- **Memory management**. Most computers nowadays are capable of holding several programs in memory simultaneously so that a user can switch from one application to another. The operating system has to allocate memory to each application – as well as to itself!

- **Resource allocation and scheduling**. In larger computer systems, which are capable of running several programs at once (**multiprogramming**), the OS is responsible for allocating processing time, memory and input-output resources to each one. While one program is executing, the operating system is scheduling the use of input and output devices for other jobs. Not all jobs are performed in the order they are submitted; the operating system schedules them in order to make the best possible use of the computer's resources.

- **Backing store management**. The OS controls the transfer of data from secondary storage (e.g. disk) to main memory and back again. It also has to maintain a directory of the disk so that files and free space can be quickly located.

- **Interrupt handling**. The OS detects many different kinds of interrupt such as for example a user pressing the Enter key on the keyboard, a printer sending a message that it is out of paper, the real-time clock interrupting to indicate that the processor should be allocated to the next user in a multi-user system, a hardware or software malfunction.

- **Allowing a user to communicate with the computer**. The user gives instructions to the computer to start a program, copy a file, send a message to another user, and so on by typing in commands recognised by the operating system or by using a mouse to point and click in a graphical user interface such as Windows XP or 2000.

Provision of a virtual machine

The operating system functions in such a way as to hide from the user all the complexities of the hardware. The average user is completely unaware of the operating system working away behind the scenes, and sees only a machine which (with luck) simply does what it is instructed no matter how complex the tasks involved. Switching from one window to another, from one printer to another, creating a new folder or making a backup is simply a matter of a few mouse clicks, as far as the user is concerned. This easy-to-use machine is sometimes referred to as the 'virtual machine'.

Operating System Classification

Operating systems can be classified into different types, some of which are described below.

Batch

The most important operating system capability for sharing computer resources is multi-programming. This permits multiple programs to be active at the same time, with the operating system allowing each one a small 'time-slice' of processor time in turn. This technique was developed when computers were operated in batch-processing mode.

Batch-processing: processing is carried out from beginning to end without user interaction.

Jobs prepared in this way have all their processing requirements defined in advance. By using multiprogramming, a batch of several jobs can be loaded so that, when executed over the same time period, the processor is kept as busy as possible by switching between the jobs as and when necessary. This increases throughput, i.e. the total number of jobs completed per unit time, and reduces the turnaround time, i.e. time between job submission and job completion. There is a significant delay of, say, several hours between submitting a job and receiving the output.

Example:
Payroll system, processing payroll data supplied as data files and printing out payslips.

Interactive

With this type of processing the user interacts directly with the system to supply commands and data as the application program undergoes execution and receives the results of processing immediately. An operating system which allows such interaction is said to support interactive processing.

Interactive processing: user and computer are in direct two-way communication.

Example:
Travel agent booking and confirming a place on a package holiday for a client waiting in the shop.

Real-Time

Real time operating systems are characterised by four requirements:

• they have to support application programs which are non-sequential in nature, i.e. programs which do not have a START - PROCESS - END structure;

• they have to deal with a number of events which happen in parallel and at unpredictable moments in time (for example, a user clicking a mouse button);

• they have to carry out processing and produce a response within a specified interval of time;

• some systems are safety-critical, meaning they must be fail-safe and guarantee a response within a specified time interval.

Example:
Process control in a chemical plant or nuclear power station – up to 1000 signals per second can arrive from sensors attached to the system being controlled. The response time must be less than one thousandth of a second.

Real-time operating system: response within a certain maximum time, suitable for control of hardware in time-critical applications.

Network

A network operating system is required when a number of computers are connected together in a network. The operating system controls who logs on to the network by means of user names and passwords, in order to protect the data and programs stored on the network. It also makes the network transparent to the user, allowing any user with the appropriate access rights to use software stored on the network's file server, and to store data either on the file server or on a local hard or floppy disk.

Network operating system: includes software to communicate with other computers via a network and allows resources such as files and printers to be shared between computers.

File Management

An important part of a computer's operating system is the **file manager** or **file management system**. A file may be a document created in a wordprocessor or spreadsheet or other software, or it may be an executable file, i.e. a program that can be executed. When the user gives an instruction to save a file, giving it a name and specifying where it is to be saved, it is the job of the file manager to find a space on disk.

The file manager will typically hold the following information about each file or folder:

- file type – e.g., folder file, system file, hidden file, batch, executable, text;
- information indicating the location of the file on secondary storage – e.g., disk address of the first block in the file;
- file size in bytes;
- access rights – who can access the file and how it can be accessed: e.g., read only, read-write, write-only, delete permission;
- date information – e.g. data of creation, date of last access, date of last amendment, purge date;

Using the access rights the file manager is able to control who can share a particular file, and protect that file against unauthorised alteration.

Drives, folders and files

A drive is the hardware that seeks, reads and writes information from and to a disk. A hard disk and its drive are one inseparable unit, unlike a floppy disk which can be removed from its drive. Drives are given letter names like A, B, C etc. Frequently a large hard disk is 'partitioned' by the user or computer technician when the drive is initially formatted so that although there is only one physical drive, there are several 'logical drives' called, for example, F, G, X, Y, Z. This is done for convenience so that different types of work can be held on separate logical drives.

A hard disk is divided into a number of **folders** (called directories in early versions of Windows). Folders can be added and deleted by the user whenever necessary, and they are used to help keep all the thousands of files held on a disk organised so that they can be quickly located when needed. Folders can contain both files and subfolders.

Folder and file names in Windows 2000 and later versions can be up to 255 characters in length. In addition, they usually have an extension, which is added automatically by the particular software package in which they were created, and which identifies them as being, for example, a Word document, an Excel spreadsheet or a Pascal program.

e.g. **BensProject.doc** (The extension .doc identifies this as a Word document.)

ProgSquares.exe (The extension .exe identifies this as an executable file.)

Pathnames

Folders (or so-called directories) are organised in a tree structure, with the folder at the top of the tree being known as the root. To refer to a particular file in a particular folder, you have to give it its full pathname, which shows exactly which folder it is in.

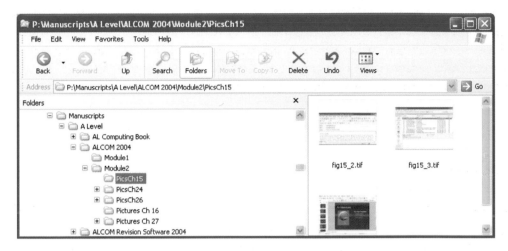

Figure 24.1: Directory structure

In the screenshot above taken from a Windows Explorer screen, the folder **A Level** is a subfolder of the **Manuscripts** folder on the **P:** drive. Within **A Level** there are subfolders named **AL Computing Book, ALCOM2004**, etc. The folder **ALCOM2004** has subfolders **Module1, Module2** etc. and Module2 has subfolders **PicsCh15, PicsCh24** etc.

The full name of the file **fig15_2.tif** is

P:\A Level\ALCOM2004\Module2\PicsCh15\fig15_2.tif

Access rights and other attributes

The file manager enables access rights to be set for particular files or folders. Depending on a user's ID and password, they may for example be given any of the following access rights to a file or folder:

Read	Allows the user to view the contents of the data file
Read & Execute	Allows the user to run a program file
Write	Allows the user to change the contents of the file
Modify	Allows the user to read, change or delete the file

Backing up and archiving

Backing up: a copy of a file is made to guard against data loss from accidents or deliberate action.

A backup is a spare copy of a file for use in the event of loss of the original. Ideally backup copies should be kept at a different site, so that data can be restored if a disaster occurs. Archiving means removing a file from the hard disk and copying it onto another medium, say on a writeable CD, which will not be changed again. For example, old invoices or purchase orders might be archived in order to make a permanent record of such documents.

Archiving: a file is removed from on-line storage and kept for longterm reference, for example on tape.

Exercises

1 (a) Distinguish file backing-up from archiving. (2)

(b) The directory structure shown in **Figure 1** contains a **root** directory (\) and four sub-directories, named **User1**, **User2**, **Project** and **Homework**.

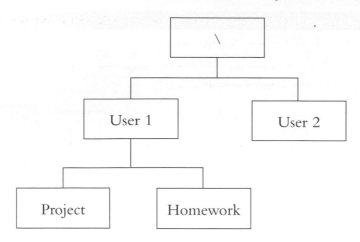

Figure 1

A file with the filename Project1.Pas is stored in the system with the directory structure shown in Figure 1. What is the pathname for Project1.Pas if it is stored in the:

(i) root directory; (1)

(ii) sub-directory Project? (1)

(c)

Field 1	Field 2	Field 3	Field 4	Field 5
Project1.Pas	rw	14286	12/12/2001	13:32
Project2.Pas	r	2560	01/01/2002	09:12

Figure 2

Figure 2 displays in five fields a directory listing of the **Project** directory. The first field is used to display a filename. What might the other **four** fields display? (4)

(d)

Field 1	Field 2	Field 3	Field 4	Field 5
	rwx	512	11/12/2001	13:32
	rwx	512	31/12/2001	09:12

Figure 3

Figure 3 shows the directory listing for the directory **User1** with the two entries for Field 1 removed. What should have appeared in Field 1 for these **two** entries? (2)

AQA CPT2 Qu 5 January 2002

2   A desktop PC has access to a *local disk drive*, C: and a *networked disk drive*, N:

(a)   What is meant by:

   (i)   local disk drive? (1)

   (ii) networked disk drive? (1)

(b)   The command "Type" lists the contents of a specified file on the desktop PC's VDU screen as shown in **Figure 1**.

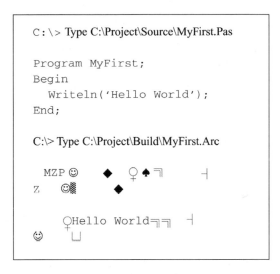

```
C:\> Type C:\Project\Source\MyFirst.Pas

Program MyFirst;
Begin
  Writeln('Hello World');
End;

C:\> Type C:\Project\Build\MyFirst.Arc
```

Figure 1

Using **only** the information contained in **Figure 1**, give **one** example of each of the following:

   (i)   a logical drive (1)

   (ii) a file pathname (1)

   (iii) a sub-directory (1)

   (iv) the filename of a text file (1)

   (v)   the filename of a non-text file (1)

(c)   Using the information contained within **Figure 1** complete the directory structure diagram shown in **Figure 2** for the desktop PC's local drive, C.

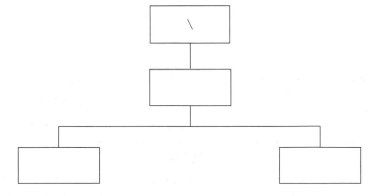

Figure 2

(1)

AQA CPT2 Qu 2 June 2003

3 For each of the following name a suitable type of operating system. Give one reason for your choice.

(a) A computer system consisting of several desktop PCs sharing each other's files. (2)

(b) A computer system dedicated to controlling the flow of chemicals in a chemical processing plant. (2)

(c) A computer system dedicated to processing, at the end of each day, a bank's transactions stored on magnetic disk. (2)

AQA CPT2 Qu 3 May 2002

4 (a) In the context of file management what is a file? (1)

The directory structure shown in the diagram contains a root directory (\ ) and three sub-directories, named **Work, Old** and **BackUp**.

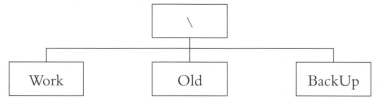

(b) The sub-directory names **Work, Old** and **BackUp** will be stored in the directory structure. In which part of the directory structure will these names be stored? (1)

(c) Two files each with the filename **MyFirst.Pas** are stored in the system with the directory structure shown in the diagram. The sub-directory **BackUp** contains one entry for MyFirst.Pas and the **root** directory contains another.

What is the pathname for:

(i) the root directory's entry for **MyFirst.Pas**; (1)

(ii) the sub-directory BackUp's entry for **MyFirst.Pas**? (1)

(d) State **three** file access rights that may be applied to files such as **MyFirst.Pas**. (3)

AQA CPT2 Qu 5 May 2001

5 For each of the following name a suitable type of operating system. Give one reason for your choice.

(a) A computer system consisting of several desktop PCs and a printer shared on-line. (2)

(b) A computer system dedicated to controlling the temperature and humidity level in a pottery kiln. (2)

(c) A computer system dedicated to processing OMR forms returned at the end of each day. (2)

AQA CPT2 Qu 4 May 2001

6 The role of an operating system is often said to be twofold:

1 To provide a virtual machine.

2 To manage the resources of the computer.

(a) What is meant by "to provide a virtual machine"? (1)

(b) Name **three** types of resource managed by the operating system. (3)

AQA CPT2 Qu 5 January 2003

2-24

Chapter 25 – Hardware Devices

In this chapter we will look at some of the common input, output and storage devices.

Keyboard data entry

The keyboard is the most common input device, suitable for a wide range of applications from entering programs to typing all kinds of documents using a word processor, or entering personal details of customers or patients at a hospital, etc. Data entered at a keyboard is commonly copied from a source document, and as such has disadvantages:

- It is easy to make **transcription** errors – that is, copy the data wrongly from the document.

- It is time-consuming.

- Data entry operators who enter data all day every day are prone to **repetitive strain injury** (RSI), a condition which renders them unable to do any further data entry or even perform everyday tasks such as pouring a cup of tea.

Microphone for voice data entry

The user speaks the text into a microphone and the text is displayed on the screen. The accuracy of the voice recognition system is improved by 'training' it to a particular user's voice – an embarrassing process of speaking a given set of a few hundred short sentences to your computer, repeating any that are not accurately interpreted.

2-25

About speech recognition

This feature is available in the Simplified Chinese, English (U.S.), and Japanese language versions of Microsoft Office.

You can use speech recognition to dictate text into any Office program. You can also select menu, toolbar, dialog box (U.S. English only), and task pane (U.S. English only) items by using your voice.

Speech recognition is not designed for completely hands-free operation; you'll get the best results if you use a combination of your voice and the mouse or keyboard.

To use speech recognition for the first time, install it by clicking **Speech** on the **Tools** menu in Microsoft Word, or by doing a custom installation. After speech recognition is installed, it is available on the **Tools** menu in any Office program.

▶ Speech recognition requirements

▼ Training speech recognition

After speech recognition is installed, you can increase speech recognition accuracy by taking a few minutes to train the computer to recognize how you speak.

When you read aloud the prepared training text, the training wizard can look for patterns in the way you speak, and gather voice data that helps interpret the words that you'll dictate into Office programs. The training session includes help with adjusting your microphone, and it should take less than 15 minutes to complete.

Figure 25.1: 'Help' on speech recognition in MS Office XP

Scanners and OCR

An optical scanner can be used to scan graphical images and photographs, and software can then be used to edit or touch up the images. Scanners can also be used to read typed or even hand-written documents and OCR (Optical Character Recognition) software can then be used to interpret the text and export it to a word processor or data file. Scanners are also used to input large volumes of data on preprinted forms such as credit card payments, where the customer's account number and amount paid are printed at the bottom of the payment slip.

Key-to-disk systems

In organisations where large amounts of data is collected on forms which then have to be keyed in for later processing (a **batch processing** system) an entire computer system consisting of a processor, dozens of terminals and central disk storage may be dedicated entirely to data entry. One terminal is nominated as the supervisor's terminal, from whose screen the supervisor can see exactly what every data entry operator is working on and how many keystrokes per hour and how many errors everyone is making. Completed batches of data are stored on disk from where they are either downloaded to the main computer over a communications link, or transferred to magnetic tape which is physically removed and taken to the main computer room.

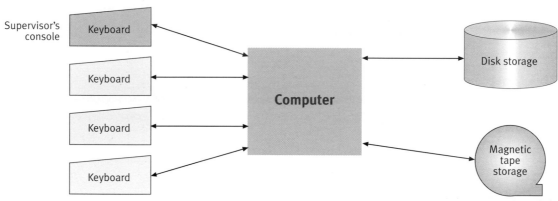

Figure 25.2: A key-to-disk system

Using a key-to-disk system, each data entry operator calls up the data entry program for their particular batch of data (e.g. payroll data entry, Council Tax payments, student grant applications) and keys in the data, which is automatically validated by the computer program.

When the batch of data has been entered and stored on disk, the source documents are passed to a second data entry operator who switches their machine to **verify** mode and keys in the data a second time. The keystrokes are compared with the data already stored on disk and any discrepancy causes the machine to beep so that the error can be corrected.

Mouse, joystick, light pen, touch screen

The mouse and its variants such as a trackball is well known to all users of PCs. A light pen is a device which incorporates a light sensor so that when it is held close to the screen over a character or part of a graphic, the object is detected and can be moved to create or modify graphics.

A touch screen allows the user to touch an area of the screen rather than having to type the data on a keyboard. They are widely used in tourist centres, where tourists can look up various local facilities and entertainments, in fast food stores such as McDonald's for entering customer orders, in manufacturing and many other environments.

Magnetic Ink Character Reader (MICR)

All banks use MICR for processing cheques. Along the bottom of a cheque the bank's sort code, customer account number and cheque number are encoded in special characters in magnetic ink. The amount of the cheque is encoded in magnetic ink when it is handed in at a bank. The cheques can then be processed extremely fast by high-speed MICR devices that read, sort and store the data on disk. MICR has several advantages for processing cheques:

- it is hard to forge the characters;
- the characters can be read even if the cheque is crumpled, dirty or smudged;
- the characters are readable by humans, unlike bar codes.

Figure 25.3: MICR characters along the bottom of a cheque

Magnetic stripe reader

Cards with magnetic stripes are used as credit cards, debit cards, railway tickets, phone cards and many other applications. The magnetic strip can be encoded with up to 220 characters of data, and there are over 2.4 billion plastic card transactions every year in Britain, with 83% of adults owning at least one card. Nevertheless, three factors threaten to destroy the lucrative business that high street banks have made out of plastic: crime, the cost of cash and competition. In 1996 card fraud cost the banks £97.1 million, with £13.3 million of it from fake magnetic stripe cards.

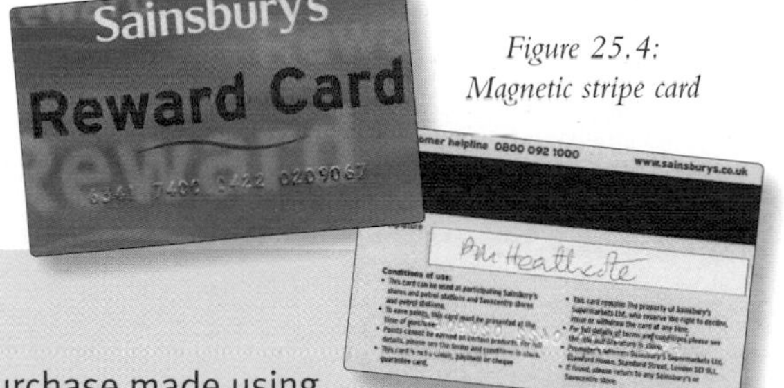

Figure 25.4:
Magnetic stripe card

Case Study: Tracking your every move

With its reward scheme, Sainsbury's records every purchase made using the reward card, including the store name, the date and time and the price paid. Over a period of time this helps them to monitor trends in purchasing, which helps the store to predict the level of stockholding required in future, and ensures that they send customers information that they will be interested in. Sainsbury's will draw conclusions from your address; are you in an area classified as "rising", "prosperous and metropolitan professional", or "gentrified multi-ethnic"?

Customers are also classified by frequency of visits, average spend per visit and the type of goods they buy. For example, you might fall into the category of customer that "buys products which suggest they enjoy trying new and different ingredients in their cooking".

Under the Data Protection Act, you are entitled to see exactly what information is held about you. For a maximum charge of £10, a company from whom you request your personal information must send it to you within 40 days.

Smart cards

The 220 characters on magnetic stripe cards are simply too easy to copy, which is why the stripes are being replaced by a chip, which is almost impossible to fake. Smart cards look similar to plastic cards with a magnetic stripe, but instead of (or as well as) the magnetic stripe, they contain a 1-millimetre square microprocessor embedded in the middle, behind a small gold electrical contact. Instead of swiping the card, you plug it into a reader.

Chip cards cost only about £1 to produce, and can hold millions of characters of data. Banks are gradually replacing magnetic stripe cards with 'chip and pin' cards which they hope will cut credit and debit card fraud. Instead of signing the credit card slip, customers type in their secret PIN.

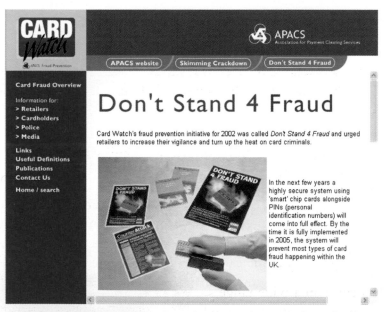

Figure 25.5: The www.cardwatch.org.uk site gives advice on combating fraud

Q1: It has been suggested that other information such as kidney donor record and driving licence could be held on the same chip card that allows you to withdraw cash and pay for goods.

What would be the benefits of doing this?

What other information would it be useful to hold on a card of this sort?

Optical Mark Reader (OMR)

An optical mark reader can detect marks made in preset positions on a form. It is widely used for marking multiple-choice exams and market research questionnaires.

Bar code reader or scanner

Bar codes appear on almost everything we buy. The pattern of thick and thin represents the 13-digit number underneath the bar code. There are four main pieces of information on a bar code.

Figure 25.6: A product bar code

The first two (or sometimes three) digits indicate in which country the product has been registered. The code for the UK and Ireland is 50.

The next five digits represent the manufacturer's code – Cadbury's, for example, is 00183.

The second group of five numbers represents the product and package size, but not the price. The last digit is a check digit, which is calculated from the other digits in the code and ensures that the barcode is keyed in or read correctly

Q2: A supermarket has a file of all stock items, which is on-line to the point-of-sale terminals at each check-out. What data is held on the stock file? What processing takes place when an item is scanned by the barcode reader? What is the output from the process?

Hand-held input devices

Portable keying devices are commonly used in such applications as reading gas or electricity meters, where the meter reader displays the next customer name, address and location of meter on a small screen, then reads the meter and keys in the reading. At the end of the day all the readings can be downloaded via a communications link to the main computer for processing.

Digitiser (Graphics tablet)

Professional quality illustrations can be drawn on a digitiser, which is a flat rectangular slab of material onto which a stylus is placed. The position of the stylus can be detected by the computer. As well as, or instead of a stylus, a 'puck' may be used to click on a special template which covers part of the tablet.

Graphics tablets come in a wide range of resolutions and types, from those used by primary school children to create drawings, to those used by engineers and architects in conjunction with computer-aided design (CAD) software. The graphics tablet shown in Figure 25.7 is a high-resolution tablet that translates x-y dimensional data into readable format and transfers it to a computer.

Figure 25.7: A graphics tablet

Digital Camera

Digital cameras convert the captured photograph directly into a digital image. It can be stored in flash memory in the camera and downloaded later to a computer.

Output devices

The most common output device for producing hard copy is the **printer**. Printers come in all shapes and sizes, and the type of printer chosen will depend on several factors such as:

- **volume of output** – for high volumes, a fast, heavy-duty printer is required;
- **quality of print required** – business letters and reports to clients, for example, will require a high quality print, probably on special headed stationery;
- **location of the printer** – if the printer is going to be situated in a busy office, the noise that it makes is an important consideration;
- **requirement for multiple copies** – some printers cannot produce multiple copies;
- **requirements for colour** – does the output need to be in colour?

Dot matrix printer

A dot matrix printer is an **impact printer**, producing its image by striking the paper through a ribbon. Its print head consists of a number of small pins, varying between 9 and 24 depending on the manufacturer. A 24 pin print head will produce a better quality of print than a 9 pin print head because the dots are closer together.

As the print head moves across the page, one or more pins strike the ribbon and make a dot on the paper. The figure below shows how the letter F is produced.

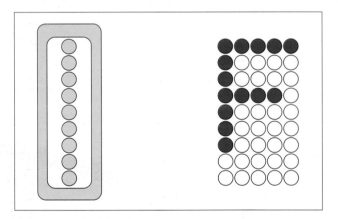

Figure 25.8: Dot matrix print head

In order to produce 'near letter quality' (**NLQ**) print, a line is printed twice, with the print head being shifted along very slightly in the second printing so that the spaces between the dots are filled in. The disadvantage of this technique is that the document then takes approximately twice as long to print. Many dot matrix printers are 'bidirectional', meaning that they can print in either direction, thus eliminating the need to start printing each line from the left hand side of the page.

Dot matrix printers are extremely versatile, with most of them able to print in condensed, standard and enlarged mode, in 'bold' or normal print. They are useful in situations where several copies of a document need to be routinely produced on 2-, 3- or 4-part stationery.

Many dot matrix printers have a graphics mode that enables them to print pictures and graphs by activating individual print head pins separately or in combination to produce any shape or line. With appropriate software any typeface can be produced, and using a special 4-colour ribbon (red, yellow, blue and black), colour output for, say, a graphical presentation can be produced. However the quality of colour is not as good as that produced by other types of colour printer.

One of the main drawbacks of a dot matrix printer is its noise; in an office environment it can be an irritating distraction. Covers can be obtained to cut down the noise, but it is still audible.

Figure 25.9: A dot matrix printer

Ink jet printers

Ink jet printers are a popular type of non-impact printer, with prices ranging between £50 and £500; a popular colour inkjet printer such as Hewlett Packard's Photosmart 7660 costs around £150. They are compact and quiet, and offer resolution almost as good as a laser printer. However, they are slow in operation; on average 3 pages per minute are printed, but a complex combination of text and colour can take several minutes for a single sheet.

Inkjet printers such as the HP Deskjet fire a droplet of ink at the page by boiling it in a microscopic tube and letting steam eject the droplet. Heating the ink can damage the colour pigments and matching the ink chemistry to the broad range of papers used in the office is a technical challenge. Large areas of colour can get wet, buckle, and the ink may smear. Printing an ink jet colour page can cost as much as 75p if all colour inks are supplied in a single cartridge; more thrifty printers will use separate red, blue, yellow and black cartridges which can be individually replaced. Although ordinary photocopy paper can be used, special smooth-coated paper may produce a more satisfactory result.

Figure 25.10: An Epson inkjet printer

Laser printers

Laser printers are becoming increasingly popular, with prices dropping rapidly to under £300 for a PostScript printer suitable for desktop publishing applications. Laser printers use a process similar to a photocopying machine, with toner (powdered ink) being transferred to the page and then fused onto it by heat and pressure. A laser printer produces output of very high quality at a typical speed in the region of ten pages per minute, and is virtually silent in operation. The main running expenses are the toner, which costs about £75 for a cartridge lasting for around 5,000 copies, and a maintenance contract which is typically up to £300 per annum.

Colour laser printers range between £600 and £5,000.

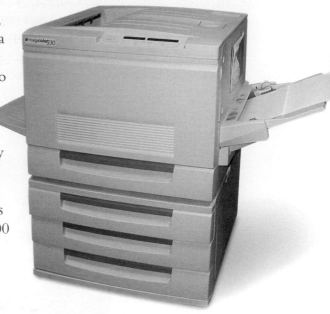

Figure 25.11: Colour laser printer

Plotters

A plotter is an output device used to produce high quality line drawings such as building plans or electronic circuits. They are generally classified as pen (vector plotters) or penless (raster plotters). The former use pens to draw images using point-to-point data, moving the pen over the paper. Pen plotters are low in price and hold a large share of the plotter market.

Penless plotters include electrostatic plotters, thermal plotters and laser plotters. They are generally used where drawings of high densities are required, for example drawings of machines, printed circuit boards or maps. Colour electrostatic plotters are increasingly being used in, for example, assembly drawings of machines and building plans, making them easier to read and understand.

Figure 25.12: Plotter

Monitor, also called Visual Display Unit (VDU)

A VDU has three basic attributes: size, colour and resolution. It has its own fixed amount of RAM associated with it to store the image being displayed on the screen, and the amount of RAM it has will determine the resolution and the maximum number of colours that can be displayed. Note that:

• the resolution is determined by the number of pixels (addressable picture elements) used to represent a full-screen image;

• the number of colours that can be displayed is determined by how many bits are used to represent each pixel. If only one bit is used to represent each pixel, then only two colours can be represented. To display 256 colours, 8 bits per pixel are required, and to display 65,536 (i.e. 2^{16}) colours, 16 bits (2 bytes) per pixel are needed. It is usually possible to adjust both the resolution and the number of colours – *if a high resolution is selected you won't be able to have as many colours because of the memory limitations of the video card.*

For example, if a resolution of 800x600 pixels is selected together with 65,536 colours, the amount of video RAM required will be 800x600x2 bytes = 960,000 bytes, i.e. almost 1Mb. If 1Mb is all the video RAM supplied by the manufacturer, the resolution cannot be increased to say, 1000x800 unless the number of bytes used to represent each pixel is reduced, thus limiting the number of colours which can be displayed.

On a PC, the number of colours and the resolution of the screen can be adjusted on the Display option of the Control Panel.

2-25

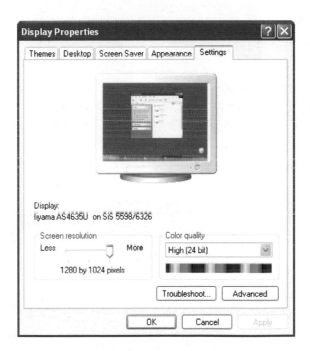

Figure 25.13: Adjusting the number of colours and resolution of a PC

Primary and secondary storage

A computer's main memory (RAM) is known as **primary storage**. In order to execute a program, the program instructions and the data on which it is to operate have to be loaded into main memory. Primary storage, however, is **volatile**; when the computer is switched off, all the contents of memory are lost. This is one good reason to perform frequent saves to disk when working on, for example, a word processed document.

A more permanent, **non-volatile** form of storage is required by all computer systems to save software and data files. Magnetic tape, magnetic disks, CD-ROM (Compact Disk Read Only Memory), and microfilm are all examples of what is known as **secondary storage**.

Magnetic Disk storage

A magnetic disk consists of two surfaces, each of which contains concentric circles called tracks. Each track is divided into sectors. If you reformat a disk that already has data on it, all the data will be erased (although you can also do a 'quick format' which erases only the file directory).

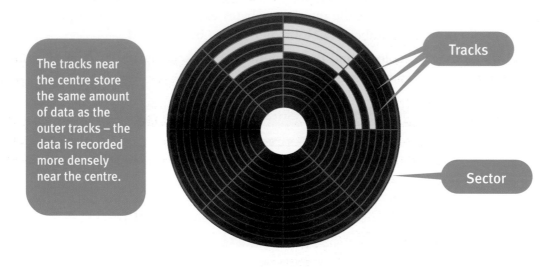

The tracks near the centre store the same amount of data as the outer tracks – the data is recorded more densely near the centre.

Tracks

Sector

Figure 25.14: Tracks and sectors on a magnetic disk

Floppy disks

The standard 3½" floppy disk is a thin, flexible plastic disk coated in metal oxide, enclosed in a rigid plastic casing. A standard high density disk has a storage capacity of 1.44 Megabytes. The disk can be removed from the drive unit and is highly portable. Floppy disks are inexpensive but easily damaged.

Hard disks for microcomputers

The hard disk used with PCs consist of one or more disk platters permanently sealed inside a casing. Hard disks typically have a capacity of between 40Gb and 160Gb.

Each surface has its own read-write head. The heads are mounted on a single spindle so they all move in and out together

Figure 25.15: A microcomputer hard disk drive

External hard drives, which can be plugged into a microcomputer, are available as extra storage.

Hard disks for minis and mainframes

For large-scale applications storing huge amounts of data, several hard disk units will be required. The disks may be either fixed (sealed inside the unit) or removable. Fixed disks are faster, more reliable, and have a greater storage capacity.

As with other types of disk, data is stored on concentric tracks, with tracks being divided into sectors. All the tracks that are accessible from one position of the read-write heads form a **cylinder**; data is recorded cylinder by cylinder to minimise movement of the read-write heads, thereby minimising access time.

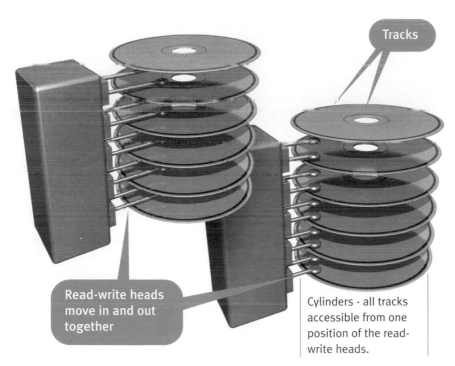

Tracks

Read-write heads move in and out together

Cylinders - all tracks accessible from one position of the read-write heads.

Figure 25.16: A disk drive

Magnetic tape

Data is recorded in 'frames' across the tape, with one frame representing one byte. The frames form tracks along the length of the tape, with 9 tracks being common, giving 8 data tracks and one parity track.

1	0	1	Track 1
1	1	1	
0	1	1	
0	0	0	
1	1	0	
1	1	0	
0	0	1	
0	0	1	
0	0	1	Parity track

Figure 25.17: Tracks on a magnetic tape

Magnetic tape is a serial medium, meaning that an individual record can only be accessed by starting at the beginning of the tape and reading through every record until the required one is found. Likewise, it is impossible to read a record, amend it in memory, then backspace to the beginning of the block and overwrite the old record. Therefore, updating a magnetic tape file always involves copying the file to a new tape with the amendments made.

Uses of magnetic tape

Tape is a cheap and convenient medium for backup, and is also used for **archiving** past transactions or other data that may be needed again, such as for example, weather records collected over a number of years.

Cartridge tape drives are in common use for backing up the hard disk of personal computers, being much more convenient than using dozens of floppy disks. A cartridge tape can store several gigabytes of data.

Figure 25.18: Cartridge tape

Q3: Discuss the relative advantages of hard disks, floppy disks and magnetic tape.

Optical Disks

Random access time is longer than that of a hard disk, but some optical storage is writeable or even re-writeable. CD-ROM, DVD-ROM (Read-only), CD-R, DVD-R (Writeable), CD-RW, DVD-RW (Re-Writeable)

CD-ROM

CD-ROMs can store around 680Mb of data, equivalent to hundreds of floppy disks. The data may be in text form, or may be in the form of graphics, photographic images, video clips or sound files. Although they do not transfer data as fast as a hard disk drive, their speed is increasing every year and is acceptable for most applications.

As the name suggests, the disks are read-only. When the master disk is created, a laser beam burns tiny pits in the surface of the disk, which (unlike a magnetic disk) has a single spiral track divided into sectors. To read data from the disk, a laser beam is reflected off the surface of the disk, detecting the presence or absence of pits which represent binary digits.

CD-ROMs are widely used for distribution of software, multimedia files, catalogues and technical manuals.

CD-R disks

Write Once, Read Many optical laser disks (WORM disks) look similar to CD-ROM disks, but they are often gold rather than silver in colour. An end-user company can use these disks to write their own material, typically for archiving or storing, say, graphic or photographic images which will not be changed.

These disks are also widely used for pirated software; whereas silver CDs are pressed in factories, gold CDs are usually written one at a time on PCs in garages and back bedrooms. A £2 blank disk can hold £20,000 worth of software and sell for £50 to £80, and they are sometimes used by less reputable PC manufacturers who install the software on their PCs to make a more attractive deal for the unsuspecting customer. However, because there is a lot of competition among pirates, these CDs sometimes carry viruses which can cause havoc on a hard drive.

CD-RW disks

These are re-writeable disks and are more expensive than CD-R. A CD writer drive costs in the region of £60 to £100. These can be used for backing up where they may need to be overwritten.

DVD-ROM

Digital Versatile Disk Read-Only Memory. These disks are the same size as CD-ROMs and are made using similar materials and manufacturing teachniques. They store about seven times as much data as a CD-ROM, because the track spacing and pit dimensions are smaller.

Figure 25.19: DVD ROM

2-25

> **Q4:** What are some of the applications of CD-ROM? Why is CD-ROM particularly suitable for these applications?

Flash memory

Flash is electrically erasable programmable read-only memory (EEPROM). It is used in memory cards for peripheral devices such as digital cameras, mobile telephones, PDAs and MP3 players. It is also available as USB memory sticks and, when plugged into a computer's USB port, behaves like an external disk drive. Flash memory is inexpensive, high-capacity storage and is rapidly replacing floppy disks as portable secondary storage. A memory stick with 1Gb capacity costs around £180.

Figure 25.20: Flash memory stick plugs into USB port on keyboard or processor box.

Exercises

1   Name the most suitable storage medium for each of the following.

   (a)   Backing up a 20Kb file.   (1)

   (b)   Backing up 1Gb of data.   (1)

   (c)   Distributing a software package requiring 400Mb of storage space.   (1)

   (d)   Transferring a 30Kb file from one stand-alone computer to another.   (1)

   (e)   A database generated and used in the course of a police investigation of a
          major crime.   (1)

   (f)   Distributing an electronic copy of an encyclopaedia.   (1)

New Question

2   A book lending library lends books to borrowers. Each borrower is assigned a unique
    borrower code. This code is encoded magnetically onto an identity card issued to
    each borrower when they join the library. The code is read from the identity card
    by swiping it through a machine connected to the library's computer system.
    The code is also printed on the card in human-readable form.

   (a)   Name the type of machine used to read the borrower code from the card   (1)

   (b)   State **one** reason for having the human-readable form of the borrower
          code printed on the card.   (1)

New Question

3   (a)   **Figure 1** shows a label removed from an item sold at a supermarket.

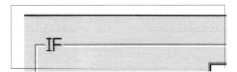

Figure 1

   What input device would have been used in the supermarket to read this label? (1)

   (b)   **Figure 2** shows a response form that customers of the supermarket have been
          asked to complete. The forms are processed using a computer system running a
          batch operating system.

Customer Survey				
Q1 – A -	– B -	– C -	– D -	– E -
Q2 – A -	– B -	– C -	– D -	– E -
Q3 – A -	– B -	– C -	– D -	– E -
Q4 – A -	– B -	– C -	– D -	– E -
Q5 – A -	– B -	– C -	– D -	– E -

Using an HB pencil place a mark through one of
the five letters for questions one to five

Figure 2

Name the most suitable input device to transfer the data on each survey form into a
computer system.   (1)

New Question

Chapter 26 – Computer Crime and the Law

Computer crime and abuse

New technologies generally create new opportunities for crime; as soon as one avenue is blocked to the criminal, another one is discovered. As information technology has spread, so too have computer crime and abuse. The Internet, for example, is used not only by innocent members of the public but also by fraudulent traders, paedophiles, software pirates, hackers and terrorists. Their activities include planting computer viruses, software bootlegging, storing pornographic images and perpetrating all sorts of criminal activities from credit card fraud to the most complex multinational money laundering schemes.

Computer abuse refers to acts that are legal but unethical.

Hacking

Hacking is defined as unauthorised access to data held on a computer system. The extent of hacking is extremely difficult to establish as it is usually only discovered by accident, with only about two percent of security breaches discovered as a result of positive action on the part of security staff. (*Digital Crime* by Neil Barrett, page 40.)

Hacking is often perpetrated by employees of a company who have acquired inside knowledge of particular user Ids and passwords. The ability of such hackers to carry out illegal actions without being detected is often hampered by the audit and monitoring software that all computer operating systems supply.

The motive behind hacking can often be mischievous rather than anything more sinister: computing students who are learning about operating systems may take delight in penetrating a university's security system to prove that it can be done, or to gain access to exam questions and answers. However, international fraudsters are constantly finding new ways of acquiring funds illegally, targeting both banks and individuals.

Case study: 'Trojan' programs

High Street banks have admitted that they are losing money to criminals who record passwords and identities using remotely operated key-logging programs. Most banks have switched their logging-in procedures for online customers to avoid the threat from Trojan programs which have been surreptitiously placed on users' computers to record keystrokes.

Instead of, or as well as, requiring customers to type in their user IDs and passwords, they are asked to select letters from a dropdown menu by clicking on them with a mouse to identify just part of their 'memorable information'.

To complete log on please enter the requested numbers and/or letters from your Memorable Information using the 3 drop down lists provided. Please click on 'Help' if you require further assistance.

Please enter characters 2, 3 and 7 from your Memorable Information

2 3 7

Continue
Cancel

Viruses

Viruses are generally developed with a definite intention to cause damage to computer files or, at the very least, cause inconvenience and annoyance to computer users. The first virus appeared at the University of Delaware in 1987, and the number of viruses escalated to over 9000 different variations in 1997. The virus usually occupies the first few instructions of a particular program on an 'infected' disk and relies on a user choosing to execute that program. When an infected program is executed, the virus is the first series of instructions to be performed. In most cases the virus's first action is to copy itself from the diskette onto the PC and 'hide' within obscure files, the operating system code or within unused disk blocks which are then marked as being 'bad' and unavailable for reuse. The virus can then proceed to perform any of a number of tasks ranging from the irritating to the catastrophic such as reformatting the hard disk.

Some viruses lie dormant, waiting to be triggered by a particular event or date – the 'Friday 13th' virus being a well-known one. The virus then infects other diskettes, perhaps by modifying operating system programs responsible for copying programs. From there, the next PC to use the diskette will be infected.

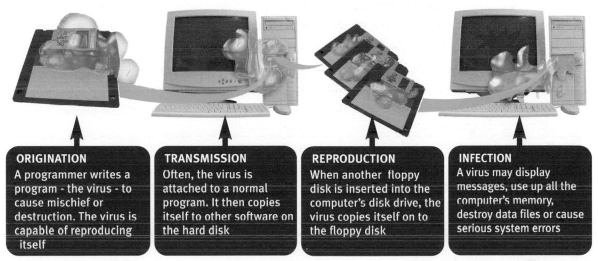

ORIGINATION
A programmer writes a program - the virus - to cause mischief or destruction. The virus is capable of reproducing itself

TRANSMISSION
Often, the virus is attached to a normal program. It then copies itself to other software on the hard disk

REPRODUCTION
When another floppy disk is inserted into the computer's disk drive, the virus copies itself on to the floppy disk

INFECTION
A virus may display messages, use up all the computer's memory, destroy data files or cause serious system errors

Figure 26.1: How a virus works

'Logic bombs' and Macro Viruses

A 'logic bomb' is similar to a virus and is sometimes delivered by means of a virus. The 'bomb' can be written to destroy or, worse, subtly change the contents of an organisation's computer systems. However, it does not begin this activity until signalled to do so by the hacker or extortionist, or it may be activated if a cancelling signal fails to arrive.

Case study: MyDoom

In January 2004 an innocuous attachment in an e-mail sent from Russia triggered a minor alarm at a leading e-mail security firm. Initially the number of copies of the new virus – christened 'MyDoom' after a misspelling of 'My domain' in its code – was small, just a few hundred. Within a few hours, numbers started to rise – to 40,000, 80,000, 200,000.

After 8 hours, millions of copies of MyDoom were circulating across the Internet. In an act of apparent terrorism, a variant of MyDoom and all its copies were programmed to attack a software company at **www.sco.com** simultaneously at 16.09 GMT on February 1st. Right on time, more than a million computers tried to load the homepage three times a second and the site had to be closed down.

MyDoom loops forever, sending more and more infected messages to every single address found on the hard drive endlessly.

Digital crime and the law

The rapid progress of computer technology has led to the need for new laws to be introduced so that all perpetrators of computer crime can be prosecuted. Laws in the US impact on computer users in this country, since the majority of systems and Internet content is American. A general approach to a common standard for Internet-related laws throughout the European Union formed part of a proposed European Commission directive discussed by member states in October 1996.

The Computer Misuse Act of 1990

In the early 1980s in the UK, hacking was not illegal. Some universities stipulated that hacking, especially where damage was done to data files, was a disciplinary offence, but there was no legislative framework within which a criminal prosecution could be brought. This situation was rectified by the Computer Misuse Act of 1990 which defined three specific criminal offences to deal with the problems of hacking, viruses and other nuisances. The offences are:

• unauthorised access to computer programs or data;

• unauthorised access with a further criminal intent;

• unauthorised modification of computer material (i.e. programs or data).

To date there have been relatively few prosecutions under this law – probably because most organisations are reluctant to admit that their system security procedures have been breached, which might lead to a loss of confidence on the part of their clients.

2-26

Case study: Online banking customers targetted

Online banking customers are being targeted by criminals who attempt to find out their passwords in a 'phishing' scam designed to persuade unsuspecting users to type in their security details into a bogus form purporting to come from the bank.

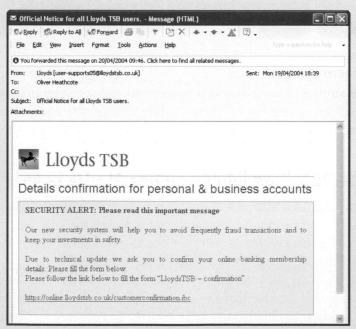

The screenshot shows the scam e-mail, which does not, of course, come from Lloyds Bank. The link takes you to a bogus website asking you to enter your security details. *Don't do it!*

Copyright, Design and Patents Act of 1988

Computer software is now covered by the Copyright Designs and Patents Act of 1988, which covers a wide range of intellectual property such as music, literature and software. Provisions of the Act make it illegal to:

• copy software;

• run pirated software;

• transmit software over a telecommunications line, thereby creating a copy.

Software can easily be copied and bootlegged (sold illegally). It is illegal to buy such software!

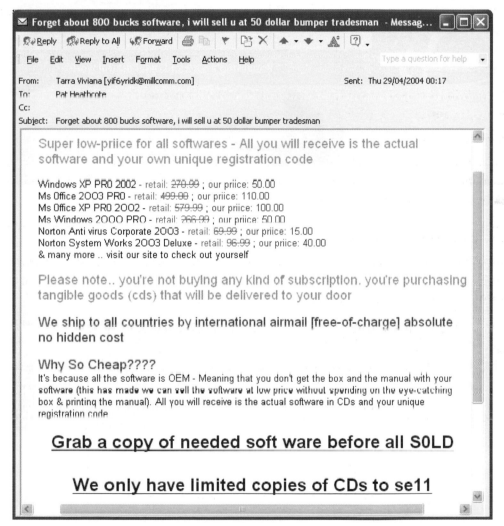

Figure 26.2: An e-mail advertising pirated software

In addition, the programming *ideas* and *methods* can be stolen by a competitor. Microsoft was sued (unsuccessfully) many years ago by Apple Computers for copying the 'look and feel' of their graphical user interface. It is possible for an expert programmer to 'reverse engineer' machine code to establish the specific algorithms used, so that they can be copied. Some software manufacturers put 'fingerprints' into the code – little oddities which do not affect the way the program runs – so that if the same code is found in a competitor's program, they can prove that it was illegally copied.

The Business Software Alliance helps companies to ensure that all software being used is correctly licensed. Offences include using 'pirate' copies of software and using software on more machines than is permitted under the terms of the licence.

Figure 26.3: The BSA website

Exercises

1 A student on work experience in the payroll department of Widgets plc, when left alone, successfully logged into the company's computer system by guessing the administrator's user id and password. The student changed the hourly rate of several employees by accessing the company's payroll file.

   (a) The Company Misuse Act defines three types of offence. What **two** offences did the student commit according to this Act?   (2)

   (b) Given that the student was left alone in the computer room, the company could have prevented or detected what happened. Describe briefly **three** methods of security that the company could have used.   (3)

   AQA CPT2 Qu 5 January 2001

2 Name the legislation that applies in the following cases.

   (a) An Examination Board allows a software reseller access to its database of centre names and addresses so that the reseller can market its products directly to centres that teach AS Computing.   (1)

   (b) A company using an encryption algorithm in one of its software products receives a demand for royalties from another software company that claims that it invented the encryption algorithm.   (1)

   (c) A user sends an attachment to an e-mail which when opened infects the recipient's computer with a virus.   (1)

   (d) A company has its computing equipment seized by the police for using unlicensed commercial software.   (1)

   AQA CPT2 Qu 5 June 2003

Chapter 27 – Data Protection & Health and Safety

Personal privacy

The right to privacy is a fundamental human right and one that we take for granted. Most of us, for instance, would not want our medical records freely circulated, and many people are sensitive about revealing their age, religious beliefs, family circumstances or academic qualifications. In the UK even the use of name and address files for mail shots is often felt to be an invasion of privacy.

With the advent of large computerised databases it became quite feasible for sensitive personal information to be stored without the individual's knowledge and accessed by, say, a prospective employer, credit card company or insurance company to assess somebody's suitability for employment, credit or insurance.

Case study: James Wiggins – a true story

In the US, James Russell Wiggins applied for and got a $70,000 post with a company in Washington. A routine pre-employment background check, however, revealed that he had been convicted of possessing cocaine, and he was fired the next day, not only because he had a criminal record but because he had concealed this fact when applying for the job. Wiggins was shocked – he had never had a criminal record, and it turned out that the credit bureau hired to make the investigation had retrieved the record for a James Ray Wiggins by mistake, even though they had different birthdates, addresses, middle names and social security numbers. Even after this was discovered, however, Wiggins didn't get his job back.

If the pre-employment check had been made *before* Wiggins was offered the job, he would not have been offered it and no reason would have been given. The information would have remained on his file, virtually ensuring that he would never get a decent job – without ever knowing the reason why.

The Data Protection Acts of 1984 and 1998

The Data Protection Act 1984 grew out of public concern about personal privacy in the face of rapidly developing computer technology. It provides rights for individuals and demands good information handling practice.

The Act covers 'personal data' which are 'automatically processed'. It works in two ways, giving individuals certain rights whilst requiring those who record and use personal information on computer to be open about that use and to follow proper practices.

The Data Protection Act 1998 was passed in order to implement a European Data Protection Directive. This Directive sets a standard for data protection throughout all the countries in the European Union, and the new Act was brought into force in March 2000. Some manual records fall within the scope of the Act and there are also extended rights for data subjects.

2-27

The Data Protection Principles

The Data Protection Act became law on 12th July 1984 and was updated in 1998.

Once registered, data users must comply with the eight Data Protection principles of good information handling practice contained in the Act. Broadly these state that personal data must be:

1 fairly and lawfully obtained and processed;

2 processed for specified purposes;

3 adequate, relevant and not excessive;

4 accurate and kept up to date;

5 not kept longer than necessary;

6 processed in accordance with the data subject's rights;

7 kept securely against unauthorised access and accidental loss or damage;

8 not transferred to countries without adequate protection for the rights and freedom of data subjects.

Useful definitions from the 1984 Act

'Personal Data' information about living, identifiable individuals. Personal data do not have to be particularly sensitive information, and can be as little as a name and address.

'Data Controllers (users)' those who control the contents and use of a collection of personal data. They can be any type of company or organisation, large or small, within the public or private sector. A data user can also be a sole trader, partnership, or an individual. A data user need not necessarily own a computer.

'Data Subjects' the individuals to whom the personal data relate.

Data Subjects

We are all 'data subjects'. All types of companies and organisations ('data users') have details about us on their computers. This growth of computerised information has many benefits but also potential dangers. If the information is entered wrongly, is out of date or is confused with someone else's, it can cause problems. You could be unfairly refused jobs, housing, benefits, credit or a place at college. You could be overcharged for goods or services. You could even find yourself arrested in error, just because there is a mistake in the computerised information.

The Information Commissioner

The Commissioner is an independent supervisory authority and has an international role as well as a national one.

In the UK the Commissioner has a range of duties including the promotion of good information handling and the encouragement of codes of practice for data controllers, that is, anyone who decides how and why personal data, (information about identifiable, living individuals) is processed.

The site **www.informationcommissioner.gov.uk** contains a lot of information on the Data Protection Act and the rights of individuals.

2-27

Figure 27.1. The Information Commissioner's Home Page

A data user's Register entry

With few exceptions, all data users have to register, giving their name and address together with broad descriptions of:

- those about whom personal data are held;
- the items of data held;
- the purposes for which the data are used;
- the sources from which the information may be obtained;
- the types of organisations to whom the information may be disclosed i.e. shown or passed on to;
- any overseas countries or territories to which the data may be transferred.

Some exemptions from the Act

- The Act does not apply to payroll, pensions and accounts data, nor to names and addresses held for distribution purposes.
- Registration may not be necessary when data is for personal, family, household or recreational use.
- Subjects do not have a right to access data if the sole aim of collecting it is for statistical or research purposes, or where it is simply for backup.
- Data can be disclosed to the data subject's agent (e.g. lawyer or accountant), to persons working for the data user, and in response to urgent need to prevent injury or damage to health.

Additionally, there are exemptions for special categories, including data held:

- in connection with national security;
- for prevention of crime;
- for the collection of tax or duty.

The rights of data subjects

The Data Protection Act allows individuals to have access to information held about themselves on computer and, where appropriate, to have it corrected or deleted.

As an individual you are entitled, on making a written request to a data user, to be supplied with a copy of any personal data held about yourself. The data user may charge a fee of up to £10 for each register entry for supplying this information but in some cases it is supplied free.

Usually the request must be responded to within 40 days. If not, you are entitled to complain to the Registrar or apply to the courts for correction or deletion of the data.

Apart from the right to complain to the Registrar, data subjects also have a range of rights which they may exercise in the civil courts. These are:

• right to compensation for unauthorised disclosure of data;

• right to compensation for inaccurate data;

• right of access to data and to apply for rectification or erasure where data is inaccurate;

• right to compensation for unauthorised access, loss or destruction of data.

Encryption technology

How secure are e-mails? When you order goods over the Internet and give your credit card number, it is obviously vital that this information cannot be intercepted by anyone. This can be achieved by **encrypting** the data. A common encryption system depends on being able to find the prime factors of two very large numbers, say 155 digits long. It is possible to devise an encryption key, which is virtually impossible to break, and this is termed **'strong encryption'**. However, there are issues here: governments are wary of allowing strongly encrypted data to circulate, fearing that terrorists, criminals and spies could transmit messages that can never be decoded. So far, for example, it has proved impossible to factor 200-digit numbers. **'Weak encryption'** using fewer digits means the code is not breakable except by organisations with massive processing power and the will to do so — organised crime presumably included. In 1999 researchers proved that they could crack a code used by the majority of major international and financial institutions, which used 155-digit numbers. *Yesterday's strong encryption is today's weak encryption.*

E-mails and privacy issues

Standard e-mail is not private. It sits around on various computers on its way to you, and even after you delete an e-mail it will still be accessible to someone with a good utility program. The only way to ensure e-mail privacy is to use an encryption program.

Many employees have their own e-mail addresses at their places of work. How private is e-mail sent to and from these addresses? Commonly, e-mails sent out from these addresses go out with the company footer, which makes it look as if they have been sanctioned by the firm.

In December 1999, twenty-three office staff from the New York Times were fired after managers discovered they had been e-mailing smutty jokes, pornographic pictures and jokes about bosses. The New York Times has a policy specifying that 'communications must be consistent with conventional standards of ethical and proper conduct, behaviour and manners'.

In 1997, Norwich Union paid £450,000 in an out-of-court settlement and had to make a public apology when an e-mail on the Intranet disparaging a competitor got out.

For information on privacy, try Privacy International **www.privacyinternational.org**.

Health and Safety (Display Screen Equipment) Regulations 1992

Occupational health and safety legislation in Britain is researched, guided and structured by the Health and Safety Executive (HSE), a government body. An EEC Directive on work with display screen equipment was completed in the early 1990s, with member states required to adapt it to become part of their own legislation. As a consequence, the Health and Safety at Work Act of 1974 incorporated legislation pertaining to the use of VDUs, and the relevant section is now referred to as The Health and Safety (Display Screen Equipment) Regulations 1992.

This legislation is intended to protect the health of employees within the working environment. Employers, employees and manufacturers all have some responsibility for conforming to the law.

Employers are required to:

- perform an analysis of workstations in order to evaluate the safety and health conditions to which they give rise;
- provide training to employees in the use of workstation components;
- ensure employees take regular breaks or changes in activity;
- provide regular eye tests for workstation users and pay for glasses.

Employees have a responsibility to:

- use workstations and equipment correctly, in accordance with training provided by employers;
- bring problems to the attention of their employer immediately and co-operate in the correction of these problems.

Manufacturers are required to ensure that their products comply with the Directive. For example, screens must tilt and swivel, keyboards must be separate and moveable. Notebook PCs are not suitable for entering large amounts of data.

Figure 27.2: Workstations must be ergonomically designed

The ergonomic environment

Ergonomics refers to the design and functionality of the environment, and encompasses the entire range of environmental factors. Employers must give consideration to:

- **lighting**. The office should be well lit. Computers should neither face windows nor back onto a window so that the users have to sit with the sun in their eyes. Adjustable blinds should be provided.
- **furniture**. Chairs should be of adjustable height, with a backrest which tilts to support the user at work and at rest, and should swivel on a five-point base. It should be at the correct height relative to a keyboard on the desk.
- **work space.** The combination of chair, desk, computer, accessories (such as document holders, mouse and mouse mats, paper trays and so on), lighting, heating and ventilation all contribute to the worker's overall well-being.

2-27

- **noise.** Noisy printers, for example, should be given covers to reduce the noise or positioned in a different room.
- **hardware.** The screen must tilt, swivel, be flicker-free and the keyboard separately attached.
- **software.** Software is often overlooked in the quest for ergonomic perfection. The EEC Directive made a clear statement about the characteristics of acceptable software, requiring employers to analyse the tasks which their employers performed and to provide software which makes the tasks easier. It is also expected to be easy to use and adaptable to the user's experience.

Exercises

1 In some countries government agencies routinely monitor the content of e-mail routed over the Internet.

   (a) Give **two** reasons why some governments may allow this to happen. (2)

   (b) Suggest **one** way in which an individual may make it difficult for any such agency to read the content of a particular e-mail sent over the Internet. (1)

   AQA CPT2 Qu 3 January 2002

2 (a) The growing level of public concern over data stored in computer systems led the government to pass The Data Protection Act 1984. The Act was introduced to protect the right of individuals to privacy.

   Give **three** reasons relating to the nature of computing systems that give rise to this concern. (3)

   (b) Name **two** other Acts that relate to computer systems. (2)

   AQA CPT2 Qu 3 January 2003

3 A well-known software company has constructed a media player to query an on-line database at the company's headquarters. It retrieves the titles of tracks on audio CDs for display in the media player's window. In the process it assigns a unique identifying digital fingerprint to the computer playing the audio track.

   In a separate transaction, the company can then link this digital fingerprint to an e-mail sent from the same computer. This links the user's e-mail address to the music interests of the user for marketing purposes.

   (a) Explain one benefit to

   (i) the user (1)

   (ii) the software company. (1)

   (b) Why might the use of the link be considered unethical? (1)

   AQA CPT2 Qu 3 June 2003

2-27

Chapter 28 – Information Processing Applications

Computing – a look backwards

Within half a century, computers and information technology have changed the world and affected millions of lives in ways that no one could have foreseen. Here are some of the things that people have said about computers:

"I think there's a world market for maybe five computers."
(Thomas Watson, the chairman of IBM, in 1940)

"I have travelled the length and breadth of this country and talked with the best people, and I can assure you that data processing is a fad that won't last out the year."
(The editor in charge of business books for Prentice Hall, in 1957)

"There is no reason why anyone would want to have a computer in their home."
(President of Digital Equipment Corporation, in 1977)

Consequences of computer failure

Individuals, organisations and society in general are totally dependent on computer systems for everything from withdrawing £10 at the local cashpoint to transferring millions of pounds' worth of shares every day of the week on the Stock Exchange. Computers play a crucial role in thousands of everyday tasks such as figuring out how many pineapples need to be imported from Kenya to meet demand in Waitrose next week, or recording £10 million worth of lottery ticket sales every week.

The consequences of computer failure, however, can be anything from inconvenient to catastrophic. When the bank's computer goes down you may be unable to withdraw cash or pay your bills. When a hospital computer monitoring a patient's vital signs fails, it may be life-threatening.

Study of one major information processing application

The AQA specification requires you to study one major information processing application. You should consider the purpose of the application and its role as an information system. You are required to examine specific user-interface needs and communication requirements of the application. You should be able to discuss the economic, social, legal and ethical consequences of the application.

To help you in this task this chapter discusses, as a case study, one of Waitrose's IT systems.

2-28

Case Study: Waitrose Quick Check System

Wallace Waite, Arthur Rose and David Taylor opened their first small grocery shop in London in 1904. One hundred years later there are over 140 Waitrose supermarkets in England and Wales. Unlike other major supermarkets, Waitrose is not owned by shareholders and the City. Instead, as part of the John Lewis partnership, it is owned by everyone who works for the Partnership.

Behind the scenes, Waitrose uses IT in its buying and distribution centres. The company web site uses e-commerce for online shopping and for dedicated services such as ordering gifts and flowers through Waitrose Direct. In their shops, Waitrose uses EPOS terminals at the checkouts and at the Quick Check till.

Quick Check is Waitrose's "Scan as you shop" service. This service is available only to account-card holders and is currently implemented in around 70 branches. As part of the service, customers are also provided with special bags, so they can pack as they scan.

Figure 28.1: Waitrose's Quick Check rack

At the entrance, the customer (we'll call her Mrs Smith) swipes her account card through the card reader (Figure 28.1 middle of picture) on the Quick Check rack, which then releases a scanner to her. You can see Mrs Smith's scanner lit up in the top row of the photograph (Figure 28.1).

Using the hand-held scanner, Mrs Smith scans each item as she places it into her shopping bag.

The price of the last item scanned is shown on the display. The controls on the scanner allow the customer to check the list of items scanned and the current subtotal.

If she changes her mind about a particular item and puts it back on the shelf, the item can be scanned again pressing the 'minus' button to delete the entry.

The scanner beeps if an item scanned is part of a multi-buy special offer, so a customer can take full advantage of these offers.

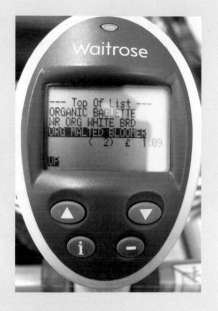

Figure 28.2: A hand-held scanner

Some items, such as freshly baked bread, do not have packaging with barcodes. The customer scans the relevant shelf edge label.

For example, if she selects 6 rolls 'Petit Pain' then the barcode shown in Figure 28.3 is scanned 6 times.

2-28

Figure 28.3: Shelf edge bar code

When Mrs Smith has finished shopping, she swipes a special barcode at the checkout.

Figure 28.4: The end-of-shopping bar code

All that is left to do is pay at the Quick Check till, without having to unpack and re-pack the shopping. If paying by debit, credit or account card the customer can save even more time by using Quick Pay. Mrs Smith simply inserts her account card to recall her bill, which is printed at the Quick Pay till.

Figure 28.5: The Quick Pay till

2-28

Purpose of the Quick Check

Waitrose introduced Quick Check as a means of gaining customer loyalty. At a time when other stores were offering loyalty cards with money-off vouchers, Waitrose was offering quality of service. The Quick Check system was introduced as a pilot scheme in one store in 1997, and it was soon evident that customers liked the convenience of scanning their own shopping and avoiding queues at the checkouts. Waitrose observed an increase in 'basket value' – that is, customers were spending more money each time they went shopping. Waitrose's original objectives were satisfied at the pilot branch, and slowly the new system was introduced at other branches. It is now a distinguishing feature of a Waitrose store.

Quick Check as an information system

This system provides excellent information to both the customer and the store.

• The customer can easily find out the accurate price of an item, even if it is misplaced on the shelf or the shelf labelling not clear.

• The customer is informed of multi-buy offers and receives an itemised bill at the end.

• Waitrose collect accurate data for stock levels.

The data for the customer's bill and for stock control are supplied by means of a barcode read by the hand-held scanner.

Each product must have a unique identifying number. Manufacturers, wholesalers and retailers need to communicate, so there is a need for a common numbering system. ANA (the Article Numbering Association) allocates numbers used in a wide range of goods. Barcoding was chosen as the best labelling system for products because barcodes are reliable. They are also cheap as they can be produced by the normal printing process used for the product labels. Note that barcodes incorporated into printed labels do not store the price of the product. Different shops, all using the same barcode, are likely to be selling the same product at different prices.

For unwrapped items Waitrose displays barcodes at the shelf edge (Figure 28.3). For produce sold by weight, Waitrose produces barcodes in the store (Figure 28.6). Networked scales with a printer produce barcodes for items weighed and wrapped at service counters, such as cheese, sliced meats, vegetables and fruit.

Figure 28.6 Barcode for weighed produce

Figure 28.7 Barcode for reduced produce

Reduced items are also labelled with a special barcode (Figure 28.7), which provides Waitrose with detailed information of what item was reduced and by how much. This is important management information.

Waitrose is planning to provide more information to customers via the scanner in the future.

Q1: What other useful information could be provided to customers?

User Interface needs

Quick Scan must be easy to use as it has a large user base and training overheads must be kept to a minimum. The scanner must be easy to operate and information on the scanner's screen must be easy to read and understand.

Communication requirements of Quick Check

The hand-held scanners need to be linked by wireless network to the Quick Check server, so that the price of an item being scanned can be downloaded from the database immediately. When the customer has finished shopping, and performs the end-of-shopping scan, the bill can be recalled by a simple swipe of the customer's account card at the Quick Pay till.

Stock levels need to be adjusted. This is done as soon as a customer ends their shopping, and at the end of the trading day the ordering system is updated. Any required price changes are also made at the end of the trading day when the product database is updated.

At random intervals shopping may be re-scanned to ensure customers do not abuse the trust. The system picks a customer completely randomly. The branch manager also has the right to request the system recalls a specified customer for re-checks.

Records of individual customers' purchases are held at branch levels, but are only used if there is a dispute with a customer. Waitrose does not collect customer profiles (customers' shopping habits).

Waitrose's and customers' needs

Waitrose needs accurate collection of data for billing and stock control.

Costs must be kept to a minimum, but the IT systems must be reliable and secure as the organisation's reputation is at stake.

Customers want to save time shopping and avoid queuing. Customers also want accurate information of the cost of items and the cost of their shopping.

Economic consequences

- The hardware required for Quick Check is expensive and Waitrose estimates that it will take 2-5 years to get a return on their investment.
- Quick Check accounts for 20% of sales. If fewer customers require EPOS checkouts, this can release floor space and increase selling space. Waitrose can save on labour costs as not as many checkout operators will be required.
- Decreasing turnaround time per customer allows more customers to be served per hour. This also makes better use of car parks.
- Waitrose needs to ensure customers are honest and scan each item as it is packed into the bags.

Social consequences

Does Quick Check result in a reduced labour force or just fewer boring jobs? Do customers find a visit to the supermarket less personal, and does this bother them? The shopping trip involves less contact with Waitrose staff because a customer can shop and pay without any human intervention at the checkout.

Legal and ethical consequences

Account card details are not held at the supermarket. The Accounts Department holds customer account details and must register the purpose of holding the names and addresses. Waitrose does not hold any personal data as a consequence of Quick Check, as there is no link made between address and account card, so there is no need to register further with the Information Registrar (Data Protection Act).

2-28

Discussion: Waitrose has a policy of not storing the Quick Check data in conjunction with account card holders' addresses, so there is no danger of breaching customers' privacy. However, other shops using similar systems might be less ethical. It would not take a lot of extra information to build up a picture of what individual customers buy, where they buy and when they buy. If the customer pays by credit or debit card the shop could also find out what bank this customer uses. The shop could build up profiles of their customers' shopping habits. How could this information be used by the shop? Would this be ethical?

The future

There is a lot of discussion in the media currently about the future development of RF ID tags (radio frequency identification tags) or 'smart tags'. Such tags are an improvement on old-fashioned barcodes because they can be read from a distance of up to 7 metres, speeding up the process of checking goods.

Currently many shops use these tags as anti-theft devices. However, some retailers, such as Tesco's, are proposing that goods will have RF tags with unique ID numbers. If these tags are not disabled at the point of sale, anyone with suitable equipment could track the movements of the item purchased. For example, if you buy a pair of shoes from Tesco's with an RF tag, your movements could be tracked whenever you enter or leave a Tesco store.

Q2: Would you consider this as an invasion of privacy? Why?

Q3: Might the retailer be in breach of any current legislation?

Q4: What are the advantages to the retailer of RF tagging?

Q5: What steps should the retailer take to avoid any invasion of privacy and yet retain the advantages of RF tagging?

Exercises

1   Players, in a national lottery, show their selection of different numbers by placing marks on an entry form similar to the one shown in Figure 1. The entry form is then inserted into a machine at the point of sale and the numbers are read.

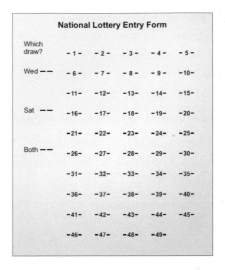

Figure 1

2-28

(a)   Name the method being used to read the data.   (1)

The data are transmitted to a central computer which allocates a unique transaction code. This code is relayed back to the point of sale where a machine prints the chosen numbers and a transaction code onto the ticket similar to the one shown in **Figure 2**.

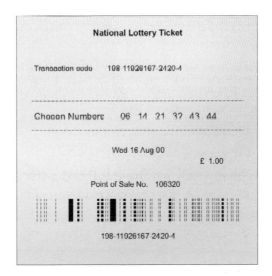

Figure 2

(b)   Each transaction code includes a check digit. What is a check digit and why is it used?   (2)

(c) Each transaction is recorded in a separate record. All transaction records for a particular lottery draw are stored in a single transaction file.

The transaction record includes the following fields:

Date of Purchase
Transaction Code
Date of Draw
Chosen Numbers
Point of Sale Identification Code

(i) What is meant by primary key? (1)

(ii) Which of the above fields should be chosen as the primary key? (1)

(iii) What would be a suitable file organisation for the transaction file if it is required that the ticket(s) with the winning numbers is to be found? Justify your choice. (2)

(iv) If individual records need to be accessed quickly what file organisation should be used? Justify your choice. (2)

(d) After a draw, some lottery prize-winners can check their tickets at any lottery point of sale machine. State the processing steps required by the lottery's computer system to check if the ticket is a winning ticket. (4)

AQA CPT2 Qu 6 January 2001

2 A publisher of a daily newspaper uses a computer system consisting of:

- Reporters' workstations.
- An image processing workstation.
- Sub-editors' workstations.
- A page make-up workstation.
- A central file store.

Each article is word-processed and stored centrally in a separate file.

(a) What type of operating system – real, interactive, batch or network – must be run at each of the workstations so that

(i) access to the central file store is possible? (1)

(ii) reporters can word-process articles? (1)

(b) The editor in charge of an edition enters the layouts of each page at the page make-up workstation. A page is divided into a number of blocks. There is one article per block.

A relational database is used to record details of the page layouts for each edition of the newspaper.

Two relations (tables) **NewspaperEdition** and **PageLayout** are used for this database:

NewspaperEdition (EditionId, Date, NoOfPages, EditorInChargeOfEdition)

PageLayout (EditionId, PageNo, BlockNo, PositionOfBlockOnPage, WidthOfBlock, LengthOfBlock, FilePathName)

Each newspaper edition is assigned a unique EditionId. There is only one edition per day. FilePathName is used to locate the word-processed article assigned to a block.

State a suitable primary key for the NewspaperEdition relation. (1)

State a suitable secondary key for the NewspaperEdition relation. (1)

Name the attribute which is the foreign key in the relation PageLayout. (1)

State a suitable primary key for the relation PageLayout. Justify your choice. (3)

(c) Word-processed articles are stored on the N: drive of the file server. Each reporter is allocated their own directory in which to store their files on the N: drive. **Figure 4** shows part of the root directory on the N: drive.

```
Reporter1      dir
Reporter2      dir
Reporter3      dir
   :            :
   :            :
   :            :
Reporter25     dir
```

Figure 4

2-28

What is the pathname for a file Cricket1.Doc that Reporter1 has written? (1)

(ii) At the end of each month all the files written by the reporters are archived. Explain what this means. (1)

(iii) Suggest a suitable cost effective medium that could be used to hold one month's archive of approximately 4GB (4 Gigabytes) of information. (1)

(d) Sub-editors use a split screen workstation with one half of the screen displaying an article for a specific page and the other half showing the corresponding page layout supplied by the editor. The sub-editor adjusts the length of the article so that it fits exactly into a block. A sub-editor's workstation can access any of the word-processed files produced by reporters as well as any of the page layouts produced by the editor.

Sketch and label carefully a possible split screen user interface for the sub-editor's workstation. Consider how this interface can:

• show the page layout and if an article is too long or too short for a block

• select a file

• indicate which article file is being processed

• indicate which page, block and edition of the newspaper is currently selected

• select editing tools/functions

• select different formats for the article

• select on-line help. (5)

(e) A block of space on a page may also contain an image.

State **two** image processing operations that an image processing workstation might apply to images. (2)

AQA CPT2 Qu 7 January 2003

3   A small film production company makes training videos for sale to schools and colleges. It uses a computer to add background music, downloaded from a particular site on the Internet, to its training videos. The editing software that it uses was found on another site on the Internet.

   (a)   Name the legislation that this company might be breaking and describe one possible way in which this might be happening.   (2)

   (b)   The company wishes to distribute its training videos in digital form so that they can be played directly through a computer system.

      (i)   State the most suitable medium for this purpose.   (1)

      (ii)   Name **two** peripherals excluding video monitor, mouse and keyboard that the computer system must use to play back a training video.   (2)

   (c)   The company also offers a microfilming service to companies dealing in personal information. The personal information is transferred to microfilm. The recording, processing and use of personal information is governed by legislation. Name this legislation and state **one** principle of this legislation that relates to the integrity of the personal data and **one** that relates to its security.   (3)

AQA CPT2 Qu 6 January 2002

2-28

Module 3

System Development

In this section:

Chapter 29	The Classical Systems Life-Cycle	172
Chapter 30	From Design to Evaluation	178
Chapter 31	Human–Computer Interface	183

3

Chapter 29 – The Classical Systems Life-Cycle

Overview of the systems life cycle

Large systems development projects may involve dozens of people working over several months or even years, so they cannot be allowed to proceed in a haphazard fashion. The goals of an information system must be thoroughly understood, and formal procedures and methods applied to ensure that the project is delivered on time and to the required specification.

The systems life cycle methodology approaches the development of information systems in a very methodical and sequential manner. Each stage is composed of certain well-defined activities and responsibilities, and is completed before the next stage begins.

There are several versions of the systems life cycle diagram; the stages include problem definition, problem investigation, feasibility study, analysis, design, construction/implementation (including programming, testing and installation), maintenance and evaluation. Most diagrams like the one below show only 5 or 6 main steps.

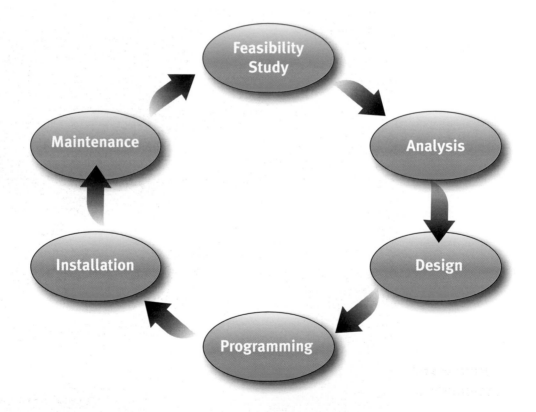

Figure 29.1: The systems life cycle

The waterfall model

The systems life cycle approach to development is also known as the 'waterfall model', and a variation on the basic diagram of 29.1 is shown in Figure 29.2.

Note that the arrows go up and down the 'waterfall', reflecting the fact that developers often have to re-work earlier stages in the light of experience gained as development progresses.

A project milestone terminates each stage of a life-cycle-oriented approach. At this stage, the 'deliverable' resulting from that stage – such as the documentation for the analysis or the design, or the program code or finished database application, is *signed off* by all concerned parties and approval is given to proceed to the next stage. The 'concerned parties' usually include the end-users, management and developers, as well as other experts such as database administration personnel. This sequence continues until the evaluation stage has been completed and the finished system is delivered to the end-users.

In this model, the end-user has very little say in the development process, which is carried out by technical specialists such as systems analysts and programmers. He or she is presented with the finished system at the end of the development cycle and if it is not quite what was wanted, it is generally too late to make changes. Therefore, it is extremely important that the system requirements are very clearly specified and understood by all parties before being signed off.

Such levels of certainty are difficult to achieve and this is one of the major drawbacks of the 'waterfall model'.

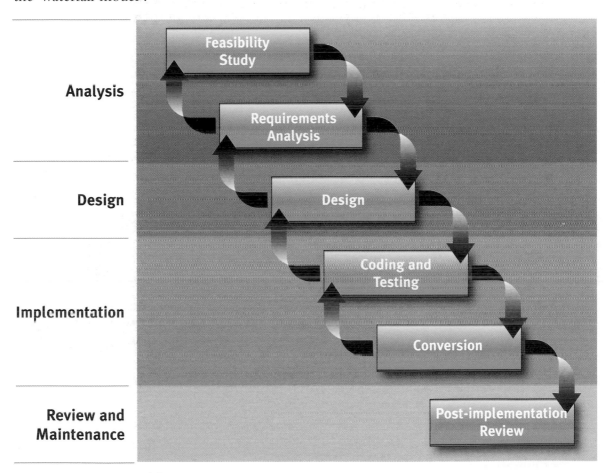

Figure 29.2: Systems development life cycle (the 'Waterfall model')

What prompts a new system?

The development of a new information system is a major undertaking and not one to be undertaken lightly. Wal-Mart, the American discount store which has recently taken over Asda, spent $700m on its computerised distribution system in the 1980s. Tesco, Sainsbury's and Marks and Spencer have spent massive sums of money on their computer systems in the past decade. Businesses must adapt to remain competitive. Some of the reasons for introducing a new system may be:

1 **The current system may be no longer suitable for its purpose**. Changes in work processes, expansion of the business, changes in business requirements or the environment in which the organisation operates may all lead to a reassessment of information system requirements.

2 **Technological developments may have made the current system redundant or outdated**. Advances in hardware, software and telecommunications bring new opportunities, which an organisation cannot ignore if it is to keep ahead of its rivals.

3 **The current system may be too inflexible or expensive to maintain**, or may reduce the organisation's ability to respond quickly enough to customer's demands.

At the end of the millennium, many businesses with old systems that were susceptible to the 'millennium bug' took the opportunity to install new systems, which would provide better information, rather than spend money on having external consultants patch up their old system.

3-29

Feasibility study

Once a problem has been recognised and identified, the **feasibility study** is the first stage of the systems life cycle. The **scope** and **objectives** of the proposed system must be written down. The aim of the feasibility study is to understand the problem and to determine whether it is worth proceeding. There are five main factors to be considered:

> **T**echnical feasibility
> **E**conomic feasibility
> **L**egal feasibility
> **O**perational feasibility
> **S**chedule feasibility

- **Technical feasibility** means investigating whether the technology exists to implement the proposed system, or whether this is a practical proposition.
- **Economic feasibility** has to do with establishing the cost-effectiveness of the proposed system – if the benefits do not outweigh the costs, then it is not worth going ahead.
- **Legal feasibility** determines whether there is any conflict between the proposed system and legal requirements – for example, will the system contravene the Data Protection Act?
- **Operational feasibility** is concerned with whether the current work practices and procedures are adequate to support the new system. It is also concerned with social factors – how the organisational change will affect the working lives of those affected by the system.
- **Schedule feasibility** looks at how long the system will take to develop, or whether it can be done in a desired time-frame.

The completion of this stage is marked by the production of a feasibility report produced by the systems analyst. If the report concludes that the project should go ahead, and this is agreed by senior managers, detailed requirements analysis will proceed.

Analysis/Requirements analysis

The second phase of systems analysis is a more detailed investigation into the current system and the requirements of the new system.

It is the job of the systems analyst to find out what the user's requirements are, to find out about current methods and to assess the feasibility of the new proposed system. Gathering details about the current system may involve:

- interviewing staff at different levels of the organisation from the end-users to senior management.

- examining current business and systems documents and output. These may include current order documents, computer systems procedures and reports used by operations and senior management.

- sending out questionnaires and analysing responses. The questions have to be carefully constructed to elicit unambiguous answers.

- observation of current procedures, by spending time in various departments. A time and motion study can be carried out to see where procedures could be made more efficient, or to detect where bottlenecks occur.

The systems analyst's report will examine how data and information flow around the organisation, and may use **data flow diagrams** to document the flow. It will also establish precisely, and in considerable detail, exactly what the proposed system will do (as opposed to how it will do it). It will include an in-depth analysis of the costs and benefits, and outline the process of system implementation, including the organisational change required. It must establish who the end-users are, what information they should get and in what form and how it will be obtained.

Alternative options for the implementation of the project will be suggested. These could include suggestions for:

- whether development should be done in-house or using consultants;

- what hardware configurations could be considered;

- what the software options are.

Data flow diagram (DFD)

A data flow diagram shows how data moves through a system and what data stores are used. It does not specify what type of data storage is used or how the data is stored.

The following four symbols are used in data flow diagrams:

External entity – data source or data destination, for example people who generate data such as a customer order, or receive information such as an invoice.

Process – an operation performed on the data. The two lines are optional; the top section of the box can be used to label the process, the middle to give a brief explanation, the bottom to say where the process takes place. An alternative convention is to use a circle for a Process.

Make the first word an active verb – e.g. **validate** data, **adjust** stock level.

Data store – such as a file held on disk or a batch of documents

Data flow – the arrow represents movement between entities, processes or data stores. The arrow should be labelled to describe what data is involved

Example:

A theatre uses a computerised booking system to keep records of customers, plays and bookings. A customer may make a booking in person, by telephone or by preprinted form. The booking clerk first has to check whether there are any seats free for the performance. If there are, the clerk reserves the seats, then checks whether the customer's details are already on file, and if not, types them in. The tickets are then printed out and handed or sent to the customer. Payment is made either in cash or by credit card.

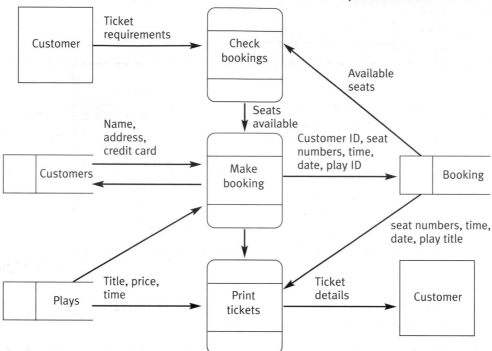

Figure 29.3: Data flow diagram of a theatre booking system

In the next chapter, the remaining stages of the system life cycle including design, implementation, testing, maintenance and evaluation will be considered.

Exercises

1   A feasibility study will often be carried out at an early stage of system development. As well as finding out if the proposal is technically possible the study will also consider economic and social feasibility.

In the context of a feasibility study describe **one** cost, **one** benefit and **three** possible social effects that would be considered. (5)

AEB AS Computing Qu 7 1996

2   State **three** different methods of fact finding available during the systems analysis stage of the systems life cycle, and for each of these three methods, give **one** reason for its use. (6)

AEB Computing Paper 1 Qu 11 1996

3   A proposed computerised information system will be used in a number of separate departments within a large organisation.

   (a)   Suggest and justify **two** criteria which the systems analyst might use when selecting the personnel to be interviewed. (4)

   (b)   State **two** disadvantages of interviewing as a fact finding method. (2)

CCEA Module 3 Qu 1 May 1999

3-29

4 During system development a *data flow diagram* may be used to represent all or part of the system. Below is an outline of a data flow diagram for a system to produce gas bills where the meter readings, having been recorded using a hand held device, are processed against the customer master file to produce the printed gas bills for the customers and a printed error report.

Give an appropriate label to **each** of the numbered elements A to E. (5)

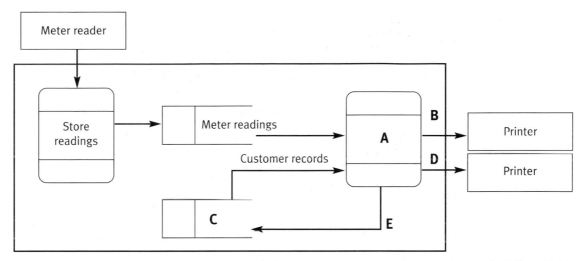

AEB Paper 2 Qu 7 1998

The following question is from the 2003 practical exercise (UKAB Re-marks)

5 This question relates to the ANALYSIS process.

(a) Candidate, Centre and Subject are three entities in this system. Draw the Entity Relationship diagrams between
(i) Candidate and Centre
(ii) Candidate and Subject
(iii) Centre and Subject (3)

(b) The analysis of this problem has already been carried out. How might the systems analyst have found out **each** of the following and from what data source? (Your two methods and two sources should be different.)
(i) The reports which were required from the system, and how frequently they need to be produced?
(ii) The volume of data the system would have to deal with? (4)

AQA CPT3 Qu 5 May 2003

The following question is from the 2002 practical exercise (Hospital Equipment Loan System)

6 This question relates to the ANALYSIS process.
When analysing the manual system, the analyst needed to gather information from a variety of sources. Suggest **two** different sources in the hospital and for each, suggest one method the analyst would use. Explain why that method would be appropriate to that source. Your two methods and your explanations must be different. (6)

AQA CPT3 Qu 8 May 2002

Note: The practical exercises may be downloaded from the AQA website **www.aqa.org.uk.**

Chapter 30 – From Design to Evaluation

System design

The design specifies the following aspects of a system:

- The hardware platform – which type of computer, network capabilities, input, storage and output devices.
- The software – programming language, package or database.
- The outputs – report layouts and screen designs.
- The inputs – documents, screen layouts and validation procedures.
- The user interface – how users will interact with the computer system.
- The modular design of each program in the application.
- The test strategy, test plan and test data.
- Conversion plan – how the new system is to be implemented.
- Documentation including systems and operations documentation. Later, a user manual will be produced.

System specification

The systems specification must describe how the new system will work. Screen layouts and report formats must be designed, file contents and organisation specified, and each program in the system must be described by means of program specifications, structure charts, pseudocode or flowcharts.

The programmers must then code, test and debug all the programs in the system. In smaller organisations the roles of programmer and analyst may overlap, and in some cases the 'analyst/programmer' may design, code and test the programs.

Program design methods

The use of structure charts and pseudocode for describing algorithms has been described in Chapter 7. An **algorithm** is a sequence of instructions to solve a given problem. **Pseudocode** is an intermediate stage between plain English and the programming language in which the solution will eventually be coded – it enables the writer to concentrate on the steps in the solution without worrying about the syntax rules of a particular language.

Prototyping

As in any other context, prototyping means building a working model of a new system in order to evaluate it, test it or have it approved before building the final product. When applied to computer systems, this could involve, for example, using special software to quickly design input screens and run a program (supplied as part of the prototyping package) to input and validate data using the screen format just created. This gives the user a chance to experience the 'look and feel' of the input process and to suggest alterations before going any further.

The prototype may then be discarded and the system built using the same or different software. This is termed **throw-away** prototyping.

Some organisations will use prototyping in the analysis stage, others in the design phase. Others may use it almost exclusively, going directly from preliminary investigation, via the prototype, to an implemented system. The analysts or programmers will simply keep refining the prototype until the user says it is acceptable. This is called **evolutionary** prototyping.

> **Q1:** What are the advantages and disadvantages of using prototyping as a tool of systems analysis and design?

Choosing a software solution

Many different solutions to a particular problem will have been looked at before a particular solution is chosen. The criteria on which the final choice is based will include:

- **Usability** – will the users find the system easy to use, will it save them time, cut out tedious repetitive tasks, give them quick access to information they need, or help them in some way? Or will it just give them extra work with no obvious benefits, or produce mountains of paperwork from which it is hard to extract useful information?
- **Performance** – will the system function in the way that was intended? Or will it suffer from 'bugs', slow access times when retrieving data from a database, screens that take minutes to change or redraw after a command is typed, hardware that is unreliable?
- **Suitability** – does the system really provide a solution to the problem, or was it considered because for example it was the 'cheapest' solution? Will it integrate with existing software, can current manual methods be adapted for the new system?
- **Maintainability** – will it be easy to upgrade the system, add new functionality, make modifications when required?

Testing strategies

When a new system is developed, it has to undergo rigorous testing before it is released. Typically, it may undergo several phases of testing including:

- **Dry run testing:** the programmer follows through the code manually using test data to check that an algorithm is correct. This technique is useful for locating run-time errors – it would normally be carried out on a part of a program rather than the whole program. A **trace table** (see Chapter 7) is useful for checking the values of variables while following through the logic.
- **Unit testing:** this refers to the testing of each individual subroutine or module in a suite of programs.
- **Integration testing:** this involves testing a complete suite of programs to ensure that they all function correctly when they are put together – for example, by being called from a menu program.

Test plan and test data

A test plan needs to be drawn up for each program in a system. This is usually in the form of a table showing each item that needs to be tested. It should cover every possible type of input including values that are too large, too small or invalid for other reasons such as an alphabetic character being entered instead of a number. The test plan needs to show for each test what the expected result is.

Technical documentation

Technical documentation helps to ensure that a system can be maintained after completion. All too often changes of staff within a company mean that no-one who was involved in the original design or programming of a system is still with the company. It is essential that proper documentation is kept to enable a newcomer to make necessary corrections, alterations or enhancements.

Contents of a documented system

- an accurate and up-to-date systems specification;
- Data Flow Diagrams showing the inputs to the system, files required, processes to be carried out, and output from the system;
- a description of the purpose of each program within the system;
- a structure diagram, flowchart or pseudocode for each program in the system;
- organisation, contents and layout of each file used;
- layout and contents of all output prints and displays;
- current version of each program listing;
- test data and expected results.

Implementation

This phase includes both the coding and testing of the system, the acquisition of hardware and the installation of the new system or conversion of the old system to the new one.

The installation phase can include:

- installing the new hardware, which may involve extensive recabling and changes in office layouts;
- training the users on the new system;
- conversion of master files to the new system, or creation of new master files.

Evaluation

When a new software system is complete, it is very important to evaluate it to ensure that it meets the user's original specifications and is satisfactory in all respects.

Minor programming errors may have to be corrected, clerical procedures amended, or modifications made to the design of reports or screen layouts.

The solution will be evaluated in terms of

- Effectiveness: does it do what it is supposed to do?
- Usability: is it easy to use?
- Maintainability: will it be easy to maintain?

Often it is only when people start to use a new system that they realise its shortcomings! In some cases they may realise that it would be possible to get even more useful information from the system than they realised, and more programs may be requested. The process of system maintenance, in fact, has already begun, and the life cycle is complete.

3-30

System maintenance

All software systems require maintenance, and in fact the vast majority of programmers are employed to maintain existing programs rather than to write new ones. There are differing reasons for this, and different types of maintenance.

- Perfective maintenance. This implies that while the system runs satisfactorily, there is still room for improvement. For example, extra management information may be needed so that new report programs have to be written. Database queries may be very slow, and a change in a program may be able to improve response time.

- Adaptive maintenance. All systems will need to adapt to changing needs within a company. As a business expands, for example, there may be a requirement to convert a standalone system to a multi-user system. New and better hardware may become available, and changes to the software may be necessary to take advantage of this. New government legislation may mean that different methods of calculating tax, for example, are required. Competition from other firms may mean that systems have to be upgraded in order to maintain a competitive edge.

- Corrective maintenance. Problems frequently surface after a system has been in use for a short time, however thoroughly it was tested. Some part of the system may not function as expected, or a report might be wrong in some way; totals missing at the bottom, incorrect sequence of data, wrong headings, etc. Frequently errors will be hard to trace, if for example a file appears to have been wrongly updated.

3-30

Exercises

1 Software developers use prototyping for different reasons in different situations.

    (a) What is prototyping? (1)

    (b) Briefly explain two reasons for using prototypes. (2)

AEB Paper 2 Qu 4 1998

2 Describe two methods of testing which will be used during the development of a new software system. (4)

AEB Paper 2 Qu 5 1997

3 A typical software system will require both corrective and adaptive maintenance.

    (a) Describe the main difference between corrective maintenance and adaptive maintenance. (4)

    (b) Explain how a software system should be developed in order to

        (i) Decrease the amount of corrective maintenance required.

        (ii) Ensure adaptive maintenance is as straightforward as possible. (6)

CCEA Module 3 Qu 4 1999

4 (a) Explain why an error in the system specification is usually more expensive to correct if it is discovered during the maintenance phase than if it is discovered during the design phase. (4)

    (b) Distinguish between evolutionary prototyping and throw-away prototyping. (4)

CCEA Module 3 Qu 2 1999

The following questions are from the 2001 practical exercise (PostQuick Parcels)★

5   This question relates to the LEGAL implications of the use of computers.

    (a) (i) Explain what legal responsibility PostQuick have for their customer data.   (3)

        (ii) Describe **one** technique that should be used to meet this responsibility.   (2)

    (b) Describe **one** further technique you would recommend to PostQuick for the security of the data against accidental or deliberate damage.   (2)

AQA CPT3 Qu 6 May 2001

6   This question relates to MAINTENANCE.

When you hand over your software to PostQuick, you include in your system documentation items that could be used for subsequent maintenance and up-dating of your solution. Name and describe **two** items which should be included for this purpose.   (4)

AQA CPT3 Qu 9 May 2001

The following question is from the 2002 practical exercise (Hospital Equipment Loan System)★

7   This question relates to the OUTPUTS.

If a piece of equipment is due for return or renewal, the patient has to be contacted. It is stated in the brief that 'there is a standard letter for this'. The hospital could use a *mail merge* process for this.

    (a) List the steps that would be required to use mail merge to produce contact letters, (even if your solution does not support this).   (4)

    (b) Explain **two** advantages of using mail merge in this situation over typing individual letters.   (2)

AQA CPT3 Qu 7 May 2002

The following question is from the 2003 practical exercise (UKAB re-marks)★

8   This question relates to the INTEGRITY and SECURITY of data in your solution.

    (a) Clearly it is essential for your data to be accurate. Describe **one** technique which might be followed to improve accuracy on data entry.   (2)

    (b) It is also essential to keep your data secure against unauthorised access. The data files could be password protected with strictly defined access rights. Describe **two** other techniques which might be followed to improve data security.   (4)

AQA CPT3 Qu 6 May 2003

9   This question relates to the EVALUATION and MAINTENANCE of your new system.

    (a) After your system has been running for a short time, it should be evaluated. Give **three** factors which could be looked at in this evaluation.   (3)

    (b) (i) Suggest **one** reason why your system may need maintenance in the future.   (1)

        (ii) Give **three** items of documentation which would be necessary for effective maintenance of your system. These may be items you have not included in your documentation for this practical exercise.   (3)

AQA CPT3 Qu 7 May 2003

★ *Note: The practical exercises may be downloaded from the AQA website* **www.aqa.org.uk.**

Chapter 31 – Human Computer Interface

Introduction

The '**human computer interface**' is a term used to describe the interaction between a user and a computer; in other words, the method by which the user tells the computer what to do, and the responses that the computer makes.

It's important not to allow the word 'computer' to limit your vision to a PC sitting on an office desk. You also need to think in terms of a person getting cash from a cash machine, a pilot of a jumbo jet checking his instrument panels, the operator of a high-volume heavy duty photocopier, a scientist monitoring a chemical reaction, a musician composing a symphony using appropriate hardware and software.

> **Q1:** Name some other tasks for which computers are used, and for which special purpose interfaces are required.

The importance of good interface design

A good interface design can help to ensure that users carry out their tasks:

- **safely** (in the case of a jumbo jet pilot, for example);
- **effectively** (users don't find they have video taped two hours of Bulgarian clog dancing instead of the Cup Final);
- **efficiently** (users do not spend five minutes trying to find the correct way to insert their cash card and type in their PIN and the amount of cash they want, and then leave without remembering to extract their card);
- **enjoyably** (a primary school pupil using a program to teach multiplication tables).

Well-designed systems can improve the output of employees, improve the quality of life and make the world a safer and more enjoyable place to live in.

> **Q2:** In the early days of cash machines, it was found that users sometimes forgot to remove their cards after withdrawing their cash. What simple change was made to eliminate this fault?

Designing usable systems

In order to design a usable interface, the designer has to take into consideration:

- **who** will use the system. For example, will the users be computer professionals or members of the general public who may be wary of computers? For an educational program, will the users be young, for example primary school children, or teenagers on an A Level course? Will the system have to cater for both beginners and experienced users?
- **what tasks** the computer is performing. Is the task very repetitive, does the task require skill and knowledge? Do tasks vary greatly from one occasion to the next? A travel agent who spends most of the day making holiday bookings will require a different interface from an office worker who needs to be able to switch between word processing, accounts and accessing the company database.
- **the environment** in which the computer is used. Will the environment be hazardous (in a lifeboat setting out to rescue a stricken vessel), noisy (in a factory full of machinery), or calm and quiet (some offices)?
- **what is technologically feasible** (is it possible to simply dictate a letter to a word processor instead of typing it in?)

3-31

Interface styles

There are a number of common interface styles including:
• command line interface;
• menus;
• natural language;
• forms and dialogue boxes;
• graphical user interface (GUI).

Command-line interface

The command-line interface was the first interactive dialogue style and is still widely used in spite of the availability of menu-driven interfaces. It provides a means of expressing instructions to the computer directly using single characters, whole word commands or abbreviations.

With this type of interface very little help is given to the user, who has to type a command such as, for example, **Format a:** to format a disk. Commands enable a user to quickly and concisely instruct the computer what to do, but they do require the user to have a knowledge of the commands available and the syntax for using them.

> **Q3:** Identify TWO situations in which a command-driven interface would be appropriate.

3-31

Menus

There are several different types of menu interface, outlined below.

1 **Full screen menu.** This type of menu is often used as the 'front end' of an application. It stays on screen until the user makes a choice.

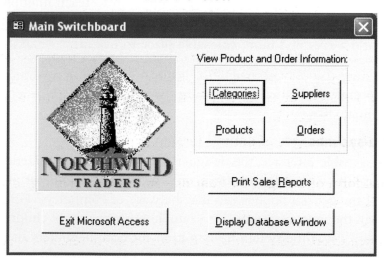

Figure 31.1: Full screen menu

2 **Pull-down menu.** This type of menu is displayed along the top of the screen, and when the user clicks on an item, a submenu appears. The menu is always present whatever screen the user is looking at in the application.

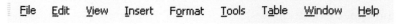

Figure 31.2: Pull-down menu

3 **Pop-up menu**. The menu pops up in response to, say, a click of the right mouse button on a particular area of the screen.

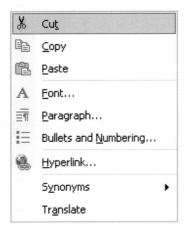

Figure 31.3: Pop-up menu

Natural language

It is a very attractive idea to have a computer that can understand natural language – 'plain English' in other words. *'How do I create an A5 folded leaflet in Word?'* is understandable to most people but does not elicit a sensible answer from the Office Assistant. (You can't, basically.) Unfortunately, the ambiguity of natural language makes it very difficult for a machine to understand. Language is ambiguous in a number of different ways. Firstly, the syntax, or structure of a sentence may not be clear – for example consider the sentences

> James and Henrietta are married.
> A salesman visited every house in the area.
> The man hit the dog with the stick.

Are James and Henrietta married to each other? Was there only one salesman involved in the house-to-house sales operation? Who had the stick?

Secondly, many English words have more than one meaning. How many ways can the word 'match' be interpreted?

Advantages and disadvantages of natural language dialogue

Advantages:
- most natural form of dialogue for humans – no need for training in a specialised command language;
- extremely flexible and powerful;
- the user is free to construct their own commands, frame their own questions, etc.

Disadvantages:
- people find it difficult to stick to grammatically correct English;
- a well designed 'artificial language' can often say the same thing more concisely than 'natural language';
- a smooth, natural language can easily mislead the naive user into believing the computer is 'intelligent'.

Forms and dialogue boxes

When a user is required to enter data such as, for example, sales invoices or customer names and addresses, it is common to have a 'form' displayed on the screen for the user to fill in. The following points should be noted when designing forms of this type:

• the form should be given a title to identify it;

• the form should not be too cluttered – spaces and blanks are important;

• it should give some indication of how many characters can be entered in each field of data;

• the user should be given a chance to go back and correct any field before the data is accepted;

• items should appear in a logical sequence to assist the user;

• default values should wherever possible be prewritten onto the form so that a minimum of data entry is required;

• full exit and 'help' facilities should be provided – for example, users could enter '?' in a field if they require more information;

• lower case in a display is neater and easier to read than all upper-case;

• colours should be carefully chosen to be legible and easy on the eyes;

• 'attention-getting' devices such as blinking cursors, high-intensity, reverse video, underlining etc should not be over-used.

Dialogue boxes are a special type of form often associated with the Windows environment; an example shown below is the dialogue box which appears when the instruction to *Print* is given in Word 2002.

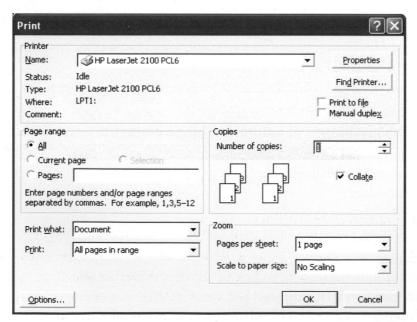

Figure 31.4: Dialogue box

The WIMP interface

WIMP stands for Windows, Icons, Mouse and Pull-down menus.

A **window** is an area on the screen through which a particular piece of software or a data file may be viewed. The window may occupy the whole screen, or the user can choose to have several windows on the screen with a different application running in each one. Windows can be moved, sized, stacked one on top of the other, opened and closed A Windows environment mimics a desktop on which a worker may have several books or pieces of paper spread out for reference.

An icon is a small picture representing an item such as a piece of software, a file, storage medium (such as disk or tape) or command. By pointing with a mouse at a particular icon and clicking the mouse button the user can select it.

Microsoft Windows enables the user to run several different software packages such as MS Word (a word processor), MS Excel (a spreadsheet), MS Paint (a graphics package) simultaneously and to move data and graphics from one package to another. Software packages written by other manufacturers, such as Aldus PageMaker, have been written to run under Windows because of the convenience to the user of this easy-to-use environment.

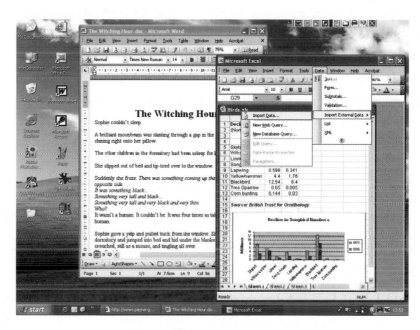

Figure 31.5: WIMP interface

Advantages of a common user interface

All the software packages mentioned above use a consistent interface and have a similar 'look and feel' so that a user familiar with one package can quickly learn a second. For example, in each package a single click of the mouse button selects an item, and a double click activates the item. In each package, the methods for opening, closing, sizing and moving windows is identical. The advantages can be summarised as:

- increased speed of learning;
- ease of use;
- confidence building for novice users;
- increased range of tasks solvable by experienced users;
- a greater range of software accessible to the average user.

Speech input (voice recognition)

The ultimate in user-friendly interfaces would probably be one in which you could simply tell your computer what to do in ordinary speech. Two distinct types of voice recognition system are emerging; small vocabulary command and control systems and large vocabulary dictation systems.

- **Command and control systems** can be relatively small and cheap because they need only a small, tightly defined vocabulary of technical terms. Such systems are coming rapidly into use as automatic call-handling systems for applications such as bank account enquiries. In PC systems, voice command can be used to bring up files, control printing and so on, effectively replacing the mouse. In some systems the computer is 'trained' by an individual user pronouncing a given vocabulary of words; it then stores a recording of the user's speech pattern for each word or syllable.

- **Large vocabulary dictation systems** can handle whole sentences and extensive vocabularies but need much greater processing power and memory space. These systems use elaborate probability distributions to estimate which word the acoustic pattern it has picked up is most likely to be, partly by looking at other words in the developing sentence and predicting what sort of word (noun or verb, for example) is likely to be used. Various voice recognition packages after suitable 'training' will take dictation at 70 words per minute and get about 97% of them correct. Voice recognition is however still an expensive technology and widespread use is some way off.

3-31

Q4: Name some other situations in which voice input would be appropriate.

Speech/sound output

A speech synthesis system works as follows:

Individual words and sounds are spoken into a microphone by a human being and recorded by the system, thereby training it to speak. Output that would normally be printed can then be spoken, so long as the word is contained in its vocabulary. A second, more flexible method uses phonemes – the individual sounds from which all words are constructed in any particular language.

Such a system has limited use but could for example be used by a bank computer connected by telephone line to customers' homes and offices. The customer could key in his account number using the telephone keypad, and the computer could then access his account and speak out the customer's account balance.

Exercises

1 You are asked to design a delivery note for registered letters delivered by courier.
Give **two** design requirements you need to consider.   (2)

Draw your design and show how you satisfied these requirements.   (2)

New Question

2 You are asked to design a standard letter for the school library to send to pupils who
have overdue books. Give **three** criteria that you need to consider for the design of
this document.   (3)

Draw your design and show how you satisfied these criteria.   (3)

New Question

3 During the analysis stage of a school Book Loan, the librarian has stated that a single
input screen should be able to accept loans and returns from pupils and staff. Initially
the book, pupil and staff identification numbers will have to be entered manually until
barcode readers are purchased.

The input screen should be user friendly and should make inputting data easy and
minimise errors. State **three** criteria you would consider in the design of this screen
and explain how each would be relevant to good user interface design.   (6)

Draw your design and show how you satisfied these criteria.   (3)

New Question

3-31

4 A company is designing a software package for use by pupils in infants' schools.

Briefly describe and justify two appropriate features of the package's human-computer
interface.   (4)

NEAB CP01 Qu 3 1998

5 A college uses a range of software packages from different suppliers. Each package has
a different user interface. The college is considering changing its software to one
supplier and to a common user interface.

(a) Give **four** advantages of having a common user interface.   (4)

(b) Describe four specific features of a user interface which would benefit from
being common between packages.   (4)

(c) Discuss the issues involved, apart from user interfaces, in the college changing
or upgrading software packages.   (8)

NEAB IT02 Qu 8 1997

Appendix A – The Practical Exercise

Introduction

The coursework for AQA AS Computing is very different from coursework you may have done for other subjects such as ICT. You have to solve a problem provided by the examination board (check the web site **www.aqa.org.uk** for this year's exercise). You must produce a solution either through programming or tailoring a database. You need to document your solution by writing up your design and provide evidence of your implementation and testing. The Unit 3 examination paper will ask you questions about how you designed and produced your implementation and you need to cross-reference your answers with evidence from your documentation, which you must hand in with your examination script.

You will be marked only on your answers in the examination script. Your documentation will not be marked as a piece of coursework – the examiner will look at it only for evidence that you refer to in your answers. It is very important that you work very closely to the specification given by the examination board, so that you have the evidence for any questions that you might be asked. Only cover the points specified in the brief.

You can either program the solution, use a relational database package, or combine the use of a database with a programming language. The solution does not necessarily require a fully automated system. Humans can form part of the system and human interaction may solve a particular difficulty you have encountered.

If you intend to solve the Practical Exercise using a programming language, you may wish to look at the book by Sylvia Langfield "Learning to Program in Pascal & Delphi" (chapters 24 and 25). Those chapters give model solutions for the 2003 Practical Exercise (UKAB Re-Marks). If you want to use MS Access, look at the book by Pat Heathcote and Alison Day "Tackling Computer Projects in Access with VBA (4th Edition)". It includes a sample solution for the 2004 Practical Exercise "Tod's Tyres".

> **The following pages explain the different stages of producing the documentation for a practical exercise. The example answers are based on a sample Practical Exercise (Book Loan System) and enclosed in frames like this one.**

Don't be tempted to write descriptions of what you want to implement. An architect's design of a building is represented by drawings, which a builder can work from. You are designing software. When you are 'building' your software, it is easier to work from drawings, lists and tables than from wordy descriptions.

Your documentation should be brief, yet include the necessary evidence, and be clearly laid out. The examination board expects fewer than 25-30 pages.

Prepare a word processed document with your name, centre number and candidate number in the header, and the page number in the footer in the right hand corner. Pages should be numbered sequentially from start to end, not subdivided into sections. It may help you to find relevant evidence during the examination, if you include a contents page. Your documentation will need to be hole-punched in the top left hand corner, so that it can be tied to your examination script.

Book Loan System

New College is a Sixth Form College with over 1000 students studying many different subjects. The library has several thousand books and multiple copies of popular books. Students can borrow books from the library.

You have been asked to create a computer application, either programmed or using a database, to replace the current manual record-keeping system. Initially there will be only one stand-alone workstation with a printer attached. This will be placed at the library counter.

Current System

1 When students first join the college, they are assigned to a tutor group. Tutor groups are known by the tutors' unique initials (three letters). Each student is given an ID card with their photo, name, tutor group and unique Student ID (a five-digit number). Each student is automatically a member of the library.

2 Each book in the library is identified by a unique book ID (a five-digit number), stamped on the inside cover of the book. The library keeps a catalogue of all the books they have, storing book ID, title, author, ISBN and book value. Each book has a record card stored inside the front cover with the book ID on the card. There is also a form attached to the inside cover where the librarian stamps the date the book is borrowed.

3 When a student wants to borrow a book, they take it to the counter and the librarian records their student ID and today's date on the book record card. The book record card is then stored in date order in a filing box. The book is stamped with today's date.

4 When a student returns a book, the librarian finds the book record card for that book and enters the date the book was returned. Then the card is stored inside the book again and the book is returned to the shelf.

5 Books are due two weeks from the date they have been borrowed. If a book is returned late, the student is fined 5p for each day late.

6 Once a week the librarian goes through the book record cards of books that are overdue and writes notes to students reminding them of overdue books. The reminder note includes the book ID, the book's title and author and the fine due. These notes are delivered via tutors.

7 When a student leaves college they must get their leaver's form signed by the librarian to prove they have no books outstanding. If they have lost any books, they are charged the value of the books, and the librarian will produce an invoice.

Testing

Test data for at least 15 students and 20 books should cover situations where some books have been returned, some are out on loan and some are overdue.

Analysis

The specification of the practical exercise is the analysis of the current system. You need to understand how the system operates, so you may need to read through the specification many times. Systems analysts use data flow diagrams to help them understand a system. Even though a data flow diagram is not a requirement of the Practical Exercise you might be asked to draw one in the exam. In any case it is a useful means by which you can get to understand the system in question. Draw a data flow diagram of the Practical Exercise. (See chapter 29 for help).

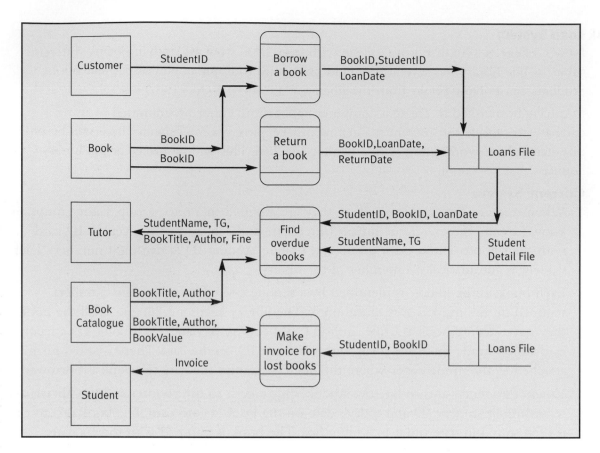

Figure A.1: Book Loan Data Flow Diagram

Design

Definition of data requirements

When you were reading the specification to draw the data flow diagram, you will have noticed what data is required in the system. Draw up a table of the necessary fields.

Field Name	Notes
StudentID	5-digit number, unique to each student
StudentName	First Name followed by Surname
TG	3-letter initials, unique to each tutor
BookID	5-digit number, unique to each book
BookTitle	title up to 50 characters
Author	author up to 30 characters
ISBN	10-character International Book Number including check digit
BookValue	replacement cost of book, between £0 and £100.
LoanDate	the date the book is borrowed by the student, default to today's date
ReturnDate	the date the book is returned by the student, default to today's date

Figure A.2: Book Loan Data Requirements

User Interface Design

Check your specification and your data flow diagram. What hard copy output is your system expected to produce? Draw a sketch of each report, noting what information is required and where on the page it ought to be placed. Think about a logical order and consider readability and sizes of fonts.

The person(s) using your system will need to communicate with the computer to input data and give commands. What screen layout(s) do you need, so all the tasks you identified while drawing the data flow diagram can be performed? Again, draw a sketch of each screen layout, considering easy operation of the interface.

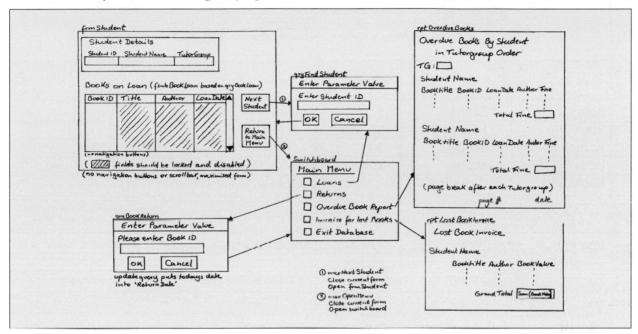

Figure A.3: Book Loan User Interface Design

Method of Data Entry

The most likely method will be entry via a keyboard. Check what validation is required by the specification of the Practical Exercise. Is there any data that can be selected from a list or a set of options?

When borrowing a book, StudentID and BookID need to be entered into the system. If these IDs are barcoded on the book and student ID card respectively, these could be read by a bar code reader. Alternatively these numbers can be entered via the keyboard. LoanDate should by default be today's date. The return date should be updated to today's date on return of the book.

Figure A.4: Book Loan Method of Data Entry

Record Structure, File Organisation and Processing

Draw an Entity-Relationship diagram of your system. This should help you decide which fields should be stored in which tables/files. Look at your data requirements (example see Figure A.2). How are you going to store these fields? Draw up a data dictionary. This should list the field name, data type, any validation rules required and any further comment you deem necessary.

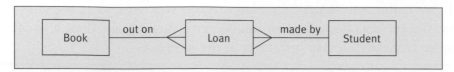

Figure A.5: Entity-Relationship Diagram

Book Field Name	Data Type	Length	Validation	Comment
BookID	String	5	digits only	
BookTitle	String	50		
Author	String	30		
ISBN	String	10		
BookValue	Currency		between 0 and 100	
Student Field Name	Data Type	Length	Validation	Comment
StudentID	String	5	digits only	
StudentName	String	50		
TG	String	3	3 letters only	Lookup
Loan Field Name	Data Type	Length	Validation	Comment
StudentID	String	5	must exist in Student table	
BookID	String	5	must exist in Book table	
LoanDate	Date/Time			today's date
ReturnDate	Date/Time			today's date

Figure A.6: Book Loan Record Structure and File Organisation

What processing does your system have to do? Check the specification. This may include

- formulae to calculate required results
- queries to find/sort records

Write down any formula you think you are going to need.

Draw a QBE (query by example) diagram or write pseudocode statements

For Fines:
Fine ← NumberOfDaysLate * 5p
For Invoice:
TotalCost ← Sum of BookValue for all non-returned books
For Reminder letters:
Find loan records, grouped by TG, student, where LoanDate <= Date() - 14

Figure A.7: Book Loan Processing Design

Query Name	Query Type	Purpose	Tables accessed	Fields accessed	Notes/Criteria
qryFindStudent	Select parameter query	Find one student by StudentID Provide data for book loans form	Student	StudentID StudentName TG	StudentID = [please enter student ID]
qryBookReturn	Update parameter query	Find loan record of book with given BookID and enter today's date into ReturnDate	Loan	BookID ReturnDate	Must find the record of the current book loan not one that has been previously returned. Criteria: BookID = [Enter BookID to be returned] ReturnDate is Null Action: ReturnDate ← Date()
qryOverdueBooks	Select query	To find all overdue book records in loan table and provide date for Overdue Book Report	Student Book Loan	StudentName TG BookTitle Author BookValue LoanDate BookID ReturnDate StudentID	Must find all books which are still out and overdue (more than 14 days out) Criteria: ReturnDate is Null AND LoanDate <Date() -14 Calculated fields: Days: Date()-LoanDate -14 Fine: Days *0.05 (Currency)
qryLostBooks	Select parameter query	Find all books a student has not returned Provide date for LostBookInvoice	Loan	BookID	Criteria: StudentID = [Please enter Student ID] ReturnDate is Null

Figure A.8: Book Loan Query Design

Test Plan

It is a good idea to think now about how you are going to test your solution. What types of tests will you need to perform?

- validation of fields works as expected
- results correctly calculated
- hard copy output includes all necessary information and is easy to understand
- Human-Computer-Interface is easy to use and allows all tasks required by the specification

Test Number	Test Type
1	Queries return correct results
2	Main Menu options go to correct forms/reports
3	overdue book report works correctly
4	Lost book invoice produced correctly
5	Loans updated correctly

Figure A.9: Book Loan Test Plan

You need to make up enough test data to fully test your solution. Make a table with sufficient records of normal data (you need to use your imagination). What specific cases do you need to test for? Have you got test data to reflect these? Also include extreme and erroneous data.

> I chose the loan data such that there are:
>
> Books which have never been out on loan (13214, 14658, 14661, 30656, 30662, 31302, 31388, 32087, 33350)
>
> Books which have been out on loan, come back and loaned out again (61234, 62345)
>
> Books which have been out on loan and come back (67890)
>
> Books which are overdue (31387, 32040, 34468, 34860, 51289, 51584)
>
> Books which are not overdue as on 11/5/2004: (14666, 52233, 61234, 62345)
>
> Some students who have overdue books, some more than one and from 2 tutor groups
>
> Loan dates so that the system tests the extreme values of overdue / not overdue (26/04/04, 27/04/2004)

Figure A.10: Reasons for choice of test data

BookID	Book Title	Author	Book Value
13214	Soul of a new machine	Kidder, Tracy	£5.95
14658	Computer Architecture	Wise, Harold	£7.20
14661	Data Structures	Bailey, Brian	£5.99
14666	Introducing Computers	Bishop, Peter	£5.99
30656	Computer Concepts	Shelly, G.B.	£7.99
30662	Computing concepts	Duffy, Tim	£12.50
31302	Mastering Spreadsheets	Gosling, Peter	£3.50
31387	Inside the Internet	Winder, Davey	£7.35
31388	Internet made simple	McBride, Peter	£5.99
32040	GNVQ core skills IT	Arden, Trevor	£5.95
32087	Essentials of computing	Capron, H.L.	£5.99
33350	Mastering Databases	Gosling, Peter	£3.50
34468	Dictionary of Computing	BCS	£12.50
34860	Road ahead	Gates, Bill	£7.99
51289	Computers and their applications	Parker, Charles	£12.00
51584	How Computers work	White, Ron	£5.99
52233	Cyberspace lexicon	Cotton, Bob	£7.99
61234	A-Level Computing	Heathcote, Pat	£16.00
62345	Programming in Pascal & Delphi	Langfield, Sylvia	£10.95
67890	Objects First with Java	Barnes, Kolling	£32.00

Figure A.11: Book Loan Test Data for Book table

StudentID	StudentName	TG
51234	Laura Saunders	ABT
51235	Andrew Stubley	ABT
51236	Katherine Tester	ABT
51237	Ross Blenkinsop	ABT
51239	Gemma Newton	ABT
51240	William Tailby	ABT
51242	Ben Brown	ABT
51249	Paul East	CDH
51250	Stuart Stanley	CDH
51251	Peter Leach	CDH
51252	Patrick Watson	CDH
51253	Simon Daynes	CDH
51255	Melanie Newton	CDH
51256	Paul Constant	CDH
51257	Heidi Robinson	CDH

BookID	StudentID	Loan Date	Return Date
61234	51234	01/04/2004	10/04/2004
61234	51253	29/04/2004	
67890	51252	20/04/2004	21/04/2004
14666	51257	30/04/2004	
62345	51252	01/03/2004	05/03/2004
62345	51236	01/04/2004	19/04/2004
62345	51253	01/05/2004	
31387	51251	22/04/2004	
32040	51240	23/04/2004	
34468	51257	24/04/2004	
34860	51240	25/04/2004	
51289	51257	26/04/2004	
51584	51240	27/04/2004	
52233	51253	28/04/2004	

Figure A.12: Book Loan Test Data for Student table

Figure A.13: Book Loan Test Data for Loans table

Security and Integrity of data

Do you need to take any precautions to keep data secure and correct? If you are setting up a database, then referential integrity and cascade deletes and cascade updates need to be considered as well as validation, to prevent loss of integrity of data. Is a password required?

> The Book Loan system is using a stand-alone workstation, which will be kept at the library counter. This database holds personal data, so it must comply with the Data Protection Act. Therefore a password should be set to allow authorised access only.
>
> To protect against data loss, regular backups would be advisable.
>
> To make sure data is entered correctly, validation should be set up wherever possible. For new book data the book value must be within range.
>
> Referential integrity is also going to be enforced to avoid loaning out books that do not exist to students that do not exist.
>
> User views will not allow changes to be made to fields, which are displayed for information only (see hashed areas in user interface design).

Figure A.14. Book Loan Consideration of Security and Integrity of Data

System Design

What hardware and software are you planning to use for the system, what are the requirements?

> I am planning to implement the Book Loan using a PC, running under Windows XP. The software to be used is MS Access 2000, a copy of which would need to be installed on the librarian's computer. Backup onto flash memory or CD-RW would be appropriate.

Figure A.15: Book Loan Design

Implementation/Testing

- Details of test plan with explanation, and evidence of testing having been carried out
- Hard copy output
- Hard copy of solution e.g. annotated program listing/database tables, forms and reports

Hard Copy of Solution

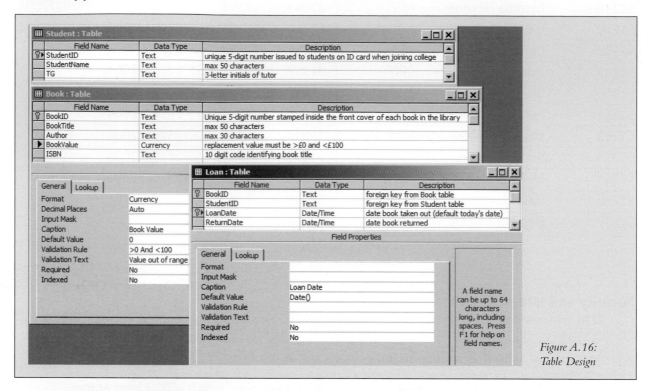

Figure A.16:
Table Design

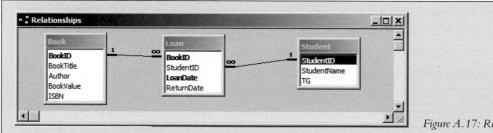

Figure A.17: Referential Integrity enforced

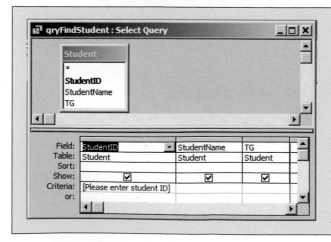

Figure A.18: qryFindStudent supplies the fields for the main form frmStudent

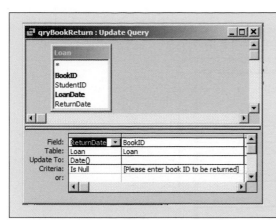

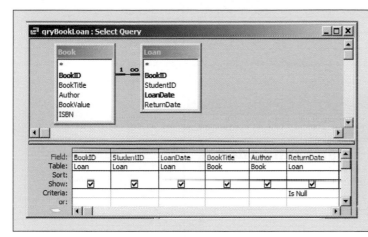

Figure A.19: qryBookLoan supplies the fields for the subform in frmStudent. The link between the subform and main form is made by StudentID

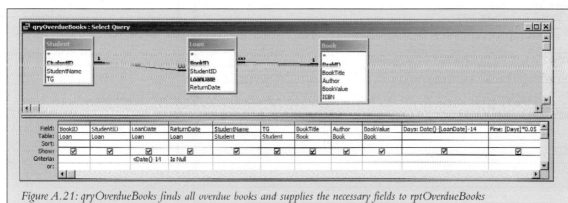

A

Figure A.20: qryBookReturn is an Update Query. It finds the record of the book with the given BookID and updates the return date to today's date

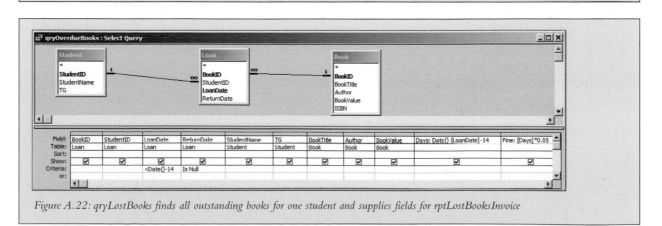

Figure A.21: qryOverdueBooks finds all overdue books and supplies the necessary fields to rptOverdueBooks

Figure A.22: qryLostBooks finds all outstanding books for one student and supplies fields for rptLostBooksInvoice

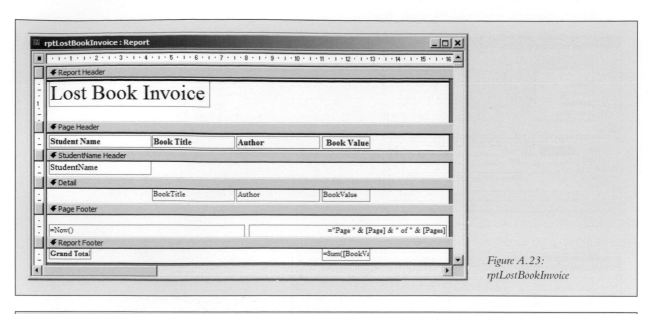

Figure A.23:
rptLostBookInvoice

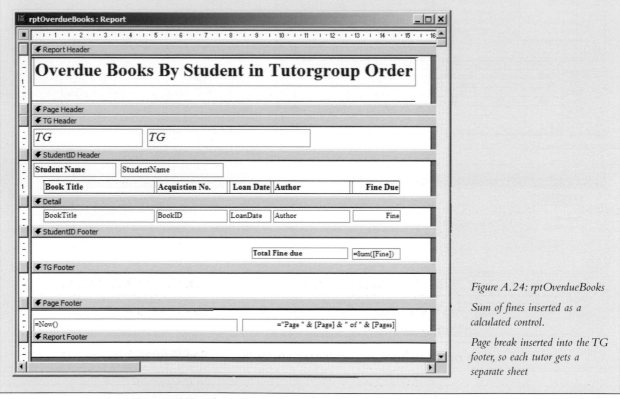

Figure A.24: rptOverdueBooks

Sum of fines inserted as a
calculated control.

Page break inserted into the TG
footer, so each tutor gets a
separate sheet

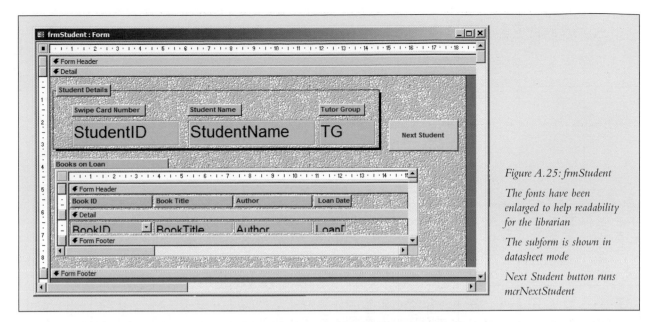

Figure A.25: frmStudent

The fonts have been enlarged to help readability for the librarian

The subform is shown in datasheet mode

Next Student button runs mcrNextStudent

A

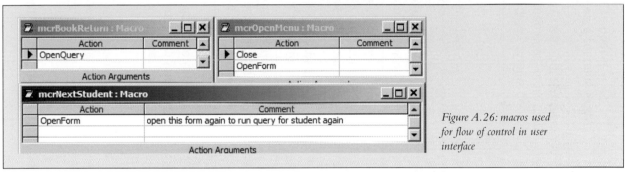

Figure A.26: macros used for flow of control in user interface

Evidence of Testing

Test Number	Test Type	Tested
1	Queries return correct results	See Figures A.28 to A.31
2	Main Menu options go to correct forms/reports	See Figures A.32 to A.33
3	overdue book report works correctly	See Figures A.34 to A.35
4	lost book invoice produced correctly	See Figure A.36
5	loans updated correctly	See Figure A.37 to A.39

Figure A.27: Test Plan with explanation

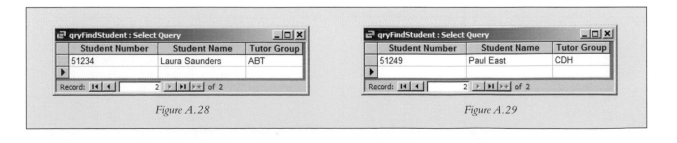

Figure A.28

Figure A.29

Test Plan

1   Overall Purpose: Test queries return correct results (Data as per tables figures A. 11-A.13)

Test Series	Test ID	Purpose	Data	Action	Expected Result	Actual Result	Evidence
	1.1	Find a student	51234	Check whether 1st student's data is returned	Return record details	As expected	see Figure A.28
	1.2		51249	Check whether student's data in the middle part of the table is returned	Return record details	As expected	see Figure A.29
	1.3		12345	Check what happens when a nonexistent swipecard number is input	Return no record	Empty table returned	
	1.4	Book return	14658	Trying to return a book	No record updated	0 rows to be updated	
	1.5		30656	Trying to return a book already returned	No record updated	0 rows to be updated	
	1.6		13214	Trying to return a book which does not exist in the book table	correct record in loans table updated with today's date	correct record in loans table updated with today's date	see Figure A.30
	1.7	Overdue books	No records in loan table	Return a book which is currently on loan	No records returned	Empty table returned	
	1.8		First 7 records only	No loan data	No records returned	Empty table returned	
	1.9		All records in loan table	Loan data contains books with loan dates older than 14 days ago, but returned	6 records returned 31387,32040,34468, 34860,51289,52233	Answer Table contains the six records	see Figure A.31

2 Overall Purpose: Test menu options go to correct form / report (Data as per tables figures A. 11-A.13)

Test Series	Test ID	Purpose	Data	Action	Expected Result	Actual Result	Evidence
	2.1	Go to loans option	51235	Press "Loans"	Window to ask for student ID then opens loans form	As expected	see Figure A.32
	2.2	Go to Returns option	14666	Press "Returns"	Window to ask for Book ID then returns to main menu	As expected	see Figure A.33
	2.3	Get overdue book report		Press "Overdue Book Report"	Print preview of a book report should be seen, when closing this, back to main menu	As expected	
	2.4	Exit the database		Press "Exit Database"	Closes the database	As expected	

3 Overall Purpose: Test overdue book report works correctly (Data as per tables figures A. 11-A.13)

Test Series	Test ID	Purpose	Data	Action	Expected Result	Actual Result	Evidence
	3.1	No overdue books	Empty loan table	Open rptOverdueBooks	No books reported overdue	One page was produced but no names or books listed	see Figure A.34
	3.2	Several overdue books from several students from different tutor groups	Loan table as p.10	Open rptOverdueBooks	2 tutorgroup lists with 6 overdue books grouped by student and TG	2 separate pages were output, one for each tutor group. This was followed by an empty page	see Figure A.33

4 Overall Purpose: Test lost book invoice produced correctly (Data as per tables figures A. 11-A.13)

Test Series	Test ID	Purpose	Data	Action	Expected Result	Actual Result	Evidence
	4.1	Student has lost overdue books	studentID 51240	Open rptLostBookInvoice	3 books reported Cost £19.93	One page was produced with correct book details	see Figure A.36

5 Overall Purpose: Test loans updated correctly (Data as per tables figures A. 11-A.13)

Test Series	Test ID	Purpose	Data	Action	Expected Result	Actual Result	Evidence
5	5.1	Loan to student without previous loans, book never lent out before	Student 51235 Book 32087	Enter student ID Enter BookID in subform	Details of book auto-complete and today's date entered in LoanDate automatically	As expected	see Figure A.37
	5.2	Loan to student with previous loans	Student 51240 Book	Enter student ID Enter BoodID in subform	Details of book auto-complete and today's date entered in LoanDate automatically	As expected, but: The books are listed in the subform by BookID order rather than date order. This could be changed by adding a sort order to the underlying query.	see Figure A.38
	5.3	Loan to student of a book which was on loan to another student and had not been returned via the system	Student 51234 Book 31387	Enter student ID Enter BoodID in subform	Details of book auto-complete and today's date entered in LoanDate automatically	Book can be lent out but the loans table now shows the book out twice. It is possible that a book is returned to the library without getting logged back in and then a student wants to borrow it. The underlying query should check that the book is not out on loan currently. If it is it needs to be returned first.	See Figure A.39

Loan : Table

Book Number	Student Number	Loan Date	Return Date
14666	51257	30/04/2004	
31387	51251	22/04/2004	
32040	51240	23/04/2004	
34468	51257	24/04/2004	
34860	51240	25/04/2004	
51289	51257	26/04/2004	
51584	51240	27/04/2004	
52233	51253	28/04/2004	
61234	51234	01/04/2004	10/04/2004
61234	51253	29/04/2004	11/05/2004
62345	51252	01/03/2004	05/03/2004
62345	51236	01/04/2004	19/04/2004
62345	51253	01/05/2004	
67890	51252	20/04/2004	21/04/2004
*		11/05/2004	

Record: 1 of 14

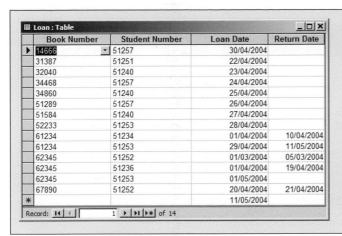

Figure A.30
Test 1.6
Returned book 61234 on 11/05/2004

qryOverdueBooks : Select Query

Book Number	Student Number	Loan Date	Return	Student Name	Tutor	Book Title	Author	Book Value	Days	Fine
31387	51251	22/04/2004		Peter Leach	CDH	Inside the Internet	Winder, Davey	£7.35	5	£0.25
32040	51240	23/04/2004		William Tailby	ABT	GNVQ core skills IT	Arden, Trevor	£5.95	4	£0.20
34468	51257	24/04/2004		Heidi Robinson	CDH	Dictionary of Computing	BCS	£12.50	3	£0.15
34860	51240	25/04/2004		William Tailby	ABT	Road ahead	Gates, Bill	£7.99	2	£0.10
51289	51257	26/04/2004		Heidi Robinson	CDI	Computers and their applications	Parker, Charles	£12.00	1	£0.05

Record: 6 of 6

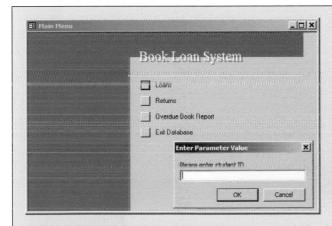

Figure A.31
Test 1.9
Five loans are overdue

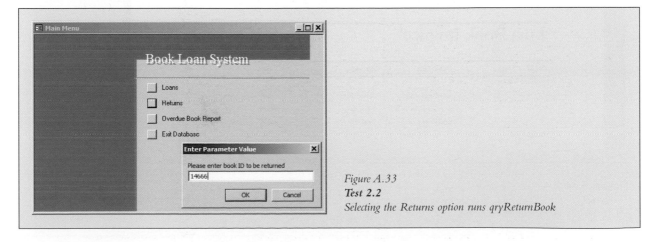

Figure A.32
Test 2.1
Selecting the loans option runs qryFindStudent

Figure A.33
Test 2.2
Selecting the Returns option runs qryReturnBook

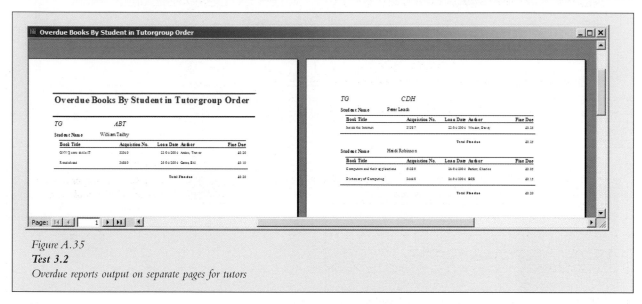

Figure A.34
Test 3.1
No overdue books found

Figure A.35
Test 3.2
Overdue reports output on separate pages for tutors

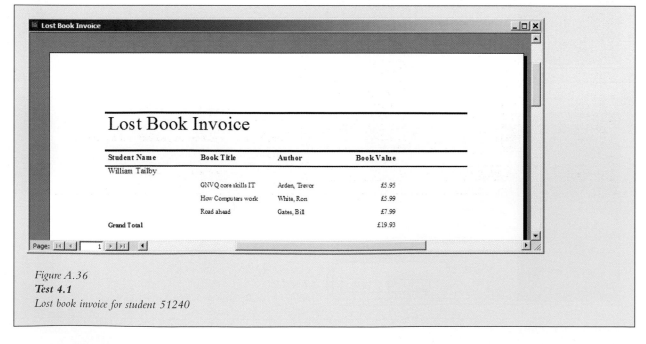

Figure A.36
Test 4.1
Lost book invoice for student 51240

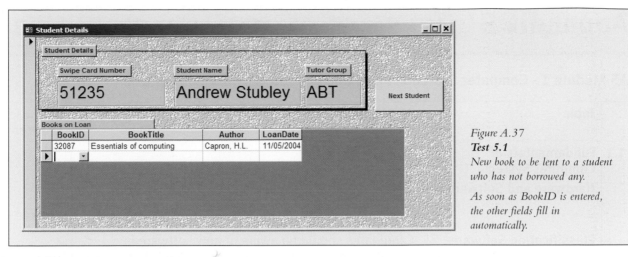

Figure A.37
Test 5.1
New book to be lent to a student who has not borrowed any.

As soon as BookID is entered, the other fields fill in automatically.

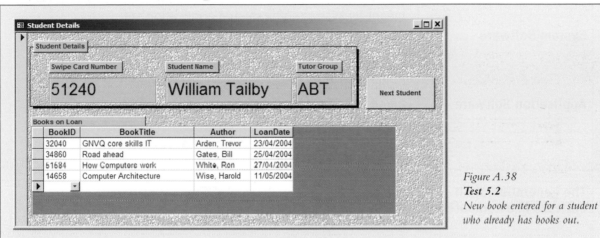

Figure A.38
Test 5.2
New book entered for a student who already has books out.

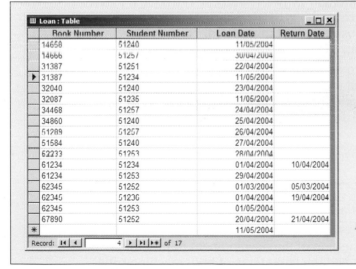

Figure A.39
Test 5.3
Book 31387 has been loaned out and has not been properly returned.

This is a problem not resolved yet.

Appendix B   AQA Specification Summary - Modules 1-3

AS Module 1 - Computer Systems, Programming and Network Concepts

	Topic	Amplification	See Chapter
1.1	**Fundamentals of Computer Systems**		
	Hardware and Software	Candidates should understand the relationship between hardware and software and be able to define both.	1
	Classification Software	Candidates should be aware of how software is classified. They should be able to explain what is meant by system software and application software.	2
	System Software	Operating system software Utility programs Library programs Compilers, assemblers, interpreters	2
	Application Software	Candidates should be able to describe the different types of application software.	2
		General purpose applications software. Special purpose applications software. Bespoke software	2
	The generation of Bit Patterns in a Computer	Explain the different interpretations that may be associated with a pattern of bits. Bits, bytes. Concept of a word. Program and data	3
	Internal Components of a Computer	Outline the basic internal components of a computer system. Processor, main memory, address bus, data bus, control bus, I/O port, secondary storage, their purpose and how they relate.	11
	Functional Characteristics of a Processor	Describe the stored program concept whereby machine code instructions stored in main memory are fetched and executed serially by a processor that performs arithmetic and logical operations.	11
1.2	**Fundamentals of Programming** **Generations of Programming Language**		
	First generation - Machine code	Describe machine-code language and assembly language	6
	Second generation - Assembly language	Some discussion of the development of programming languages and the limitations of both machine code and assembly-language programming would be useful.	6
	Third generation - imperative high level language	Explain the term 'imperative high level language' and its relationship to first and second generation languages	6

Types of Program Translator Assembler, compiler interpreter	Define each type of language translator and illustrate situations where each would be appropriate or inappropriate	6
Features of Imperative High Language Data types Built-in, User defined	Illustrate these features for a particular imperative, third generation language.	6
Programming Statements Type definitions Variable declarations Constant definitions Procedure/ Function declarations Assignment Iteration Selection	Describe the use of these statement types.	6
Procedure and function calling	Explain the advantages of procedures/functions.	6
Constants and variables	Explain the advantages of named variables and constants.	6
Procedure and function parameters	Describe the use of parameters to pass data within programs.	6
Fundamentals of Structured Programming	Candidates should be familiar with the structured approach to program construction and should be able to construct and use structure charts when designing programs, use meaningful identifier names, procedures/functions with interfaces, use procedures that execute a single task, avoid the use of GoTo statements. Candidates should be able to explain the advantages of the structured approach.	7
Abstract Data Types Binary tree Stack Linear queue	Candidates should be able to recognise and use these in very simple ways. They will not be expected to have knowledge of how to implement these in a programming language. Uses of these should include a binary search tree and using a stack to reverse the elements of a linear queue.	9, 10
Data Structures One and two dimensional arrays	Candidates should be familiar with each of these and their uses.	6
Simple Algorithms	Candidates should understand the term algorithm and be able to hand trace simple algorithms	8

B

1.3	Fundamentals of Information and Data Representation Relationship between Data and Information		
	Data. Sources of data	Explain the term data. Consider sources of data, both direct and indirect.	4
	Meaning of the term information	Consider data as an encoded form of information and as any form of communication that provides understandable and useful knowledge to the recipient.	4
	Number Representation Systems Binary number system		
	Pure binary representation of decimal integers	Describe the representation of unsigned decimal integers in binary. Perform conversion from decimal to BCD and vice versa. Explain advantages of BCD.	4
	Information Coding Schemes ASCII EBCDIC Unicode	Describe standard coding systems for coding Information expressed in character form and other text-based forms. Differentiate between the character code representation of a decimal integer and its pure binary representation.	4
	Representing Images, Sound and other Information Bit-mapped graphics Vector graphics Sampled Sound Sound Synthesis	Describe how bit patterns may also represent other forms of information including graphics and sound.	5
	Analogue and digital signals Analogue to digital converter (ADC)	Differentiate between analogue and digital signals. Describe the principles of operation of an analogue to digital converter.	5
1.4	**Communication and Networking** **Communication Methods**		
	Serial data communication Parallel data communication	Define both serial and parallel methods and illustrate where they are appropriate. Consider the effect of distance on the transmission of data.	12
	Baud rate, bit rate and Bandwidth	Define these terms. Differentiate between baud rate and bit rate. Consider the relationship between bit rate and bandwidth.	12
	Asynchronous data transmission	Define	12
	Start and stop bits	Describe the purpose of start and stop bits in asynchronous data transmission	12
	Odd and even parity	Explain the use of parity checks	12

Handshaking in parallel data transmission and meaning of the term protocol	Explain what is meant by a protocol in this context.	12
Modem	Describe the purpose and the method of operation of a modem.	13
Networking Network	Define these networking terms.	13
Local area network (LAN)	Candidates should be familiar with LAN topologies but will not be required to know details of their operation.	
Bus, Ring and Star LAN topologies	Candidates should be aware of the advantages and disadvantages of each LAN topology. Candidates should be able to compare local area networking with standalone operation.	
Wide area network (WAN) The Internet Intranet Network adapter Leased line networking Dial up networking		14
Uniform Resource Locator (URL)	Describe the term URL in the context of Internetworking.	14
Domain names and IP addresses	Explain the term domain name and IP address. Describe how domain names are organised	14

AS Module 2 - Principles of Hardware, Software and Applications

	Topic	Amplification	See Chapter
2.1	**A study of one Major Information Processing Application of Computing**	Consider the purpose of the application. Discuss the application as an information system in the context chosen. Examine specific user-interface needs. Examine the communication requirements of the application. Discuss the extent to which the given system satisfies both the organisation's and users' needs.	28
		Discuss the economic, social, legal and ethical consequences of the application.	
	General Purpose Packages Database, spreadsheet, word-processing, Desk-top publishing, presentation package, e-mail	Candidates should have experience in using a database and a spreadsheet package as part of their skills' development. In addition, they should be aware of how the listed packages facilitate the execution of particular tasks. Candidates should be able to assess the suitability of a given package for a particular task as well as its limitations.	15, 16
	Social, Economic and Ethical Consequences of Current Uses of Computing	Discuss the social and economic implications for an individual in relation to employment, government, education and leisure.	26, 28
		Discuss issues relating to privacy in the context of electronic mail and data.	26
		Consider the impact of encryption technology on the privacy of the individual, organisation and the state.	
	Legal Implications of the Use of Computers	Discuss issues of ownership of information and programs, and protection of data. Consider current legal controls on computerised data and programs and the implications of current legislation.	26, 27
2.2	**Files and Databases** **File Types**		
	Text and non-text (binary files) files.	Define a file. Describe the meaning of the terms, text and non-text files.	17
	A file as a collection of records.		
	Records and fields (data Items), primary and secondary key fields.	Illustrate how key fields are used to locate and index heterogeneous records.	17
	Fixed and variable length records.	Describe the use of fixed and variable length records. Consider the advantages and disadvantages of each.	17
	File structure	Define what is meant by the structure of a file.	
	File size		
	File Organisation Serial	Describe the organisation of these files.	18
	Sequential	Explain hashing.	19
	Direct access		

File Processing	Explain the principle of master and transaction files methods used to retrieve, insert, edit and delete data	18, 19
Security and Integrity of Data in a Data Processing Environment		
The meaning of the terms Security Integrity	Define these terms	20 21
File Security Methods Backing up strategies Encryption	Describe hardware and software protection of online files against unauthorised access and system failure.	20
Data Processing Integrity Methods	Explain how corrupted data can be detected and prevented using techniques such as batch totals, control totals, hash totals, check digits, virus checking, parity checking, check sums.	21
Database Concepts Data sharing Data consistency Primary key Alternate key/ Secondary key Indexing Secondary index Validation	Consider a database as an integrated collection of non-redundant, related data accessible from more than one application and stored in different record types together with a mechanism for linking related records. Consider how data inconsistency may arise in an application based on a separate file approach and how this is avoided in a database approach. Consider why indexing is used and how databases support multiple indexes. Describe typical built-in validation controls.	23
Relational Databases	Explain the concept of a relational database. Define the term attribute.	23
Querying a Database Querying by Example (QBE)	Illustrate the use of QBE to extract data from several tables of a relational database	23

B

2.3	**Operating Systems**		
	Role of an Operating System Provision of a virtual machine	Candidates should understand that the role of the operating system is to hide the complexities of the hardware from the user.	24
	Resource management	In addition, it manages the hardware resources in order to provide for an orderly and controlled allocation of the processors, memories and I/O devices among the various processes competing for them.	24
	Operating System Classification Batch Interactive Real time Network	Define each type of operating system and explain their operational characteristics	24
	File Management File, Filename, Directory, Pathnames, Directory structure, Logical drives,	Define the term File, Filename and Directory. Describe the use of directories. Explain the relationship between the root directory and sub-directories and the use of pathnames.	24
	Access rights Backing-up, Archiving	Explain the term access rights in the context of file management. Distinguish file backing-up from archiving.	24 24
2.4	**Hardware Devices**		
	Input and Output Devices	Consider how the application and needs of the user affect the choice of input and output devices. Candidates should be able to make appropriate selections based upon knowledge of the usage of contemporary devices. Principles of operation will **not** be required.	25
	Secondary Storage Devices	Explain the need for secondary storage within a computer system and discuss the difference between archived data and directly accessible data. Compare the capacity and speed of access of various media including magnetic disk and tape, optical media and CD-ROM storage. Give examples of how each might be used.	25

B

AS Module 3 - System Development

	Topic	Amplification	See Chapter
3.1	System Development The Classical Systems Life-cycle Problem definition/ Problem investigation/ feasibility study, analysis, design, construction/ implementation and maintenance	Describe the stages of development and maintenance of a hardware/software system including evaluating the operational, technical and financial feasibility of developing a new system. The importance of testing the specification, design and implementation.	29 30
	Evaluation	The importance of evaluating the effectiveness of the implementated solution in meeting the users' needs.	30
	Analysis	Describe methods of deriving the user and information requirements of a system and its environment.	29
	Methods of gathering Information Data flow Diagrams	Evaluate the feasibility of a computer-based solution to a problem, specify and document the data flow and the processing requirements for a system to level one and identify possible needs for the development and maintenance of the system.	
	Entity-Relationship Diagrams	Produce a data model from the given data requirement for a simple scenario involving two or three entities.	22
	Design Module and top-down Design Pseudo-code Simple algorithm design	Specify and document a design that meets the requirements of the problem in terms of human computer interface (usability and appropriateness), hardware and software, using methods such as structure charts, hierarchy charts pseudo-code, relations.	30
	Prototyping	Define prototyping.	
	Human Computer Interface	Examine and document specific user interface needs.	31
	Testing Strategies	Dry run testing. Unit testing. Integration testing. suitable test data. Test solution.	30
	Construction/ Implementation	Make use of appropriate software tools and techniques to construct a solution to a real problem.	
	Maintenance	Understand the need for and nature of maintenance. Understand how technical documentation aids the process of maintenance.	30
	Evaluation	Evaluate methods and solutions on the basis of effectiveness, usability, and maintainability.	30

Index

Access
directory   107
rights   107, 131
Address bus   53, 55
Algorithm   178
Alternate key   90
Analogue to digital
converter   20
Antivirus software   114
Archiving   131
Arithmetic logic unit   53
Array   28
ASCII   12
Assembler   8, 24, 26
Assembly code   24
Asynchronous transmission 60
Attribute   116
Auxiliary storage   5
Backup   108
Bandwidth   69
Bar code reader   139
Baseband   59
BASIC   25
Batch
processing   112, 136
operating system   129
Baud rate   59
BCD *See* Binary Coded Decimal
Bespoke software   10
Bidirectional   140
Binary
Coded Decimal   18
number system   12, 13, 17
tree   49
Biometric security
measures   108
Bit   12, 89
Bitmapped graphics   21
Boolean
value   19
Bootstrap loader   4
Broadband   59
Bus   52, 53
address   55
control   54
data   55
network   65
Business Software Alliance 154

Byte   3, 12, 89
Cache memory   4
Carrierband   59
CD-ROM   147
Central Processing Unit   52
Chart   84
Check digit   113
Checksum   114
Child nodes   49
Collision   100
Command and control
system   187
Command-line interface   184
Communications
media   68
satellite   68
security   106
Compiler   8, 27
Composite data types   44
Computer
abuse   150
crime   150
failure   161
Misuse Act   152
Conceptual data model   116
Contents of documented
system   180
Control
bus   54
unit   53
Copyright Designs and
Patents Act   153
CPU   52
Crime   150
Cylinder   145
Data
bus   53, 55
compression   69
direct collection of   16
encryption   106
flow   175
flow diagram   175
hierarchy   89
indirect collection of   16
integrity   110
Protection Act   155
Protection Registrar   156
security   105

sources   16
store   175
structure   44
subjects   156
transmission rate   69
validation   112, 120
Data type
composite   44
elementary   44
structured   44
Database   89
approach   119
relational   120
Degree of a relationship   116
Deliverable   173
Denary number system   14
Design, top-down   31
Desktop publishing   77
Dialogue boxes   186
Dial-up networking   71
Digitised sound   20
Digitiser   139
Disaster planning   108
Disk
cylinder   145
floppy   5, 144
hard   145
magneto-optical   147
sector   144
storage   5
track   144
Domain name system   72
Dot matrix printer   140
Drives   130
Dry run testing   179
DVD-ROM   148
EBCDIC   12
Electronic mail   77
Elementary data types   44
E-mail   77
and privacy issues   158
Embedded computers   6
Encryption   106
strong   158
weak   158
Entity   116
Relationship Diagram   116
Ergonomic environment   159

index

Evaluation 180
Evolutionary prototyping 179
External entity 175
Feasibility study 174
Fibre optic cable 68
Field 89
File 89, 130
   access methods 102
   direct access 100
   hash 100
   lookup check 112
   management 130
   manager 130
   master 93
   transaction 93
   updating 97
File organisation 93
   random 100
   relative 100
   sequential 94
   serial 94
Firmware 6
Fixed length record 91
Flag 101
Flash memory 148
Floppy disk 144
Folders 130
Foreign key 122
Format check 112, 120
Full-screen menu 184
Gates, Bill 4
Gb 3, 14
Generations
   of files 98
   of programming language 24
Generic software 10
Geosynchronous orbit 68
Gigabyte 3
Grandfather, father, son 98
Graphics
   bitmapped 21
   tablet 139
   vector 22
GUI 184
Hacking 105, 150
Hand-held input devices 139
Handshaking 61
Hard disk 145

Hardware 2
Hash file 100
Hashing algorithm 100
Health and Safety 159
   Executive 159
   Regulations 159
High level language 25
Hit rate 102
Human computer interface 183
I/O controller 52, 55
I/O port 52
Icon 187
Impact printer 140
Imperative high
   level language 25
Implementation 180
In situ 101
Indexed sequential files 93
Indexing 121
Ink jet printers 141
Integration testing 179
Integrity of data 110
Interactive processing 129
Interface 55
Internet 70
Interpreter 8, 27
Interrogating files 96
Interrupt
   handling 128
Intranet 73
IP address 73
ISDN line 69
Iteration 32
Jackson structure diagram 31
Joystick 137
Kb 3, 14
Keyboard data entry 135
Key-to-disk system 136
Kilobyte 3
LAN See Local Area Network
Language
   high level 25
   low level 24
Laser printer 142
Last In First Out 45
Leaf nodes 49
Leased line networking 71

Library programs 8
LIFO 45
Light pen 137
Linking database tables 122
Local Area Network 63
Logic bomb 151
Low level language 24
Machine code 24, 26
Macro 85
Magnetic
   Ink Character
   Recognition 137
   stripe 137
   tape 146
Magneto-optical disk 147, 148
Main memory 3
Mainframe computers 3
Maintenance
   adaptive 181
   corrective 181
   perfective 181
Master file 93, 96, 98
Mb 3, 14
Megabyte 3
Memory 3, 14
   cache 4
   management 128
   Read Only 4
Menu
   full-screen 184
   interface 184
   pop-up 185
   pull-down 185
MICR 137
Microprocessor 3
Microsoft Windows 187
Microwave 68
Modem 69
Modular programming 37
Module 31
Monitor 143
Mouse 137
Movement files 96
Natural language 185
Near letter quality 140

INDEX

Network
  Local Area 63
  topology 64
  Wide Area 68
NLQ 140
Object code 26
OCR 136
OMR 138
Operating system 8, 128
  batch 129
  interactive 129
  real-time 129
Optical
  Character Recognition 136
  Disk 147
  Mark Recognition 138
Overflow error 46
Parallel
  data transmission 58
Parent node 49
Parity 60
  bit 114
Pascal 25, 27
Password 106
  protection 106
Pathnames 131
Periodic backups 108
Peripherals 52
Personal privacy 155
Picture
  check 112
  element 21
Pixel 21
Plotter 142
Pop-up menu 185
PowerPoint 79
Presence check 112, 120
Presentation graphics
  software 79
Primary
  key 90, 121
  storage 144
Printer
  dot matrix 140
  ink jet 141
  laser 142
Privacy 155
Process 175

Processor 3, 53
Program
  constructs 32
  design 31
  structure 31
Programming
  modular 37
Protocol 61
Prototyping 178
  evolutionary 179
  throw-away 179
Pseudocode 36, 178
Puck 139
Pull-down menu 185
QBE See Query by Example
Query by Example 123
Querying a database 123
Queue 44
Quick Check 162
RAM 4
Random
  Access Memory 4
  files 100, 103
Range check 112, 120
Read Only Memory 4
Real-time 129
Record 89
Recovery procedures 109
Reference file 96
Regulations
  Health and Safety 159
Relation 120
Relational database
  design 120, 121
Relationship 116
Relative file 100
Repetitive strain injury 136
Requirements analysis 175
Resolution 143
Resource allocation 128
RF ID tags 166
Ring network 66
ROM See Read Only Memory
Root 131
RSI See Repetitive strain injury
Satellite 68
Scanner 136
Secondary key 90, 121

Sector 144
Security of data 105
Selection 32
Sequence 32
Sequential file 94, 102
Serial
  data transmission 58
  file 94, 102
Service providers 70
Signalling methods 59
Simulation 44
Smart card 138
Software 2
  bespoke 10
  copyright laws 153
  general purpose 9
  generic 10
  off-the-shelf 10
  special purpose 10
  systems 8
Sound 20
Source code 26
Spam 78
Special purpose software 10
Speech input 187
Speech synthesis system 188
Spreadsheet 80
Stack 45
Star network 64
Storage
  auxiliary 5
  primary 144
  secondary 144
Stored program concept 53
Structure chart 33
Structured program 32
Supercomputers 3
Synonyms 100
System
  buses 54
  design 178
  maintainability 179
  maintenance 181
  performance 179
  specification 178
  suitability 179
  usability 179

Systems
  life cycle 172
  software 8
Tb 3
Technical documentation 180
Terabyte 3
Test
  data 179
  plan 179
Testing
  dry run 179
  integration 179
  strategies 179
  unit 179
Text file 90
Throw-away prototyping 179
Time-slice 129
Top-down design 31
Topology (of networks) 63
Touch screen 137
Trace table 39
Track 144
Transaction file 93, 96
Transcription errors 111, 135
Transmission
  asynchronous 60
  errors 114
  rate 59, 69
  synchronous 60
Turing 53
Underflow error 46
Unicode 17
Uniform Resource Locator 71
Unit testing 179
Updating
  by copying 97
  by overlay 101
  files 97
  in place 101
  in situ 101
URL 71
User ID 106
Utility programs 8
Validation checks 112, 120
Variable
  length records 91
VDU 143
Vector graphics 22

Verification 114
Virtual
  machine 129
Virus 151
  protection 114
Visual display unit 143
VLOOKUP function 82
Voice
  data entry 135
  recognition 187
Volatile 76
von Neumann machine 53
WAN *See* Wide Area Network
Waterfall model 173
What If 80
Wide Area Network 63, 68
WIMP 187
Windows 187
Word processing software 76
Word size 14
WORM disk 147

index